Remembering Leningrad

Remembering Leningrad

The Story of a Generation

MARY McAULEY

The University of Wisconsin Press

The University of Wisconsin Press
1930 Monroe Street, 3rd Floor
Madison, Wisconsin 53711-2059
uwpress.wisc.edu

Gray's Inn House, 127 Clerkenwell Road
London EC1R 5DB, United Kingdom
eurospanbookstore.com

Printed in the United States of America

This book may be available in a digital edition.

Library of Congress Cataloging-in-Publication Data

Names: McAuley, Mary, author.
Title: Remembering Leningrad: the story of a generation / Mary McAuley.
Description: Madison, Wisconsin: The University of Wisconsin Press, [2019]
Identifiers: LCCN 2018056728 | ISBN 9780299322502 (cloth: alk. paper)
Subjects: LCSH: Saint Petersburg (Russia)—Biography.| Saint Petersburg
(Russia)—History—1917- | McAuley, Mary.
Classification: LCC DK543 .M33 2019 | DDC 947/.21085—dc23
LC record available at https://lccn.loc.gov/2018056728

Imagination and memory are but one thing, which for diverse considerations hath diverse names.

Thomas Hobbes

Contents

Part 3
St. Petersburg
The New City, 1995 to 2017

Illustrations

Acknowledgments

Conversations, reminiscences, and letters need no references but diaries and excerpts from published memoirs should have an acknowledgment. El'mar's autobiographical essay "В миру и наедине с собой" written in the mid-nineties is available at http://samlib.ru/s/sokolow_e_w/memory .shtml#_Toc42652481. My account of Andrei Alexeev's actions and thoughts in the period from 1960 to 1990 come from published and unpublished materials that were in his archive in the Institute of Sociology in the 1990s. Many were subsequently published or republished (in edited versions) in his *Драматическая социология и социологическая ауторефлексия*, vol. 2 (St. Petersburg: Norma, 2003–2005); see in particular 438 and *Из неопубликованных глав*, vol. 1, 378–79. Both volumes are available at http://www.socioprognoz.ru/publ.html?id=216. I have his permission to include the occasional quote that does not appear in the published edited materials.

Many of Vilen Ochakovsky's comments are taken from his unpublished manuscript "Выродок или Антигерой нашего времени 1955–1992" and from a chapter in Alexeev, vol. 2 (cited above), 422–33, which includes a commentary by Gennadi Khoroshikh. Quotations by Liuba Myasnikova appear in her "Блокада," *Звезда* 9 (2012): 167–80, and in her "Почему милые девушеи рвутся в науку," in *Из истории отечественной науки (женщины-ученые в Физтехе)* (St. Petersburg: Изд. Политехнич. Университета, 2008), 120.

Parts of chapters 1 and 2 appeared in my "Дети Сталина: Ленинград 1960-х," *Социологичеслий журнал* 4 (2005): 103–16; and some paragraphs in chapter 7 in my *Human Rights in Russia: Citizens and the State from Perestroika to Putin* (London: I. B. Tauris, 2015).

I use a modified Library of Congress system of transliteration in the text, adopting -*y* for names ending in -*ii* and -*yi*. I use *x* in names such as Alexander, Alexeev, and Felix in place of *ks*, and keep *ye* only for the initial letter of a name (hence Yevgeny, Yeltsin). Where a name is already well known in the west (e.g., Tolstoy, Herzen, Dostoevsky, Tchaikovsky), I use the usual spelling. All the translations are mine.

✳

I make no claim that the characters you will meet are representative of their generation, but from their actions, and from the letters and diaries they wrote, they bring their peers and the city to life. I have included a list of those who appear more than once, and they are there in the photographs, most of which come from my personal collection. I am grateful to Alexandra Veselova, whom I commissioned to draw the maps. Of course, the description is mine, the lens through which my friends, acquaintances, and colleagues and Russia itself is viewed is that of an English observer. My response to shopping in Prism, the Finnish supermarket on Vasilevsky Island, is not the same as Galina's. This is my Russia, not theirs. It is not written for my Russian friends, although it is dedicated to them. A few may read it with interest, or wryly, or shake their heads, and reflect on how their perceptions differ from mine.

To all those who read the manuscript at different stages—Catriona Bass, Vladimir Gel'man, Rose Glickman, Patricia Harris, Oksana Mamyrin, Marion McAuley, Gary Yershon—I am truly grateful for corrections and comments. My sincere thanks to the three reviewers for the University of Wisconsin Press, and to Gwen Walker, editor, whose comments and suggestions persuaded me to make changes, to delete or to add more details, to edit the style in places, and to think again about potential readers.

I end with a special word of thanks to my seventeen-year-old grandson, Joe, who ended his page-long review with "There are two huge gaping holes in the book however: 1) Zenit play in blue and white not red and white 2) Your darling grandson Joe is not mentioned once." I have, I hasten to say, made the necessary corrections.

Dramatis Personae

This is a list of those who reappear more than once at different times and in different contexts. It does not include those who appear only once, not because they are less valued but because no reminder is needed.

El'mar and His School Friends (all born in 1932)

El'mar Sokolov (d. 2003), philosopher, lived in the Botanical Garden, taught at the Herzen Institute, then the Institute of Culture; m. Albina, son Andrei; m. Tamara, daughter Ekaterina

Vladimir (Volodya) Frolov (d. 2018), scientist, Technological Institute

Oleg Konrady (d. 2006), medical doctor

Lef (Leva) Osipov, medical doctor; m. included to Valya, daughter Masha, and to Gabriella

Dmitry (Dima) Glebovsky, chemist, St. Petersburg University

Yury (Yura) Smirnov (d. 2004), scientist, Technological Institute

Other St. Petersburg Friends and Colleagues
Who Appear First in the 1960s

Vera Kamyshnikova (Fedotova) (b. 1937), history student, Leningrad University, then teacher in Sakhalin, in Tambov, and retired to St. Petersburg; daughter Olga

Galina Lebedeva (b. 1937), history student, then graduate student in Byzantine history, professor, history faculty, Leningrad–St. Petersburg University

Leonid and Liuba, the Romankov twins (b. 1937), both scientists; Leonid was elected to the City Council from 1990 to 2002 and Liuba Myasnikova continues to hold a research position at the Ioffe Phys-tech Institute, Academy of Sciences

Alexander Stepanovich Pashkov (1921–96), chair, Labor Law Department, Law Faculty, Leningrad University in the 1960s, then director of the Labor Relations Centre, Bobrinsky Palace

Vladimir Yadov (1929–2015), sociologist, Leningrad University, then the Institute of Social and Economic Problems, Leningrad; in 1989 moved to head the Institute of Sociology, Academy of Sciences, Moscow

Friends and Colleagues from the 1980s and 1990s

Andrei Alexeev (1934–2017), journalist, lathe operator, sociologist; m. Zina

Boris Firsov (b. 1929), district party secretary, head of Leningrad TV, sociologist, director of the St. Petersburg Institute of Sociology, Academy of Sciences, then founder and rector of the European University at St. Petersburg; m. Galina

Vilen Ochakovsky (b. 1937), journalist, Komsomol activist in Yakutia, Ukrainian miner, detained in a psychiatric hospital 1982–86

Vitaly Startsev (1931–2000), historian, Institute of History, Academy of Sciences, then Herzen University

Remembering Leningrad

Prologue

Zhivkov's Geranium

I am very sad," said seventy-something Galina Yevgenevna. "Zhivkov's geranium has died." It was 2014. We were having our weekly telephone call. She, standing at the kitchen window of her St. Petersburg apartment, was looking out at the courtyard, its children's playground and the tall ash trees to which the cawing black-headed crows return each evening at six o'clock. I, at my study window in Bloomsbury, looked across the street at the Edwardian mansion block, its spikes to keep the pigeons from laying eggs on the balconies. Our windowsills share some of the same plants. Hers have the edge in light and sun. But now Zhivkov's geranium, brought to Leningrad more than fifty years ago by a Bulgarian graduate student, had drooped and died. "Don't worry," I said. "Although mine rarely flowers, I'll bring a cutting on my next visit." And a year later, as though happy to be back, the geranium on her windowsill in St. Petersburg was producing fronds of little blue flowers.

There are threads, some short, some longer, some with knots, which link thoughts of today with memories of the past. A telephone conversation, a chance meeting, a place or an old photo tugs a long-forgotten incident, shelved somewhere in memory, back into the present. What did that conversation bring back?

In 1961 Galina Yevgenevna and I lived on the same floor of a student hostel, four to a room, across the river from the Winter Palace, the home of the Hermitage. The view from our fifth-floor windows, particularly when the evening sun caught the palace windows and burnished them golden, was spectacular. Dina, from Sofia, lived there too. She had previously had a work assignment in the office of Todor Zhivkov, first secretary of the Bulgarian Communist Party and head of government from 1954 to 1989. Zhivkov, remarkably long-lived, believed that geraniums, with a strong camphor scent, were good for the heart. His office was full of them, and one day Dina, finding herself alone there, took cuttings. She brought these with her to Leningrad—as the city was known from 1924 to 1991—to the hostel, and thence to Galina. Since then Zhivkov's geranium has accompanied the two of us during our more than fifty years of friendship.

Galina, a final-year student in the medieval history department at Leningrad University, was from Tula, a town famous before the revolution for its samovars. I was a visiting graduate student from Oxford, writing a thesis on labor disputes, attached to the university's law faculty. I was busy with visits to factories and courts. No "politics" or "sociology" was taught then; one might add that there was no sociology at Oxford.

By 1992 Leningrad was again St. Petersburg, Galina was a professor in Byzantine studies at St. Petersburg University, I was on research leave from my Oxford college and attached to a new Institute of Sociology in St. Petersburg, studying the dramatic political change engulfing the country. Galina had privatized her well-built postwar apartment on Vasilevsky Island and, with her help, I had bought a two-room apartment in a 1970s "cooperative block." Or had I? Not quite clear. But, owner or not, I was now living just off Sredny Prospect, almost in the middle of the island, but with a feeling of openness and being near the sea. Zhivkov's geranium took its place on my windowsill, followed me a few years later to Moscow, and from there in 2002 to London. When Galina visited, she could always find her way back to my Bloomsbury apartment, she said, by looking for its window box. It reminded her of the flowerpot whose presence on a windowsill, in the famous Russian TV serial of the 1970s, *Seventeen Moments of Spring*, starring Vyacheslav Tikhonov as a Soviet spy in Germany in the Second World War, indicated that it was safe to visit.

In 2016 we were in a hospital on the outskirts of the city. Galina had an appointment for a checkup. We collected blue plastic shoe bags at reception—we put them on over our boots—negotiated the stairs and lift, and sat down to wait. Dmitry Ivanovich, a young doctor in a white coat, invited her in. I thought of the time in 1961 when I had found myself in the "Sverdlovka," the hospital for Old Bolsheviks, and an object of great interest to the doctors and to elderly patients walking up and down the corridors in their pyjamas. After all, they had never seen an English person before—and the English are known to be prim or stuck-up (*choporny*). I felt terrible but somehow I must not be stuck-up. In the pages that follow you will hear the term used more than once. Not this time, though, when Galina and Dmitry Ivanovich came out together, and Galina, smiling, holding his arm, introduced me. "This," she said, "is Mary, whom I told you about, a professor from Oxford, we've been friends for more than fifty years." So, for the reader who wants to know what lies ahead, this is the story of a friendship. But it's not only that. It's the story of a city, St. Petersburg, told through the memories and experiences of a particular generation.

For whom am I writing? Primarily for younger readers, for those who are studying or interested in Russia. For them I offer a past and present, an everyday history to accompany the more serious books they read about the city. Perhaps I can tempt them to make a visit. But it is also for those from the west who spent time in the city when it was still Leningrad, or who arrived in St. Petersburg in the turbulent nineties. For them it offers an opportunity to place themselves, and their experiences, within a narrative that starts with the blockade of 1941 and ends today. And, finally, it's for the curious traveler, about to visit the city for the first time.

But how to tell the story of the city's transformation, of its several transformations since the Second World War, how to give the visitor of today a grounding, a sense of where the city and its people are coming from? I may have lived in Leningrad in the early sixties and in St. Petersburg in the early nineties; I may have made more visits than I can remember—research visits starting in the late seventies; visits to introduce students or children to the city in the eighties; then, as the nineties turned into the new millennium, visits as a grantmaker from the Ford Foundation, or to act as a consultant, or simply to see old friends—but my memories are not enough. To tell the story of the city from the perspective of a particular generation, I need their voices—the conversations, letters, diaries, notebooks, published and unpublished memoirs of those who knew it as children during the Siege or were teenagers when Stalin died in 1953; of those, including the newcomers, who as adults experienced the hopes under Khrushchev, the disillusionment under Brezhnev, and then the giddying changes of the nineties. The early sixties and the early nineties take pride of place in the story, not just because these were the years I lived in the city but because they were years of dramatic change for our generation.

Politics at times intrudes, the way the system of rule, or type of government, affected everyday life. Sometimes it is in the forefront, sometimes as a backdrop. But I am not here offering the reader a political history. This is history of the everyday. Certain themes dominate: a place to live, hostels, apartments; everyday living—especially food and clothes; trains, traffic, arriving and departing from St. Petersburg to the rest of Russia and, for some, visiting foreign countries. Then there's the world of culture—theater, libraries, museums—and the world of science and higher education. In the early years the threat of surveillance is ever-present; in the nineties the old world falls apart. There's love, marriage, and divorce in the sixties, ill health and death as the years pass by. Letters give way to mobile phones and the internet. And now, in their old age, my friends try to make sense of their lives in St. Petersburg today and of the role that Russia is playing in the world. Disagreements run deep.

We shall leave St. Petersburg to make two trips—to a nature reserve in the south, on the edge of the North Caucasus, and to Mirny, the diamond capital of northeast Siberia. If by the 1990s Galina and other St. Petersburg friends could come to Britain and simply stay as guests—something unimaginable even in the mid-eighties—I too could now explore Russia, travel to cities, towns, forests and lakes, far from Moscow, St. Petersburg, and the carefully restored architectural gems of Pskov and Novgorod. Today airfares match their European counterparts, and the smart Sapsan train speeds you to Moscow in four hours.

In the early nineties travel was absurdly cheap—an air ticket to Siberia cost the same as a ballpoint pen, the overnight train to Moscow from St. Petersburg was less than a dollar—although getting tickets was a problem, and overnight trains could be dangerous places. But there were buses, boats, even helicopters to distant places. I could take you to the Solovetsky Islands in the White Sea where so many died in the camps, or to Yekaterinburg and Perm in the Urals, down to Astrakhan on the Caspian Sea, or to Kazan, capital of Tatarstan, and, of course, Moscow beckons. But all of that will have to find a place in another story. The justification for taking you away from St. Petersburg, albeit briefly, is that its unique combination of western architecture, culture, Russian traditions, and modernity shines out even more brightly when set in the context of the huge country that is Russia. So, at one point, we shall set out and come back—to take up a story that starts in Leningrad in the 1930s and ends in St. Petersburg today.

Part
1

Leningrad

From the Siege of 1941 to 1991

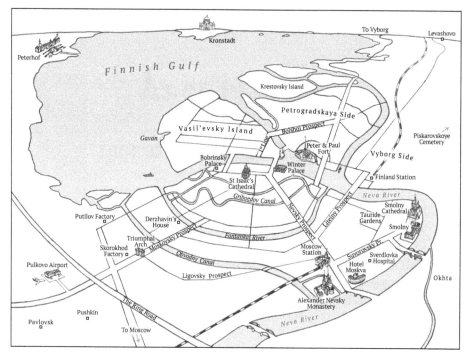

The city on the Finnish Gulf.

1

Stalin's Children

The Leningraders

In 1703 Peter the Great built St. Petersburg to give Russia a window on Europe. Yet, despite its elegant buildings and waterfronts, often the work of Italian architects; despite its "English embankment," home to English and Scottish ship owners; its German community on Vasilevsky Island; and its wealthy and well-educated families where French was spoken as easily as Russian, St. Petersburg remained a city apart from Europe. Diderot might visit Catherine the Great (herself from a German family), its ballet and opera might be the talk of Europe, but when the snow came in early November, and the days drew in, the dark city attracted few visitors. It grew silent as the snow muffled the sound of sledges; all that remained was the military music as the regimental bands marched out each day, and the cannon sounded the midday from the Peter and Paul Fortress. Wealthy families headed for Europe for shorter or longer breaks.

Renamed Leningrad in 1924 in honor of Vladimir Lenin, the Bolshevik leader at the time of the 1917 revolution, the city had become a very different place. The wealthy had gone for good or had been expropriated. The state had taken over housing, the metalworking factories, the locomotive plants, shipbuilding, the porcelain and confectionery factories, the universities, schools, and institutes, medical care, transport . . . and the shutters gradually came down. Foreigners became suspect and, by the thirties, the only Soviet citizens who traveled abroad were the sailors on the boats and the occasional official delegation. Then came the arrests and executions during the purges of the late thirties, the devastating Siege of 1941–44, and, after the war, further political purges.

It was 1960 before the casement window on the west was eased open a crack. Very few Leningraders made trips abroad. Occasionally the Kirov ballet or the Philharmonia appeared on stage in the capitals of Europe. But now tourists, in their organized groups, were coming to Leningrad from Europe or America, and a handful of students and scholars from the west were studying in the libraries and archives. They found a city of islands, rivers and canals, elegant eighteenth-century embankments, shipyards, tall tenements and untidy courtyards, red brick nineteenth-century factories, and the odd gleaming golden spire. Leningrad was still one of the world's most beautiful cities. It had palaces and grand townhouses, huge wide streets, and city parks where the old women sat on the benches and the children played in the sand. The palaces, museums, and institutes were pale green and white, or yellow and white, or occasionally a pinky red. They were painted every spring, covered with birds' nests of thin wooden scaffolding up which the women painters, in their boots and white headscarves, lugged the buckets of paint. But the shadow of the Siege and the war still hung over the city and lay on the buildings. And the greater part of the population still lived in communal apartments, a room to a family, with all sharing a kitchen and bathroom.

"*Veterany?*" asked the cashier in the art gallery in 1990 when Galina and I reached the head of the queue. "No," we replied, offended to be thought old enough to have fought in the war, but we could have been *blokadniki*, children during the Siege. They too are entitled to free entry to museums and to larger pensions. Several of my friends are *blokadniki*. But for all my generation, those born in the 1930s, whether in Leningrad or elsewhere in Russia, the war stamped itself on their early lives. For the Leningraders, it was the Siege. The long grassy mounds, the communal graves at the Piskaryovskoe cemetery, are the physical monument to the thousands of its victims while the stories, the memories of the survivors, were still part of everyday conversation in the sixties. Even in the 1980s, when interviewing elderly Leningraders for memories of their childhood in the 1920s and 1930s, I found that almost all wanted to talk about the Siege, that was what had seared into their minds. "Next time," I would say, aware that if we started on the Siege I would never get them back to the 1920s.

The children who survived the Siege recognize each other as sharing a common past. The wartime experiences of the students who came from across Russia to Leningrad in the fifties may have been just as brutal as those of their Leningrad peers, but they were different, and for them Leningrad wasn't home. They, and the foreign students, were birds in transit. For them, Leningrad was a treasure house of culture and scholarship where they would spend five years studying and partly studying, surviving on their modest monthly stipends, fall in and out of love, and then depart to faraway places. This at least was true of the students of the history faculty who lived in Mytny, the hostel on the banks of the Neva. The only way to stay in the city was to get one of the scarce places as a graduate student (as Galina did), or to marry a Leningrader. All who were born in Leningrad had resident permits and could, with a little persistence, find employment once they graduated. But for those from the provinces there were two obstacles: first, the system of "redistribution" which obliged graduates to work two or three years in allotted rural schools or small towns and, second, the lack of a residence permit. Devised to counter the magnetic pull of the two capitals, Moscow and Leningrad, the system of residence permits resulted in a subtle social stratification: there were the native Leningraders, who thought of the city as their home by right, knew it and each other; and there were those who, even after twenty years in the city, were still conscious of their provincial roots.

But despite the differences, the generation born in the 1930s had much in common. They had all experienced the war, whether as teenagers or children, and then the hard and hungry postwar years. They were at school or students when Stalin died in 1953, still studying when, in 1956, Khrushchev gave his Secret Speech with its denunciation of Stalin, and they were the first student generation to feel the thaw and the tentative openings in the iron curtain. Among my friends in the early sixties, only one, Volodya Smirnov, was old enough to have fought in the war. It seems appropriate then to begin with his experience of the

Siege before moving on to those too young to have fought, again a marker for those born in the 1930s.

The Siege

Volodya's clothes were of the shabbiest, he had a scar on his head, messy blond hair that I doubt he ever combed, and he lived on a shoestring: his war invalid's pension and intermittent work at a literary archive. His one preoccupation was literature, Russian and French, and this had brought him contacts with the occasional western visitor. He had a curious group of friends, one of whom was a theater-ticket seller who might turn up with, say, five tickets, but if we were six we would swoop in a noisy, bustling group on a helpless theater attendant, confuse her with numbers, and crowd our way in.

One beautiful early summer evening when the pale green Winter Palace and the yellow Admiralty Buildings looked their most serene, with the river in a gentle mood and the lilac out, we were sitting in the Admiralty gardens. I asked him about the Siege. This is what he told me. He was fifteen in 1939 when the Soviet Union declared war on Finland; vodka disappeared from the shops and his father, an alcoholic, drank himself to death on methylated spirits; his mother worked as a conductor on the railways but once the Germans advanced on Leningrad in the summer of 1941 the trains stopped running, she remained at home, in the room they shared in a communal apartment. He lied about his age, enlisted, and was sent to defend the "pocket handkerchief," the tiny scrap of land across the river outside Leningrad now surrounded by the German army. He was lucky to be lightly wounded and was ferried back across the river before the Germans overran the remaining defenses. Then came the Siege and the terrible winter of 1941/42. As a young soldier he had better rations than civilians—a piece of bread and watery soup, another piece of bread and a scrap of salt herring, and a piece of chocolate—and an elderly Jew who lived in the communal apartment used to save him a piece of his even more miserly bread ration. The young soldiers' job was to patrol the streets and see that order was maintained in the bread queues. Sometimes a man or woman, driven mad by hunger, would seize a ration from someone leaving the queue and stuff it in their mouth. The soldiers took such people and shot them down by the river.

The soldiers' billet was in the Alexander Nevsky monastery, at the end of old Nevsky. His mother lived down Ligovsky. On New Year's Eve Volodya went to see her and found her dead, from hunger. The elderly Jew was dead too, and all the furniture (including all his books), except for the bed on which his mother lay, had been burned by a neighbor for fuel. He took his mother's body downstairs, out onto the street, and not wanting her to lie in a communal grave he found a sledge and set out for the churchyard. It was a long walk, bitterly cold, but the priests had a fire and vodka to keep them going; once warm again, he set off to walk back through the night to the barracks. But with still half a mile to go, his legs folded; a man came by, pulled him to his feet, telling him to keep walking or die. He made it to the monastery, dragged himself up the stairs to the room where the soldiers slept. Some were playing cards, and when he appeared a shout went up, and the betting took a new turn—on how long he would live, with his coat and boots as the stakes. That was the custom.

He decided to make one last bid for survival. He got himself downstairs and across the courtyard to a nearby hospital where he lay down in the corridor together with others. A harassed doctor, nurse, and hospital administrator, desperate over the overcrowding, decided to send as many as possible to another hospital. He remembers being loaded as part of a pile of bodies onto an open lorry, whose two drivers tried unsuccessfully to find a hospital willing to take them in. The only course of action, they decided, was to tip the people out in front of a hospital, ring the bell, and drive off fast. And so he ended up, by great good fortune, in a hospital for war-wounded where there was food. But, by now, he could no longer eat, his tongue had swollen up, and he was slowly dying. A huge and very hungry Georgian who occupied the neighboring bed told Volodya, too weak to resist anyway, that he would cure him in return for his food. He seized Volodya's jaw, held his tongue, and forced a piece of salt herring and a slug of vinegar down his throat, then held Volodya's jaw tight shut while he retched, and retched. He repeated the treatment at intervals, and in the meantime ate Volodya's gruel and bread and soup. After a few days he stuffed a piece of bread down, and then Volodya began to eat again. The doctors never knew. When Volodya recovered, he was sent out of the city to the front, and fought through the war, receiving wounds that gave him a full invalid's pension. Back in Leningrad, he worked in a factory for two years before getting a place at the university to study French literature. Although more critical of the Stalinist past, and of the Soviet present, than my student friends, Volodya never doubted that the October revolution had brought enormous benefit to the poor and that the ideal of socialism was good, while the reality of capitalism left much to be desired.

El'mar and His Friends

In the late fifties contact between the Soviet Union and the west was cautiously reestablished. In 1957, at an International Youth Festival held in Moscow, for the first time since the 1930s young Russians could meet and mingle with foreign students from the west. El'mar Sokolov, a young philosopher from Leningrad, blatantly ignoring the conventions of the time, took a British student back home with him to stay for a fortnight. When they eventually went to register with the police, Jim was given a ticket to leave the following day and a KGB colonel came to visit the family apartment. Thus began El'mar's acquaintance with visiting British students. The National Union of Students began to organize trips. In September 1959, after working for a month as shop assistant and waitress to earn the £30 it cost, I went on a three-week visit to Moscow, Leningrad, and Kiev. It was on that trip, introduced by an Oxford friend, that I met El'mar, "small, fair, with screwed-up eyes," I wrote in my diary. He took three of us out on the train to Pushkin to walk in the park, and then home to the family apartment in the Botanical Garden where we drank Moldavian wine and ate cabbage pies.

Over the next two years we corresponded—I wrote about visiting workers' councils in Yugoslavia, about Marx's 1844 manuscripts and Isaiah Berlin's *Two Concepts of Liberty*. He asked if I could get him a copy. We discussed George Orwell and what a communist society might look like. In subsequent years our correspondence would avoid such dangerous topics. Letters from abroad were opened and read. However, had anyone suggested to either of us, when we met again in the early sixties, that twenty years later the possession of Orwell's *1984* would feature in a KGB indictment we would have laughed. Similarly, the idea that contact between the two sides would, for the next thirty years, be limited to official exchanges would have seemed absurd.

In 1941, with the German advance on Leningrad, El'mar's parents had moved the family into the city, into the Botanical Institute. Upon the death of the director, El'mar's father took his place. This gave them a large three-room apartment on the top floor of the old building that stands just inside the Botanical Garden. El'mar was eight, his sister six, and there was also their grandmother. Both parents, born into lower-middle-class families in provincial Russia before the revolution, had joined the party before arriving as botany students in Leningrad in the late twenties. They never doubted the rightness of Communist Party rule and the superiority of socialism over capitalism. They did not register their marriage (an unnecessary bourgeois convention) until the 1950s, and they named their son, born in 1932, El'mar, in honor of Engels, Lenin, and Marx. Among his colleagues El'mar's father was referred to as "a real communist": by this they meant his dedication to furthering the study of botanical science in the interests of mankind and his helping people in need. He supported the relatives of those arrested and sought ways to send any colleagues at risk out of the city on research assignments. When, in response to a campaign from above, party members in the institute submitted critical comments on the political awareness of fellow colleagues, he simply locked the fat dossier away in a cupboard. He refused the offer of a dacha: it was too much like private property. And when, in the course of an argument about marital fidelity in which he referred to communist morality, El'mar responded angrily with "to hell with your party," he sat down on the bed and wept.

By that time, 1960, El'mar himself was a party member, that was part of the problem. But what of his childhood? Living in the Botanical Garden, given over to gardening allotments during the war, surely contributed to the family's survival, and school provided a close-knit group of lifelong friends. By the time I met this group of friends in 1961, all scientists except for El'mar, all had been married but they frequently changed their wives or girlfriends and spent little time with their children. As boys during the blockade, teenagers during the postwar years,

The boys from Petrogradskaya. Dima is sitting second from left and El'mar and Volodya are third and fourth from left. (courtesy of Tamara Sokolova)

and students when Stalin died, they grew up under conditions of great hardship. El'mar was from the most privileged family. Yury, whose father was killed in the war, was solid and quiet. Both he and dark-haired Volodya, who sang hauntingly, played the guitar. Dima, who looked like the young Maxim Gorky, had lost both parents. He lived with an aunt and was too poor to buy boots for winter. Leva's father was an engineer who talked of writing his memoirs: *The Grimace of Communism*. Perhaps it was from him that Leva, as a boy, became critical of the regime. One day during the war he tore all the pages out of his notebook and wrote fascist anti-communist slogans that he then distributed. He spent two days in the KGB headquarters, where he was given hot meals. His parents were summoned, but all were then released. Subsequently the head teacher would periodically summon him, hit him on the side of the head, and say he hoped he had not been writing any more propaganda. After the war they were joined by Oleg, trimly turned out in gaiters and very proud in a new jacket, until El'mar reduced him to tears by squirting it with ink. How could he now go home, he wept, as his mother had spent their savings on it? El'mar felt not contrite but embarrassed, and took him home, where his grandmother scolded him roundly, cleaned the jacket, and sent a note to Oleg's mother.

The boys from Petrogradskaya. El'mar is second from left and Leva and Yury are fourth and fifth from left. (courtesy of Tamara Sokolova)

When the war ended, they were bored and restless teenagers, facing extra years at school because of wartime interruptions. In the Botanical Garden there were fruit trees. El'mar would report to the group when he heard that the fruit was to be picked and that night they would strip as much as they could. Once they climbed into the conservatory and were bathing naked when a commission, headed by El'mar's father, walked in; they scampered out of the windows and fled through the park, causing consternation. Leva's favorite game was to lie on a step of a dark staircase, terrifying a pensioner as she trod on the soft body. Another prank involved blocking the pensioner's path by tying a piece of thin wire between the letterboxes on two front doors facing each other on the landing; as she moved onto the landing and the wire tightened, the letterboxes clattered down. After three attempts she would be assailed by the householders, furious that a pensioner was knocking at their doors. Yury and Volodya would walk down the street a few paces apart with a thin piece of wire tying the earflaps on their hats together and catch unsuspecting pedestrians across the face.

But the postwar years were a rough and brutal time. The boys fought the gangs from the other side of the river. Together they traveled out of the city and exploded the old bombs or barrels of gunpowder they came across. They took the revolvers they found back to school and fired at the blackboard when the teacher was not looking. (In the thirties the kids of their age hid on darkened landings in apartment blocks and used catapults to break the windows of apartments across the courtyards.) They celebrated the end of exams by drinking in the beer bars on Nevsky Prospect. On one occasion El'mar was picked up by the police and spent the night in the police station; Leva wandered off and fell into the frozen river by the Hermitage. Luckily he kept his head and shoulders above the ice, and a man pulled him out. On another, celebrating El'mar's birthday, they raided his grandmother's chest and threw all the jars of preserves down the backstairs.

In 1952 El'mar and Dima went to Leningrad University to study chemistry, Volodya and Yury to the Technological Institute, Leva and Oleg to medical institutes. In 1955 El'mar, Dima, and a group of women students were told they were being transferred to the Technological Institute. Outraged, they wrote complaints. For three months El'mar collected his stipend but refused to attend classes. When, finally, one of the girls' fathers used his Moscow connections, all were allowed to return to the university. Why had El'mar and Dima been picked for the transfer? Perhaps because they were not good students, but perhaps because they were the only two in their course who had refused to specialize in secret work.

With the exception of El'mar and Oleg, all were living in very cramped conditions. Yury's were perhaps the worst: not only did he live with his mother and sister in one room in a communal apartment but, to supplement the family income, his mother rented out a corner to a young woman lodger. Housing was scarce in Leningrad even before the war, much scarcer afterwards. The apartments in the old buildings gradually became home to several families, each with a room (often divided up with bookcases and wardrobes) but sharing the kitchen (with more than one stove), one toilet, and bathroom. Queuing for the lavatory in the morning was a fine art. The entrance hall was a common space; usually the telephone was there. There was little privacy in a communal apartment. Leva used to send Yury postcards, requesting him to come for his second checkup for venereal disease—postcards that would be read by all the apartment's inhabitants, as would the summons to appear in court that they sent each other.

If (a rare occurrence) the apartment housed one family (as did El'mar's), there were often three generations—grandmother, parents, and when a child married, he or she brought husband or wife in too. El'mar married a fellow chemist, Albina. She moved in, and they had a son, but Albina and El'mar's parents did not get on and the young family moved to her mother's communal apartment. But before long El'mar had moved back to live with his parents. Dima, the orphan, met and started going out with the daughter of a wealthy cultured professor who had a seven-room apartment. Her family did not approve of Dima but his friends had already decided how they would allocate the rooms between them once the apartment belonged to him. Alas, after four years, she met a man who, unlike Dima, wanted to take her to the theater. Everything fell apart, she married him, Dima wept.

The shortage of housing both encouraged early marriages and made them fraught affairs. Yury had married, got a single room, but once divorced he and his ex-wife had no option but to remain in the single room. When Leva's girlfriend was thrown out of the room she was renting and had nowhere to go, he gloomily moved her and her bags into his room, and a month later they married, but not for long. By 1961 he was parting company with his second wife and child, and by 1963 living in a two-room apartment with his third wife, Valya, and her mother. Very often an elderly mother was part of the household, helpful when it came to child minding but often critical of the new son- or daughter-in-law.

While still studying chemistry, El'mar realized it was philosophy that interested him and he signed on as an external student at the university. But upon graduating, with two degrees, he had difficulty finding a job. Yury signed him on as a lab assistant. He never actually went to the institute, except to collect the wages that he shared with Yury. But then he struck lucky. The Herzen Institute, the pedagogical institute, offered him a post in the philosophy department, which was where he was teaching when I came to Leningrad as a graduate student in 1961.

Now we talked about more lighthearted things, but I was puzzled that he was a party member. He had not joined, he said, from a sense of commitment to a cause but because the head of his philosophy department, an old party worker, suggested he should; to refuse was difficult and could well put obstacles in a philosopher's career, and, anyway, why should it affect his actions? I was slightly shocked when he said to me "I don't really feel myself to be a communist, but I do feel Russian." An impractical and errant philosopher, eternally inquisitive about all things, his main concern since childhood had been to be free to do what he wanted. In the sixties he largely achieved this. He could read the books he wanted, he had access to the "special collection" of closed books, those that the censor had deemed unacceptable for the everyday reader; he had time to write, and the critical official reception of his book *Culture and Personality* only added to his reputation. His party membership required little more than attendance at meetings. He was fortunate to be employed in departments where his unorthodox views were forgiven — although, on occasion, when he defended colleagues or students accused of politically unacceptable behavior, his mentors rounded on him for his political stupidity.

El'mar was not concerned to do battle with the system. There were, he argued, ways to get round it. The system was like a Soviet fence — there always hung an "Entrance Forbidden," but if you walked on a little you could find a hole. From him I learned that party membership said little about political views. Who but he would choose, when lecturing to Intourist guides in 1962, to talk about Orwell's *1984*, and when approached afterwards by a young man from the censor's office, ask if he would lend him *Animal Farm*? And he would take risks. He lent me a copy of the transcript, a highly sensitive document, of a meeting that had been organized by one of the university departments to discuss the theme "Fathers and Sons" and which had got out of control. Students had voiced their criticisms of the older generation for failing to speak out earlier and of being insufficiently critical of the political present. It was a time when those in the prison camps, upon receiving a pardon for a political crime they had not committed, might return to a department, still peopled by colleagues who had denounced them. On principle, they would vote against whatever such colleagues proposed. Sometimes the ashtrays flew.

El'mar Sokolov.

El'mar and his friends rarely talked about politics but I was aware they were more critical than my younger hostel friends. They would tease El'mar on account of his party membership. Leva was the most openly critical, and to an extent that shocked me. When camping out in the woods held by the Germans during the Siege, he would argue the good points of Nazism compared with Stalinism. Traveling out to the forest in winter to ski through the pine forests and over the bumpy frozen sea, and in spring and summer to walk, make bonfires, camp by the lakes and catch crayfish, in autumn to gather mushrooms and berries, this was an important part of their existence. We would travel out to the Finnish gulf, to wherever someone had rented a room in a dacha. We drank a great deal. These excursions always involved lengthy telephoning, catching the train after the one intended, then sometimes standing, sometimes sitting on the wooden seats, among old and young, reading newspapers, clasping saplings ready for planting or skis, holding rucksacks, sturdy baskets, and enamel buckets. Forty minutes out of the city, the train was traveling past woods and small villages and dacha colonies in the huge snowy fields. The dacha in which El'mar and friends had rented a room in the winter of 1961/62 had a huge stove in each room, to be lit on arrival, a kitchen with a gas stove, but no water. Two big beds and a table, chairs, and a cupboard completed the furnishings. We skied through the woods and down the hills, everyone on the long light Finnish skis. It's very beautiful in the pinewoods. One evening, we all went to walk on the frozen sea, covered over with snow, under a shining moon.

Later, in the seventies, when the city shops were barer, we would buy anything the local shop had, not just bread, alcohol, and salami. If, on a summer's day, they were selling frozen whitefish by the kilo, each of us would take it in turns to carry two kilos of defrosting fish wrapped in newspaper in a rucksack. But that is to run ahead. For the moment we are still in the early sixties.

The Romankov Twins

Liuba and Leonid Romankov, twin brother and sister, also Leningraders, born into an academic family in the late thirties, spent their childhood in the large family apartment on Tchaikovsky Street in the city center. Their father and mother both worked in the Technological Institute, whose staff and families were due to be evacuated as the Germans approached. At the last moment the large families were crossed off the list. So, together with parents, grandparents, and older sister, the four-year-old twins remained in the city. Evacuation sometimes split up families, children from parents, and some never found each other again. When the factory where Galina's father worked was evacuated from Tula to the Urals and families went too, her parents smudged her passport to make her the same age as her older sister, in the hope that this would at least keep the children together. By the time they returned, after the war, it was easier to leave the passport smudged as it was.

Marina, another St. Petersburg friend, evacuated with her kindergarten, was only found by a stroke of good luck by her parents who had lost hope as they searched for her.

The Romankov twins were too young to understand the dangers and the horror of the first winter of the Siege. They played in the yard with the other children, greeted the whistle and thump of a shell in a neighboring courtyard with a joyful cry, and rushed to see who could find the largest fragment of hot shrapnel. Liuba kept her trophies in a large box but, alas, one day she added something that ticked and, that night, her mother threw the whole box in the Neva. Their mother changed her job, to work in a maternity hospital nearer home, but that still meant she was out all day and the children were left to their own devices. When a bomb hit the block of apartments next door, the children scavenged. Liuba's trophy was a pair of elegant silver candlesticks. Occasionally their mother would bring something home for the children. They hated cod liver oil. They loved wood glue, a prized possession in the Siege. They had a stock of it, from which their mother would dole out a spoonful, like a medicine. They swapped their cat for a loaf of bread. Cats and dogs disappeared, rats flourished.

For a while the family, together with others from the courtyard, used a suffocating underground shelter at night. The children hated this and would grow hysterical. At some point it was abandoned, and Liuba and Leonid slept in a cupboard, convinced it was safer. The windows of one room of their apartment had been blown out. However, as the months dragged past, as food grew scarcer and scarcer, and the temperature dropped and dropped, they and their older sister spent the day cuddled together in a bed in the one room they could heat. They were waiting for their mother's return from work. They were fortunate to have some fuel. Each apartment had its storehouse in the yard, and their grandfather had laid in a store of logs in the summer. No one stole from it.

By the spring the water supply and sanitation had failed. They fetched water from the Neva, and all the residents deposited their night soil in a large pit dug in the courtyard. In the summer of 1942, when the worst was over, they were allocated an allotment in the Field of Mars, the huge park-parade ground not far from where they lived, and here

Leonid Romankov. (courtesy of Leonid Romankov)

they planted vegetables. Alas, when they came to dig up the carrots, they found that someone had done it the night before. They spent the next three years undernourished, but surviving. Their grandparents were evacuated by plane to Moscow, but not before grandmother had taught the children to read. This was something that their mother always found time for. When schooling started again, after the war, they were way ahead.

By the early sixties, when I met them, both Liuba and Leonid were physicists, engaged in research. Sheelagh, a graduate student from Glasgow with whom I shared a room in the student hostel, had become part of their close-knit circle of friends. We celebrated the New Year of 1962 way out in the country, beyond the 40 kilometer limit for foreigners. Once back in England I wrote,

Liuba Romankova. (courtesy of Liuba Myasnikova)

Siverskoe is a big straggling village with a collective farm and fenced in market but, beyond the frozen lake, rows of little dachas are set in small gardens. We all sat in one room and tried to keep warm by smoking cigarettes and telling anecdotes. There were two girls with black sweaters and heavy eye shadow looking very decadent and western who sat on the bed, idly thumbing a Polish film magazine. The electricity found it a strain to feed the lights, the tape recorder, and the rotating Christmas tree machine, and once every half-hour everything fused. By quarter to midnight we were starving hungry. There were eleven bottles of champagne, perhaps seven of vodka, and ten of wine for the fifteen of us. At midnight, as the salute from the Kremlin cannons came over the wireless, we drank the champagne with the lighted Christmas tree rotating wildly. Then the jazz was on full blast, the vodka opened, and there were sausages and hot potatoes and pickled gherkins. Everyone got drunk very quickly and jived madly. Someone threw a volleyball through one of the windows. One of the girls, with a weak heart, had hysterics when she found her boyfriend kissing another girl and had to be put to bed. I got more drunk than I have ever been. I threw up and then went to sleep on one of the couches. Some went to bed and some didn't.

By ten next morning everyone was as spry as could be, playing volleyball, and the boys went to have baths in the snow. All the empty bottles were taken off to the village and exchanged for more red wine and vodka, so for breakfast it was vodka and tea. I felt awful. Bob and I went for a walk through the village and ended up at a beer shack where he nearly had a fight with two men for no reason. At the age of fifteen he had a fight with three policemen outside the Velikan cinema, broke the wrist of one and the jaw of another who, unfortunately, swallowed his whistle. Bob only got off from a heavy prison sentence because his mother, an old Party member and a doctor, provided a medical certificate stating that a boy of fifteen could not have done that much damage, and she paid the judges. Several have had scraps with the police. Little Vitya Rimsky-Korsakov who is very dapper and whose aim in life is to look like Anthony Eden (once he saw a photograph of him in a white dinner jacket and has never got over it), recently asked a man in a telephone kiosk if he would hurry up and finish his conversation. When the man came out he hit Vitya, who naturally hit him back. A crowd collected, the police came, and the man accused Vitya of insulting him, a Jew; this enraged Vitya because he is one of the few who always object to anti-Semitic remarks.

This, and my accounts of El'mar's friends, makes it sound as though drinking and socializing together was the main preoccupation or pastime of this generation. But that of course was not true. They were all engaged in research or teaching in different scientific fields, but I knew nothing of science, or of their work. Abstract art, jazz, Hemingway, Salinger were the aspects of the west that interested them, not its politics. Liuba and Leonid took sport seriously, and Liuba became interested in ballet. When Rudolph Nureyev came as a seventeen-year-old to the ballet school in 1955, his teacher Alexander Pushkin and his wife gave him a

Mary and Bob celebrating the New Year on the Finnish gulf.

home and wanted him to have friends. They asked the Romankov parents to introduce him to the twins. They became a second family to him. His flight to the west in the summer of 1961 was still major news when we were there and, when we returned to the UK in the summer of 1962, Sheelagh brought a large soft toy for Nureyev from Pushkin. We delivered it to the stage door with a message. Many years later Liuba told me that Pushkin's wife used to receive phone calls from Nureyev— she was not afraid to speak to him—and sometimes she would alert Liuba that a call was coming. But, as Liuba said, she and Rudik, as they called Nureyev, could not say anything interesting to each other. It was 1987 before they saw each other again.

In the early sixties most of those whom I met took it for granted that the Soviet system led the world in its free medical care, education, and absence of unemployment, and that the aim of its leaders' foreign policy was to promote peace and provide aid to underdeveloped countries. The conviction that, despite its faults, the social and political order in the USSR was "more progressive" than that in the west was probably shared by the great majority of Russian students in the 1950s and 1960s. The Stalinist past was past. The west was a strange, exotic place, a place they wanted to visit, but it was not seen as a model. Very few protested, even silently, against the Soviet intervention in Hungary in 1956. At a meeting in the hostel organized by the students from East Germany, everyone present recognized the building of the Berlin Wall was a necessary measure. It was a time when spies and foreign agents were taken very seriously, a time when, for its youth, the country was perceived to have a future—a different and better future. No one among my new friends, Russians in their twenties, took seriously Khrushchev's promise of reaching communism by 1980, but improving the standard of living and doing things differently seemed quite feasible. It was not that anyone expected sudden change. Certain things, everyone recognized, such as freedom to travel to the west, would take a long time in coming. But when I said to El'mar in 1961, at the time of the new Communist Party program that announced communism by 1980, as we stood on our skis in a snowy forest: "Well, at least under communism you will be able to travel," I was only joking. It could not take *that* long. Gagarin flew into space, students cheered and hung sheets out of the hostel windows.

And that brings us to those who came from across the Soviet Union, and from abroad, to study in Leningrad. How had I come to be there in 1961?

2

Stalin's Children

Birds in Transit

My interest in Russia had first been awakened at school, through history and literature. My sympathies were firmly with the radicals, wherever they appeared, and the Russian revolutions of 1905 and 1917 were even more exciting than the French revolution. I explained this to the tutors at my Oxford interview and graduated with my interest in Russia undiminished, but now it was the Soviet present that had captured my attention. The literature was sparse. American textbooks suggested a society of terrorized and indoctrinated individuals, whereas in Soviet publications a society of equals worked, danced, and improved their educational levels. Both versions seemed to me highly dubious, and there was, I felt, no way I could discover the truth at Oxford.

My time at Oxford coincided with the emergence in Britain of the New Left: a broad intellectual coalition of socialists of different generations and persuasions, some Marxists, others not, but all committed to the idea of creating a democratic socialist order in place of the existing capitalist west and communist east. Khrushchev's Secret Speech of February 1956 denouncing Stalin, and then the Polish and Hungarian uprisings, produced a rethinking and realignments. But what kind of a society and politics was that of the Soviet Union? I had returned baffled from that first visit in 1959. "I had hoped," I wrote, "to get my ideas clear but this proves impossible. If only I could talk Russian." I bought a copy of *Teach Yourself Russian*, arranged with a fellow student for a lesson each week in return for half a bottle of whisky each term, and learned to read Russian.

I was fairly clear that both western capitalism and Soviet communism were deeply flawed. I was not sure about Yugoslavia. Perhaps with their workers' councils the Yugoslavs had found the way to end alienation, bureaucratization, and a hierarchical system of power? In 1960, a chance meeting in the Yugoslav consulate with a Serb engineer, who gave me his family's address in Belgrade, gave me the opportunity to find out. With a friend I hitchhiked down through Italy and over to Greece, and while he went to Mount Athos to look at monasteries I headed for Belgrade and its factories. I sat, sipping *slivovitsa* and Turkish coffee, discussing industrial production and the workers' councils with their representatives, taking notes before touring the plants. By now I knew the question I wanted to answer—was Marx right in claiming that the type of ownership and control in the workplace determines the character of the social and political order? I would study the settlement of labor disputes in Russia and find out.

In 1959 the British Council and the Soviet Ministry of Higher Education had agreed on ten-month research visits for graduate students. "Somewhere beyond the Urals," I wrote in my application in 1960, which was rightly rejected—foreigners only went to Moscow or Leningrad, and anyway I needed to come to grips with the literature and to improve my Russian. I approached St. Antony's, a graduate college where the Russia specialists in Oxford were to be found and whose Monday evening seminars I had attended as an undergraduate. I had learned little from hearing elderly émigrés discuss issues with (as I learned many years later) British academics with histories in the security services and did not mind their turning me down—on the grounds that I was a woman. There was nobody there who could supervise a graduate student with a thesis on labor disputes in the USSR. I stayed at my women's college, Somerville, and was given Hugh Clegg, a labor relations specialist at Nuffield College, as my supervisor. By 1964, when Sheila Fitzpatrick enrolled at St. Antony's as a graduate student studying Soviet history, the policy had changed, but she still referred to it as "the spy college" and when, later that year, I was invited to give a talk on my research in Leningrad, and Hugh Clegg came and sat in the front row, I felt a frisson run through the St. Antony's audience. I didn't understand why, not even afterwards when I heard one of the regulars say to another, "He certainly *was* a member of the Communist Party."

In 1961 I was given a place on the British Council exchange. By now I had worked out my thesis topic, could read Russian, and had started on the literature. In September 1961 I packed a large tin trunk with all my clothes, my mother's old fur coat, a catering size tin of Nescafé, and a year's supply of Tampax (neither instant coffee nor sanitary towels were available in Russia), and sailed, with the other graduate students, in the prestigious Soviet cruise ship, the *Baltika*, from Tilbury to Leningrad.

Mytny

The hostel on the Neva known as Mytny had been home to students from across Russia, from Central Asia and the Caucasus, since the 1920s. With an unrivaled view of the Winter Palace and within walking distance of the main Leningrad University building, the humanities faculties, library, cafeteria, and the Academy of Sciences with its library, it was prized accommodation. The memoirs that exist of life in its early years portray individuals and concerns that I can recognize from the early sixties: the apolitical students, the homesick ones from far away, and older activists committed to the cause. By the sixties life was easier, everyone knew something about politics and no one whom I knew was quite as dedicated as those early civil war communists. There were a few who organized the *subbotniki* (spring cleaning), but they were not among my friends nor did they tend to mix with students from the west. East Europeans had appeared in the 1950s and in 1961, under the new cultural exchanges, a handful of western graduate students—ten Americans, four Brits, and two French—found themselves in Mytny. We were the only people from the west in the city. A year later the Americans and Europeans were moved out to a new brick-built hostel at the far end of Vasilevsky Island, now two to a room but still with hot water for just a few hours once a week. A new contingent of students from Africa took our places in Mytny.

The hostel's entrance lobby with its heavy drapes and heavy arm-chairs, a bronze cupid, a great gilt mirror, and pots of huge aspidistras had probably changed little since the twenties. A white bust of Lenin, a red banner proclaiming *Lenin lived, Lenin lives, Lenin will live*, and a poster of the Politburo members greeted all seeking access to the stairs. The three porters worked shifts, kept a tally of visitors, and handed out mail from pigeon boxes. There was a public phone box, from which, for the standard 2 kopecks, calls could be made and calls could come in—but whether messages were received depended upon whether someone actually answered the phone and was prepared to go up to the room in question. Visitors were meant to leave by 10:30. The heavy outer door was locked at 1 a.m. Hammering on the door might wake the porter sleeping in a chair, or it might not. Enterprising students climbed up and in through a first-floor window. But this was only possible in late spring and summer. When the cold weather came we padded and taped up the big double windows in our rooms, leaving only a little window to let fresh air in from time to time.

Sheelagh and I, the only two women on the British Council ex-change, were allocated beds in a large room on the fifth floor, looking out over the river. Our room had four beds instead of the more usual six (hospital beds with springs and thin mattresses, and clean sheets issued once a fortnight). The floor was painted dark red, the walls green and white. Twice a year we repainted the floor. There were large brown wooden cupboards, small cupboards by each bed, a bookcase, a large table, usually littered with crockery, four chairs which laddered our stockings, and a very large mirror. Oh, and the wireless on the wall. This shut down at midnight after the national anthem and Kremlin chimes, only to come on again with a repeated musical chime at 6 a.m. if we had forgotten to turn it off. Sometimes we did. Then it was usually Sheelagh who, in a rage, got out of bed to silence it. And, once we had taped up the windows, leaving only the little window for air, a further bone of contention arose. Should it be left open at night? Strongly held competing opinions sometimes produced a silent war between tiptoeing opponents at two in the morning.

The lavatories were unspeakable and washing facilities minimal: hot water on Tuesdays and Thursdays from 2 to 4 p.m. For washing we usually used the public baths. Most of the Leningrad population made use of the public baths. Washing facilities, whether in a communal apartment or in a hostel, were minimal. And men would make it a social occasion because a good bathhouse had a beer bar too. The one Sheelagh and I went to had a huge cloakroom for coats and boots, great leather chairs, the cashier's booth, a beer bar, and a place to buy soap, towels, or vests. There were tickets for the public bath, for a private room, the showers, the steam room, or even for the hairdresser. The first room of the public bath, with its white benches and mirrors, was where you undressed and left your clothes. The underwear and the size of huge Russian matrons was a sight to be seen. Then, clutching your bit of soap and back scratcher, you passed through the double doors into a red-tiled inferno full of steam and marble benches. It was vital to commandeer a tin basin, to be filled from a tap of boiling water, and a marble bench because that allowed the ritual of soaping and scrubbing to begin. The firmly held belief was that if you soaped all over five times, you were cleaner than if you did it only twice, and that it took at least three-quarters of an hour to get clean. (The cloakroom attendants would upbraid you for slovenliness if you emerged too soon.) You moved on to the steam room, the higher you climbed the steps, the hotter it became (I could never manage more than two steps) and those with experience beat each other with bunches of birch twigs.

But we still smelled. We may have had our Odorono, the only deodorant available in Britain at the time, but the rooms were overheated, we had very few clothes, and washing was a luxury. Russians, living in communal apartments and with no access to a deodorant, could not but smell. For my younger readers, I add that it was not until the 1970s in Britain (yes?) that washing habits began to change and this, together with a range of deodorants, washing machines, and cheaper clothes, gradually brought into being today's odorless population. The Americans got there sooner. They had deodorants and washing machines, and washed frequently in the sixties. I remember being surprised when I first visited the United States.

The hostel had a buffet where rye bread, pale frankfurters, and eggs were almost always available. On each floor there was a kitchen with gas stoves where we cooked and heated up water for washing ourselves or

Vera Kamyshnikova. (courtesy of Galina Lebedeva)

Galina Lebedeva. (photographed by Nikolai Akimov, courtesy of Galina Lebedeva)

clothes. (Where did we put our clothes to dry? Presumably on the radiators.) Men and women lived on alternate floors and some married students had children who rode their tricycles up and down the wide corridors. Although it was not uncommon to see a drunk student struggling up the stairs, past the large white spittoons and receptacles for cigarette ends, the fights were few and far between. It was a sociable and safe place.

That first Sunday night only Sheelagh and I were in our room. At 6 a.m. Vera, a final year history student, arrived, as surprised to see us as we were to see her. She was back from taking a coach tour to Riga, acting as excursion leader, something she did on alternate weekends. She liked the radio left on so as to wake her at 6 a.m. Usually it only woke us, and we then had to wake her. She stumped about the room making breakfast for her boyfriend, Vitya, who would arrive shortly before seven. On

Mary in the Botanical Garden.

her return two days later, she would make breakfast, and only take her-self to bed by eight to sleep for three hours. By this time both Sheelagh and I would be thoroughly awake and bad tempered. The ability to sleep through noise and bright light is something that Russians, many Russians, possess to a high degree. Our fourth roommate, Lilya, was extraordinarily placid but Vera too could sleep with all three naked light bulbs blazing and the wireless playing.

Lilya was one of five children of a rural schoolmaster and his wife. Her mother worked cleaning floors in a hospital, and only after her husband died had she learned to read—so that she could reply to Lilya's letters coming from faraway Leningrad. Lilya herself had two interests in life: sleeping and makeup. She slept through her final year at university, rising at about midday to apply a heavy coat of makeup. Then, after carefully arranging her headscarf so that little was visible except her eyes and lips, she would go for a short stroll along Nevsky, from whence she would return, sighing over the lack of attractive men (her favorite quotation was from Ilf and Petrov, referring to the streets of Rio de Janeiro, where the men wore white trousers), and, after flicking idly through a copy of *Vogue*, she would have another sleep. Lilya did her hair in a beehive. She might put her curlers in at two in the morning, which required three-quarters of an hour of studious application in front of the mirror. Admittedly she draped the table lamp with a towel or scarf; it usually scorched. She was quite unperturbed when she featured in the photographs that members of the Komsomol committee took in response to complaints from the faculties that students were failing to make even the ten o'clock lectures. Occasionally the committee did a tidiness check and awarded marks or left critical comments: "Comrades, this room is a disgrace! Please clean it up! You are not meant to remove crockery from the buffet!" Specializing in archaeology, Lilya somehow got her diploma and opted for work in a museum in faraway Dushanbe because, given that the work involved dangerous chemicals, it meant a short four-hour day.

If Lilya was easy to live with, Vera from Tambov, who became my closest friend, was less so. Her family had barely made it through the war. Both parents were schoolteachers. Her father returned from the front, half-blinded, in 1943; her mother worked a twelve-hour shift, six days a week, sewing army greatcoats. Her older sister, suffering malnutrition, was sent to grandparents. Vera, three years old when war broke out, spent hours on her own, wrapped up in outdoor clothing, waiting for her mother's return from work. In the late fifties she repeated the entrance exams to Leningrad University to get the sought-after place. Temperamental, self-righteous, a born schoolteacher but endlessly casting herself as a tragic heroine, she would sit till three in the morning, with a towel shading the table lamp, either revising for an examination or writing yet another twenty-page letter of "explanations" to Vitya, who lived on the floor above. My struggle to improve my spoken Russian delighted her. At two in the morning, from her corner of the room would come a drowsy voice: "Merinka, say something," and angry ripostes would follow from Sheelagh and Lilya. She had a good voice, and would practice arias from *Carmen*, striking poses in front of the mirror. Although by nature an optimist, she swung between optimism for the future and predictions of doom. As a historian, job allocation meant either teaching in a school in rural Russia or a far-distant "hard assignment," where the pay would be higher. Having persuaded Vitya to marry her (the wedding party in our room was far from joyful), they departed for Sakhalin, the island off the east coast of Russia. Five years later with a child, Olga, from a second marriage, she returned to Tambov.

Galina, pretty, whose brown eyes and reddish-brown hair brought her the nickname Squirrel, was a few doors down, sharing a room with another history student and the two French students. Dina and Zhivkov's geranium were further down the corridor.

A Student Existence

The student stipend was 29 rubles a month, 35 for an outstanding student, such as Galina. On this you could live—just—by eating in the student cafeteria and cooking frankfurters and potatoes, or cabbage, only splashing out occasionally for a birthday or celebration; parents sent food (preserves, bottled mushrooms) in parcels. Vodka was cheap and the only other alcohol sold in bottles was a horrible port wine or reasonable Georgian wine. By the end of the month, hot water with sugar substituted for tea. You couldn't buy clothes or shoes on your stipend (but then there wasn't anything you wanted to buy in the shops—on one of her trips to Riga, Vera managed to buy me a pair of boots for skiing) but you could afford the cinema, theater, or even the ballet. Transport was cheap: 5 kopecks for the bus, 4 kopecks for the trolleybus, and 3 kopecks for the tram. In winter the tram windows were frozen over, sitting next to them was hazardous, better to stand in the crowded aisle. Not surprisingly, students found work on the side. The occasional

Vera, Galina, Ira, and Lilya outside Mytny.

student worked nights on the trams, but most only looked for a white-collar job. Had I, a university student, really worked as a shop assistant, a waitress, and cleaned floors, they asked in disbelief?

It's a mistake to try to buy anything in the Soviet Union, I wrote in 1962, and an even bigger mistake to try on a Sunday on Nevsky Prospect. (Shops were shut on Monday, not Sunday.) The wide pavements were crowded with people just taking a walk, with the large ice cream sellers in their padded coats and white overalls selling Eskimo ice creams on sticks, sometimes so cold they froze to your tongue, and the lottery ticket sellers were there even when it was snowing, clothed in their thickest fur coats, hats, and huge felt boots with galoshes. The carts selling colored drinking water and the booksellers would disappear, but the pie sellers and the shoe cleaning booths, blocking up the pavements, were there in the worst of weathers. The pre-revolutionary shopping arcade, Gostiny Dvor, with its alleyways and staircases, could defeat even the most committed shopper—booths might shut for a lunch break at any time, and the directions as to where to find particular goods were less than helpful. Who would have thought that zips would be on a leather counter in the electrical section?

Basic foodstuffs—from bread, cheese, and salami to tea and tinned goods—could be bought across the street from the hostel. But it took time. First you would identify what you wanted, then get a price from the assistant, then stand in the queue for the cashier, pay and return with the receipt to queue again, and, finally, collect your purchase. The markets where the collective farmers sold meat, curd cheese, pickled cabbage, and honey and where the Georgians and traders from Central Asia sold fruit, nuts, and spices were, in comparison, Aladdin's caves, but students could not afford the prices. Shoe menders built little booths into the market fences. I eventually found one who agreed to mend my shoes, as a great concession, because I was English. He wrote "Anglia" on a large piece of paper and stuffed it inside them. But when I went back to collect them on Monday, his door was nailed up. He was usually shut on a Monday, the woman in the next-door beer kiosk explained, because he drank himself blind on Sundays. On Tuesday, clasping a bottle of beer, he was there.

We, the westerners, had stipends three times the size of the Russian students. We could shop in the market and buy pork chops from a cafeteria at the back of the Main University Building. We could buy milled coffee from a shop on Nevsky, Bulgarian cigarettes from the cafeteria in the Astoria Hotel, and have coffee and cakes in the new café, Sever, on Nevsky. But so could our older friends, Leningraders, already earning as young scientists, often still living at home with their parents. They lived as well in terms of food and drink, albeit differently, as their counterparts in Britain. They might decide to celebrate a birthday at the Astoria or in the Hotel Europa (two of the prestige hotels in the city), occupy a large table, order more and more food and drink, and then, finding that they did not have enough money for the bill, send one or two of the party home to borrow it, while consuming more. Years later in the nineties none of my friends could afford to drink even tea in these hotels.

In the 1960s there were very few private cars, and none of them were western makes. The British ambassador, Sir Frank Roberts, had the only Rolls Royce in Russia (apart from Lenin's, in a museum). In 1961 he and his wife paid a visit to Leningrad and invited the four British students to lunch in the Astoria, then the grandest hotel. The chef made Baked Alaska to mark the special occasion. "Would you like to borrow the Rolls for the afternoon?" asked Sir Frank. Imagine! Sheelagh and I leapt at the offer and into the car, gave the driver his instructions — Nevsky Prospect, of course. We waved, pretending to be royalty, went to collect a skirt from a dressmaker in a back street, and had the driver circle the student hostel, slowly, in the hope that someone we knew would see us.

We had no contact with the British Embassy in Moscow, or indeed with anyone else from Britain, except at Christmas when we were invited to Moscow to stay with Embassy families, and from where we could make a three-minute call, booked in advance at the main post office, to our families in the UK. There was no telephone connection from Leningrad to the UK but, in an emergency, a telegram could be sent from the main post office. Letters came and went regularly, within a week or two, but they had always been opened and clumsily stuck up again.

What did we bring with us? Women brought Tampax. I had brought some knitting. I taught Vera to knit. *Burda*, a German magazine, was accessible. My mother sent more wool. Vera became a brilliant knitter and, later, as different yarns became available, designed and knitted wonderful jackets. We could receive monthly British journals — *Punch*, whose cartoons of Khrushchev would cause great merriment, and *The Economist*. That was our only access to the western media. What did we buy to take home? Fur hats, gramophone records, a camera, books — I found a map of St. Petersburg from 1914 in the secondhand book shop on Liteiny — oh, and we took black caviar, it cost hardly anything.

Clothes represented a difference. It was not so much that students from the west had more clothes than our Russian peers, but that ours were brighter with variety in design, color, and style that was missing from the Russian clothes. Hence the passionate interest in fashion magazines, in Polish and Hungarian magazines, in shopping in the Baltic states. It was sadly true that winter coats came in one of five colors — brown, black, maroon, navy, and dark green — unless you could afford a fur coat. Clothes were dull. The dazzling contrast between the costumes at a ballet on the Kirov stage and the coats, as the audience queued to collect them at the end of the performance, made the everyday world seem even more drab.

Within a few months both Sheelagh and I had groups of friends, born and brought up in the city, with whom we spent most of our free time. But with friends from the hostel I went to what were probably the most popular theaters or shows in the early sixties. One was the stand-up show by the comedian Arkady Raikin, a brilliant and versatile mimic who took on the absurdities of life and of Soviet bureaucracy. To our huge delight, Sheelagh and I were asked by the university's Foreign Department (responsible for foreign students) to meet with Raikin, who had been approached by a British theater agent, and to help him with his English. We marveled at his ability, with no knowledge of English, to listen and repeat phrases. But, alas, when the BBC brought him to London in 1965 for a television performance we were both in Glasgow.

The students' (and not only the students') most popular theater director of the time was Nikolai Akimov, director of the Comedy Theater on Nevsky. He put on plays that earlier would have been banned and gave students free tickets to the previews. Perhaps the most famous play of the time was Yevgeny Shwartz's *Drakon*, which features a community in thrall to and enthralled by a dragon who exacts a tribute of young virgins. Akimov staged Byron's *Don Juan* and brought onto the stage Tatyana Gnedich, the elderly woman who, sitting in solitary confinement in a prison, had translated Byron's poem from memory into Russian. We clapped every other line. Akimov had a penchant for pretty girls, and Galina found herself invited to his social gatherings or parties. In 1963 even a quite traditional theater staged *Woe from Wit*, a famous Russian classic, in contemporary dress, as a slightly veiled take on the contemporary political scene. A British film, dubbed into Russian, might appear on the cinema screen. *Kind Hearts and Coronets* was prefaced by a short introduction that came over the speakers—a warning not to be beguiled by the humor into thinking the class system was not oppressive—a warning that was met by booing from the audience.

Leningrad was a magical city. In the winter the Neva froze, and a track worn by boots would wind across the ice to the bank on the Hermitage side. In spring as the ice melted, coming downstream from Lake Ladoga, the huge crackling, jostling mass sailed past the hostel windows. The drainpipes on the outside of the buildings discharged, with a

On the frozen Neva outside Mytny.

roar, the snow and ice from the roofs onto the pavements. In June, when the sun never sets, we might spend the night walking the embankments, watching the bridges open. The cemeteries, even the Alexander Nevsky Cemetery with its graves of famous people, were untidy green places; children played round the overgrown graves between the birch trees in the Smolensk graveyard. And outside the city were the famous tsarist palaces with their parks—at Pushkin, Pavlovsk, and Peterhof—destroyed during the war, still being rebuilt in the 1960s, but again places of great beauty and easily accessible by train.

Being English

If someone fell sick, a roommate would ring the medical center and a stout little doctor, all in white, with little boots, would come to check out the patient and write a prescription for someone to take to the chemist. We were all hit with flu in early spring. This was when Leva and a fellow doctor took me to the Sverdlovka for Old Bolsheviks to be treated with hot weights and sandbags on my nose and cheeks, and where I tried my best not to be a stuck-up Englishwoman.

Perhaps now I should explain. There's a short story, "A Daughter of Albion," in which Chekhov, the famous nineteenth-century novelist and playwright, writes of an irascible Russian landowner sitting, fishing without success, on the banks of a river. Beside him, also fishing, is Miss Twice, the children's English governess. He can't stand her. She does not speak a word of Russian and refuses to understand his entreaties to turn her back when he takes his trousers off and, naked as Adam, wades into the water to disentangle his fishing line. Joined by a neighbor, he calls her, among other things, a Triton, with a nose like a hawk . . . the word *chopornaya* does not appear but, for later generations of schoolchildren who read the story, she became the prim and proper, the stuck-up Englishwoman. Only very recently did I come across the story. Just as well, I find myself thinking, the thought of Miss Twice might have made me hesitate before going fishing with Russian friends.

I used to keep my monthly stipend in a card index box. One day it was stolen. Vera's 10 rubles were missing too. Angry and upset, she summoned the police. "Why have you not brought tracker dogs?" she upbraided the two tired detectives who turned up and took away my card index box. Some days later I received a note asking me to come round to the police station—not, as was explained when I arrived, that they were any further forward but that the head of criminal investigation wished to see me. Whether one or both of the two gentlemen who rose to their feet and bowed when the inspector proudly introduced me—"This is Mary"—were from criminal investigation or from the KGB, I do not know. Then, for about two hours, we discussed Chekhov, the Russian character, crime, the British police, and my research. The more senior explained to me that he had wanted to meet me for two reasons: first to suggest (and this was done most delicately) that I should not pass the story of the theft on to any journalists and, second, because he had never met an English person. An hour and a half into the conversation, he confided that he had always thought the English were stuck-up but I wasn't a bit. I gave him a weary smile. How many times had I been told this by different people, each of whom thought he or she was the first to say it? At last, when I was nearly dropping off the chair with exhaustion, we finished the conversation with the hopeful thought that under communism there will be no crime and, as we laughingly agreed, they would be out of jobs. I had hoped they would send me back to the hostel in a police van but, alas, it was a large yellow car with a driver. The Foreign Department reimbursed me, and I gave Vera ten rubles.

Stuck-up. Hmmm . . . fast-forward fifty years. I was in Moscow, taking a taxi. I suggested to a friend, an energetic Russian activist who was late for a meeting, that we could drop her off first. She gladly agreed and scrambled into the back from where, more than once, she treated the driver to bossy and condescending instructions. I, sitting in the front, tried to counter this with sympathetic and friendly interjections. Once she had left us, the driver asked me, "And where are you from?" "I am from England," I replied. "Yes," he said. "As I thought, a stuck-up Englishwoman."

But sometimes I was rewarded. For example, once, in 1962, sitting at a desk in the clerks' room in a district court, working through court cases, I was approached by a burly citizen whose case involved snow falling off his lorry and damaging another vehicle. Clutching his file, unable to decipher the judge's handwriting, he turned to me: "Young woman, please help me, I can't make heads or tails of this." "Well," I said, "please forgive me but I am English." "So what?" he said in exasperation. "Does that mean you can't read?" For once, I was being treated as "one of us," and I happily tried my best. But, of course, I wasn't one of us, and we, the foreign students, and our friends and colleagues knew that too.

KGB

Officially western students were allowed to travel only inside a 40-kilometer limit of the city. Usually, but not always, I kept to it. We accepted that our movements were watched and all our acquaintanceships were known. We also took it for granted that some of the Russians who sought us out had been assigned to befriend us and to report. We did not talk about one set of friends to others. The less one person knew about others, the less he or she would have to hide if questioned.

The KGB kept El'mar under surveillance. Perhaps his father's party reputation gave him some protection. Occasionally he would be called in for a discussion; he would tell me beforehand. Despite keeping his watch a half-hour fast, he was usually a half-hour late for any appointment, but on one such occasion he was over an hour late. I grew more and more anxious and, fearful that my hair was going white, looked every ten minutes in the large mirror, but he had just been standing in a queue somewhere. I had told him about my dealings with MI6, an unnerving story, just in case it was part of my dossier.

In 1959, when the first two graduate students from the Soviet Union came to study at Oxford, one of them to Somerville, a friend who was studying Russian received a letter from the War Office (a government department, incorporated into the Ministry of Defence in 1964) asking if she would be prepared to discuss "a certain matter." We were all intrigued, and when we heard that a fellow student in one of the men's colleges had received a similar letter, we guessed that the matter concerned the Soviet students. My Somerville friend, about to leave for America, suggested that I take her place and I agreed. On the appointed day, a woman arrived from London. With little beating about the bush, she explained that the British government was interested in the type of young Soviet citizen picked to go abroad to study. Would I be prepared to meet, from time to time, with a representative of the War Office and pass on relevant information about "our Soviet friend"? My reaction to the request was mixed. Learning that MI6 also used informers hardly surprised me and I had no desire to be one but, if I refused, the War Office would find someone else in my place. I reasoned that perhaps it was better to agree and then to do nothing. I revealed my naïveté when I virtuously announced that I would not of course repeat anything said to me in confidence.

When Galina, a literature student, arrived, and I invited her to have coffee, I quickly realized that my position was untenable. I would have liked to practice my Russian with her, but felt impossibly restrained and made no attempt to further our acquaintance. Had George Audley, the War Office representative from whom once a term I received an invitation to lunch in the Roebuck or tea in Fullers, been interested in Galina, the fact I barely knew her would have been readily apparent. However, and this puzzled me, he was far more interested in what I and fellow students thought of contemporary politics. I enjoyed instructing, as I thought, a member of MI6 on the need to abolish nuclear weapons. Only at the end of our meal would he say, "And how is our Soviet friend?" and I would answer with something quite empty. Galina left at the end of the year and the War Office never again approached me.

Three years later, to my total consternation, I learned from a friend in the Diplomatic Service that George Audley was none other than George Blake, now serving a forty-two-year prison sentence as a Soviet double agent. The photographs in the press had borne scant resemblance to the man I knew. In 1966 he would escape over the prison wall and make his way to Moscow, but it was 2016 before the story was told on British television and a very elderly and portly George Audley appeared in the snowy lane outside his dacha.

In the early sixties the KGB targeted several British and American students in Leningrad. Typically, the students would receive both subtle blackmail threats (concerning what might happen to their Russian friends) and enticements (a visit to a closed collection in the Hermitage) but, in the cases I knew of, what was required of them remained unclear. I was spared this kind of attention. Why, I don't know.

Many years later, in the cloakroom of the House of Writers, I caught sight of a dapper individual with wavy white hair in air force uniform whose face seemed familiar. Suddenly I placed him: it was Yury, the teacher of English in the Airforce Academy, owner of a car, who in 1961 used to play me old dance records, 78s from the thirties, and fed me cream cakes in the heavily curtained apartment of his parents, who were actors. He gave me two of the records: "Don't Stick Your Nose In, Samurai" and "My Machine-Gun." He used to gaze at me sadly and propose traveling "far far away into the forest where it is calm and quiet." I was not enthusiastic but a drive out of the city was a nice proposition and I didn't know anyone else with a car. I agreed, on condition my friend Sheelagh came, and off we went one Sunday in spring. But instead of the forest we ended up in a garrison town, Luga, far beyond the 40-kilometer limit for foreigners. A few days later Sheelagh was called in by the KGB who suggested that the trip to Luga had been planned. When, at a second meeting, she told "our comrade" (names were never given) that she had told me, he said he would speak to me. A few days later I had a message that "our comrade from the visa department" wanted to speak to me in the university's Foreign Department. At the meeting a middle-aged man gave me a half-hearted ticking off for going outside the limit. He ended the conversation by saying that, should I at any time need help, I could turn to him. I told Yury, and I saw little of him after that. And now, here he was, still fluttering in the way he used to around a woman, holding the red carnations, and checking his trim appearance in front of a big mirror.

Very different was my experience with Sergei who, I learned many years later, was used by the KGB to report on foreigners. On November 7, 1961, I went with Vera to join the parade in Palace Square in memory of the 1917 revolution. We walked past the nameless and faceless party leaders, standing on the podium in their overcoats and neat trilby hats. My friends from the hostel went partly because it was expected of them but also because for them, from the provinces, it was an occasion not to be missed. Later that evening, however, as we sat at the window watching the fireworks display light up the river and the Winter Palace, and as Lenin's head appeared shining brightly high up in the sky, I began to cry from confusion and bewilderment. The evening before Sergei, thin, hollow-cheeked, with his share of steel teeth, in shabby clothes, who used to come to the hostel to borrow English books, had taken me to the celebrations at the Kirov plant. I was terribly excited. My research after all was on labor relations and the Kirov, the famous Putilov factory in 1917, was still the biggest in the city. I don't know quite what I had expected. The evening, held in a large hall, was for all the workers of the shop where Sergei worked as a lathe operator. There was decorous ballroom dancing, lemonade and biscuits, and a general knowledge competition, which Sergei won. Then we wandered off and sat on a park bench in the dark, and I got colder and colder as Sergei told me how, as a student in 1956, he had been arrested and sentenced to a camp for two or three years for quoting "There is something rotten in the state of Denmark" at a student meeting following Khrushchev's Secret Speech. He talked about the camp and others who had been arrested. All next day I felt a heavy stone inside me, and tried, to no avail, to understand how the world of the camps could coexist with the celebrations, the parade, and the lighthearted participation in the festivities by so many, myself included. I lost touch with Sergei. I think he stopped coming to the hostel. But what, I still wonder, was the intention behind the visit to the Kirov, and on whose part? Was Sergei meant to have told me what he did about the camps?

In 1963, when all my requests for permission to go camping with Leva and his wife, Valya, in the Pskov countryside had been turned down, I asked whether I could speak to "our comrade, who offered help in case of difficulty." I was just trying it on, hoping to discomfort the official in the Foreign Department. But he just looked at me calmly before replying, "I am sorry, Mary, but that's not possible. Our comrade has died—you see how stressful it is to work with foreigners."

We traveled, in those years, to the Baltic States, to Novgorod and Pskov, to Moscow, and down to the Black Sea, to Odessa and Yalta, across to Georgia, and then to Tashkent, Bokhara, and Samarkand, but always in an organized group, and always staying in the Intourist hotels. The Russia that stretched to the Urals and on to Siberia remained out of reach, and traveling with a rucksack on one's back was something only my Russian friends could do. El'mar wrote of whitewater canoeing and camping in the northern forests, Volodya of meeting a mother bear and her cubs in a Siberian forest, the twins left for archaeological expeditions and sports training camps in the mountains in the south. Vera left for the islands of Sakhalin. I envied them.

Back to Mytny and on to Gavan

It was a time of more open discussion, and experimentation with forbidden themes, than had been known for the past thirty years. In the hostel we followed the revelations of the 22nd Party Congress, where Khrushchev reopened the theme of repression under Stalin; we read the articles and camp stories, the rehabilitations; with our Leningrad friends we sang the songs of Okudzhava (the most famous ballad songwriter of the period) and told political anecdotes outside of listening walls. Occasionally, in the hostel, we would discuss the latest developments. On one occasion Vera announced that if it were up to her to recommend someone for party membership, she would recommend me—I took my research so seriously—and an awkward silence fell. There were those who refused at first to believe that Stalingrad had been renamed Volgograd and had mixed feelings about the removal of Stalin's body from the mausoleum. But most of the students had no wish to get involved in politics, and it was perfectly clear that it was foolhardy to do so. A student from the Far North was expelled for his careless, critical comments but, if anything, the feeling was that he had been foolish.

I read Solzhenitsyn's *One Day in the Life of Ivan Denisovich* in the public library in the spring of 1963. You had to ask for the copy of the journal *Novy mir* at the desk, sign for it, and read it sitting at a table just in front of the librarian. The pale blue cover was grimy, and the now black-edged pages made the story stand out like a memorial piece. But by then my hostel friends, with the exception of Galina, had graduated and left the city and I, having returned in December 1962 for a further six months, was living in a new graduate hostel in Gavan, at the end of Vasilevsky Island.

Our places in Mytny went to the first cohort of African students, from Nigeria, Mozambique, Tanzania, who came to Leningrad to study for five years. An exception was made for Patrice Lumumba's nephew, who had a room to himself in the graduate hostel and made himself unpopular by his self-importance. Unfortunately relations between the Africans and the Russians deteriorated in Mytny. The Russians were quite unprepared for the African students being smartly dressed and "western." The Africans, who like the students from the west received stipends three or four times those of Soviet students, compared conditions in the hostel unfavorably with those back home, criticized the food, and asked to live apart from Russians. They organized a committee and held a meeting to voice their demands. Many were model hostel inhabitants, but they took their holidays in Paris or London. Russians responded at first with bewilderment, then rationalization ("they must all be the sons of very rich Africans"—perhaps in some cases true), and then with racism. I found myself sharing at least part of a common culture with some of the English-speaking Africans. The Nigerians (I think) wanted to talk about cricket; they asked if I would pass on any British newspapers and *The Economist*. Russian students were confused. Surely I was one of the oppressors? While I was pleased that a simplified picture of imperialism had come under question, I was uncomfortably aware that I found it easier to establish ordinary friendly relations with the Africans in Leningrad than in Britain.

But you, the reader, may be saying in surprise and perhaps irritation, "This is all quite interesting, but were you doing any work?"

3

Studying Labor Disputes in the 1960s

Apart from El'mar, and a little with Leva, political discussion—even of an intellectual kind—almost never featured. The camps and Stalinist repression came on the agenda but the questions that exercised us in the west—Had the Mensheviks been right, or Trotsky? Was there a new class? How did one move beyond state socialism? How did one prevent a meritocracy arising?—simply had no place. Neither a politics nor a sociology faculty existed. Given that my thesis topic was labor disputes in industrial enterprises, I was sent to the law faculty, housed out at Smolny, not far from the prestigious girls' school taken over by the Bolsheviks in 1917, which became the city's Communist Party headquarters. The blue and white Smolny cathedral still stood, adjacent, and the Tauride Palace was just down the road.

In early September 1961, still an inadequate linguist, I took the number 7 bus, found the building, negotiated the cloakroom, and made my way, with some trepidation, to the dean's office. The dean himself led me though the winding corridors to the labor law department and handed me over. Concerned surprise greeted my unexpected arrival in the middle of a department meeting, which, I subsequently learned, could last several hours. On that first occasion I sat on a chair and smiled, uncomprehendingly, for about an hour. Then silence fell and one of the members turned to me. "Please," he said, "tell us about English law." I tried, in my halting Russian, to explain that I was not a lawyer.

The Law Faculty, Factories, and Courts

I was fortunate that the department was concerned with improvements to the Labor Code and with strengthening the role played by the trade unions and the courts at a time when such issues were on the political agenda. It was standard practice for law students to spend time observing and collecting data in factories, courts, and the prosecutor's office. My topic was a straightforward one and my supervisor, Alexei Stepanovich Pashkov, treated me as though I were one of his graduate students. I had to master the legal literature and then I would do my practical work in the courts, and in the factories. I learned how a small department with five faculty members and three graduate students worked, and how it set itself collective projects. For example, in honor of the Party Congress we did a study of illegal overtime in Leningrad enterprises. I grew used to enormously long meetings held to discuss teaching timetables, a recent piece of legislation, or each other's work. We discussed the new Communist Party program, and Pashkov jovially countered my skepticism that in the course of twenty years differences between urban and rural Russia, and mental and manual labor, would be done away with in the USSR, but we did not pursue points such as these. There were rules for public discussion and I knew that, even privately, he would feel it to be his responsibility to defend the party line to me. It did not affect our working relationship nor did my presence affect the discussion at department meetings. What was said subsequently at party meetings or reported to the Foreign Department may have been another matter.

Because our command of Russian was poor, a fellow student, Barry, and I had intensive Russian classes. We had to make it across the bridge from Mytny, past the maritime museum, the Kunst Kamera, Academy of Sciences, and the Main University Building to the philology faculty for conversation, composition, essay writing, reading, and phonetics classes. Our phonetics textbook had been designed for Chinese students. I struggled. Our elderly phonetics teacher praised Barry's good pronunciation while she kept me on the first verse of the same Lermontov poem for three months. However, I got my own back with literature, where the task was to read a novel a week and recount the storyline. Someone told me how to do it. "Read the last paragraph on every tenth page, and see if that doesn't enable you to follow the story." Amazingly, it worked. But we were also in demand as the only native English speakers in the city. "Would you not, please," asked an elderly philologist, "make a recording?" Reluctantly I agreed, and found myself in a booth faced with a book whose first exercise began with the line "The wee greedy bee sat on the bleeding keeper's knee." The recording was not, I fear, a success.

Much of my time was spent in the public library, reading the legal journals and books. It had an excellent catalogue and book reserve system. The only hazard was to find the cloakroom full and thus have to queue until one of the disabled war veterans who staffed it could hand you a token in return for hanging up your coat. The reading room was always full, sometimes pensioners had a nap, heads on their books. But every three hours the huge windows would be opened to air the room and in winter icy blasts sent everyone scurrying for the smoking room (with its dense fog of cigarette smoke), the cafeteria, or simply to stand in the corridors and talk.

Labor disputes in the Soviet Union were regulated by law. A Labor Code of 1922 with its subsequent amendments, and industry-wide collective agreements, specified or laid down rulings on job description, rates of pay, overtime, disciplinary sanctions, or redundancy. At factory level disputes commissions and trade union committees took up the cases that employees brought before them—effectively claims that the rulings had not been correctly applied. A dispute might involve a single employee or a group of employees. If dissatisfied with the decision at factory level, the claimant could turn to court: he or she should not have been made redundant, overtime was not being paid appropriately, or a disciplinary censure was unwarranted. There was an extensive legal literature on the legislation, its interpretation, court practice, and proposals for change.

In the spring Alexei Stepanovich decided that I had mastered the literature, my spoken Russian was good enough, and I should begin my work in the district courts and then the factories. Sitting in the clerks' offices, going through court files and attending hearings, both civil and criminal, spending time in different factories (Karl Marx—heavy machine building; the Instrumental'ny—precision instruments; Skorokhod—boots and shoes; the Kotlyakov factory—originally made horseshoes for cavalry but after the war shifted to escalators and used the spare metal to make tricycles, hammers, and training weights), reading materials from the labor disputes commission in the trade union office or the labor and wages department, and talking to those who worked there—all of it was enthralling. I loved every minute of it. "Where else would you like to go?" asked Alexei Stepanovich. Prompted by my hostel friends, I suggested a confectionery factory and perhaps a vodka distillery? "Hmm," he said, with a quick look at me. "We'll settle for the Mikoyan chocolate factory."

A graduate student from the department, Lucia, was in charge of organizing the factory visits. By this time we were friends. Together we set out for Mikoyan. She was wearing a loose top with a broad belt round her quite ample waist, "just in case" she said. And indeed, while working in the labor and wages department and going past the conveyor belts, we were encouraged to try a variety of chocolates, far more than we could eat. Somehow a sizable number vanished into Lucia's ample bosom, escaped surveillance as we went through the checkpoint, and were shared out once we were back in her apartment.

Lucia was an able graduate student and, I think, a good lawyer. She, her husband, their little boy, and her mother, who taught me how to make more than one kind of soup, lived in a large room in a communal apartment on Fontanka. Her father no longer lived with them but had retained the right to a corner of the room, fenced off with tall bookcases and cupboards. Her husband worked in a laboratory, which gave him access to distilled alcohol, simply known as "spirit," and this we drank with tomato juice. On one occasion we had left a meeting with a prosecutor specializing in labor cases, saying that we must hurry to an important conference in the trade union headquarters. Instead we went home and drank Bloody Marys before setting out, unsteadily but very cheerful, to put in a token and late appearance at the trade union conference. Unfortunately the prosecutor was there. He simply smiled knowingly as he greeted us.

Lucia was my only woman friend with a child and, from her, I first learned just how hard it was to be a wife, a mother, and work full time in Russia. Without a grandmother in residence and grandparents somewhere in the country to whom the child could be sent for the long summer holidays, there was no way a woman could keep up with her male colleagues. The one-child family was the pattern among my Leningrad friends and this could all too often be accompanied by abortions, still illegal, as they were in the UK. Contraceptives for women were not yet available in Russia while sexual relations—at least within the student body and between students and faculty—were accepted as part of everyday life. Short-lived marriages, affairs on the side, casual encounters—all characterized this generation's life in the sixties, while their parents seemed much more conventional. But perhaps this is how an older generation always looks to the young? I am tempted to tell the stories that circulated, and sometimes from firsthand experience, of individual professors, but they were little different from those that circulated at Oxford.

When visiting the factories, I was always introduced to one of the brigades of communist labor, whose members helped each other and whose workplace would be decorated with little red flags, perhaps slogans, and posters listing the members' responsibilities. Were they really a shining example of committed collectivism or were they all for show? Neither conclusion seemed right but, if this was so, what did their members think they were doing? I was skeptical of the claims—the labor disputes that I followed in the factory and court records revealed a work force concerned with much more humdrum issues—and had my suspicions confirmed by one of the first sociological surveys carried out, in 1963, by the fledgling sociology section in the philosophy department. The survey on workers' motivation revealed little difference in the responses of those who were and were not members of brigades of communist labor. A copy was given to me by Vladimir Yadov who, upon graduating and much to the surprise of his university teachers, had gone to work as a lathe operator in a factory. In the spring of 1963 he was setting up a new sociology section in the philosophy faculty.

A chance meeting brought me to him. My application to spend a further six months at the labor law department was approved by Leningrad University, I received a visa, Somerville gave me a research grant of £250 to pay for my fares and my upkeep in Leningrad. When I reached Leningrad I put the bulk of it in a post office account and drew it out as I needed it. I was not charged for my hostel accommodation or tuition. But how and where did I change the pounds into rubles? Surely I did not have them in my suitcase when in late December 1962 I was traveling back to Leningrad by train from London? Standing in the corridor, I got into conversation with a passenger who had joined the train at Warsaw. Hearing what I was working on, he gave me his card—he was Anatoly Kharchev, from the Academy of Sciences—and told me he would put me in touch with Vladimir Yadov. Back in Leningrad I attended Yadov's occasional seminars, but it was in 1963-64, when he came to the UK on the British Council exchange to study public opinion surveys, that I got to know him as colleague and friend. Where, I asked him, was the Iron Curtain? A labor lawyer from Poland who had arrived at the department in Leningrad in 1963 had acted as though he and I were partners in an alien environment and should make common cause. I was puzzled. Surely Poland was part of the communist block? Yadov smiled. "The Iron Curtain," he said, "is at Brest-Litovsk."

I had returned in July 1963 to England, and by September I had a job at Glasgow University as assistant editor of *Soviet Studies*, working under Alec Nove, who had been born into a Menshevik family in St. Petersburg before the revolution. A lively and imaginative economist ("He reminds me of a Moscow economics professor," said Yadov, when he came up to Glasgow to give a seminar), Alec was at heart a social-democrat. Thirty years later, he would come to St. Petersburg, and we would go to the Mariinsky to hear *Yevgeny Onegin*. He left his library to the Academy of Sciences' Institute of Economics and Mathematics. But in 1963 I was in Glasgow and still writing up my thesis.

I was now far more critical of Soviet policy and politics. Certain features of Soviet society appealed: greater educational opportunities, the range of jobs open to women, the absence of the conspicuous consumption or the social snobbery of British society. While the bureaucracy and the inability to keep to any previous arrangement drove me to despair, I liked the untidiness, illogicality, and emotional warmth that accompanied all activity. Reality was more complex than portrayed in either the standard western or Soviet analyses, and I had become less interested in Marx. The task, as I put it in the preface to my book on labor disputes, was not for west and east "to indulge in comparisons between existing societies as though they provided the only alternatives in social organization," but to improve on each other. I dedicated the book to "The Petrograd Factory Committees of 1917 in the hope that their ideals may one day be achieved." The editor at Oxford University Press wrote to ask me to change it—the press felt it was too provocative—and, unsure of the outcome, I cut out the second half of the dedication.

England through Russian Eyes

Unknown to me, a young journalist, who would subsequently follow Yadov's path to work in a factory and to sociology, was convinced that the brigades of communist labor were a key to the future. It was 1990 before we would meet and become firm friends. His name was Andrei Alexeev. His mother, born into an upper-class St. Petersburg family, had met his father, from a peasant background, at the institute where they studied engineering at the end of the twenties. She taught Andrei French and English before he went to school but, thereafter, left him to form his own opinions about the society in which he lived. There was no discussion at home about the family past or political present. Andrei became an ardent member of the Komsomol. Upon graduating from the journalism faculty in 1956, he went to work for two years in Samara, then returned to Leningrad to work for *Smena*, the Komsomol paper.

In 1958 a campaign had been launched to encourage work brigades to work and live in a collective "communist" way. Not only would the members strive to over-fulfill work targets but they would help each other to improve their qualifications and to cope with domestic problems, while participating in social and cultural activities. These nuclei of the communist future would set an example for all. In 1959, in an article on the brigades, Andrei was arguing: "It is time we asked ourselves: but what, after all, will communism be like? We need not seek some extraordinary features. Communism is within us and around us, in the achievements and characteristics of our contemporaries. . . . As of now it only exists in individual shining examples but in the future it will exist as a whole beautiful system." He felt it was his responsibility to test out his beliefs and "with his own hands" to participate in the building of communism. In 1961 he joined the party and began an apprenticeship as a rolling mill operator at one of the enterprises that had pioneered the communist brigade movement.

Before starting work, however, he was chosen to join a group on a two-week trip to England. Had we met then, would we have found a common language? I doubt it. I found believers hard to take, whether it was the moral superiority of capitalism or socialism that formed their creed, and I did not share his belief that the Soviet system was, however slowly, moving forward toward communism. His diary reveals how alien Britain seemed to some of the Soviet students and the relief with which they departed for home. They felt baffled, they could not reach the "real England" (they were like flies on the glass and England was on the other side). This was just as I had felt in 1959 on my student trip to Russia. Both we and they shared a concern with foreign agents. No sooner had the Russian group crossed the frontier into Poland than they were on the lookout for foreign agents. Was the German girl they met on the boat really what she claimed? Was it not suspicious that the two students . . . ? But, as well as the similarities, there were differences. I doubt that any members of a British student group were concerned to create "a good friendly collective," something that Andrei proudly noted they had succeeded in doing.

They were prepared for the provocative questions they encountered—about democracy ("the English seem to be obsessed with democracy"), freedom, and Pasternak—because they knew that these were attempts to trap them. They grew tired of their student guides only ever giving them the most favorable information about Britain (just as British students grew tired of their Soviet guides' presentations). When they visited the National Gallery, however, Andrei noted the tour leader's argument, that art always sought new means of expression. Whether he, William, liked or understood abstract art (which he did not) was not the point; his irritated responses—"I am giving you my personal view, why do you always reply 'We'?" and "I may hate your ideas but I shall defend to the end your right to express them"—made Andrei describe him as "a worthy opponent."

Although Andrei found attractive certain buildings, the Leicester University library, its swimming pool, and aspects of the countryside, as a society England remained alien and unappealing. He was shocked by student behavior—rock and roll, drunkenness, and kissing at the Saturday night students' union—disappointed by how little interest the students showed in Russia, and dismayed by how little the tourist guides seemed to know. "To be quite honest," Andrei concluded, "the Soviet citizen, although our own propaganda dulls his wits, is a head higher than his counterpart in bourgeois society. That's what the comparison should be and not the metro or the poor on the streets. After all one can find the poor both here and at home." "Of course," he added, "the spontaneous internationalist which exists inside each of us cannot but see something good in the life of each and every people." However, he was unable to specify what *was* the good he had managed to see. "Each of us," he wrote, "returned a more convinced, international communist."

How true this was of the other members of the group we cannot know, and Andrei, in his thoughts and actions, was always a singular individual. Soft spoken but utterly stubborn, with a gentle smile and a penetrating gaze, his newspaper articles and diary reveal an individual who is prepared to take responsibility for his actions; words without actions are not merely irresponsible, but damaging. In 1962 he wrote a major article criticizing the campaign for communist brigades as little more than a campaign to raise output. In his personal diary, in 1961, he was seeking an explanation for the workers' dissatisfaction with the Khrushchev leadership. "What has Khrushchev achieved, what has he given the people?" he asked himself. To suggest that one could take pride in the arrests and executions being a thing of the past was absurd. Promises of a communist future? But the reality of the present jarred. "Not to have to stand in a queue for milk would seem a sufficient feature of a communist society for today's children." Future promises were being used as a substitute for real changes. Yet the leadership was not stupid. Did it not realize the damage that it did? Perhaps, he wondered, he should write a letter to Khrushchev.

Twenty years later Andrei would be in deep trouble, subject to a search by the KGB and expelled from the party. Thirty years later, as Communist Party rule was falling apart, we met in a new Institute of Sociology and became colleagues and friends.

4

Zastoi or Stagnation, 1965 to 1985

What did those twenty years—from the mid-sixties to the mid-eighties—hold for our young Leningrad intellectuals as they moved from youth to middle age? Many, but not all, found themselves marking time. Khrushchev was ousted in 1964. Brezhnev ruled as first secretary of the Communist Party until, ailing and elderly, he died in 1982. I was in Leningrad at the time and went straight to Dom Knigi, the bookshop on Nevsky, to buy, before they vanished, a set of posters showing him at work and at play. The artists had failed to make him an inspiring figure. An anecdote current in the Brezhnev period had Stalin, Khrushchev, and Brezhnev traveling together in a train. The train stops. Stalin sticks his head out of the window and shouts "Shoot the driver!" Khrushchev follows with "Rehabilitate him!" But Brezhnev says "Comrades, comrades, draw the curtains, and let's pretend the train is moving." Not for nothing did those years acquire the moniker "stagnation." The hopes and dreams of the Khrushchev period quietly faded away. For me those years produce the fewest memories, not only because my visits, for family reasons, were infrequent and short but also because, looking back now, those years seem like a wasteland between two periods of dramatic change. Not entirely true, as we shall see, but cast into shadow by the years that followed.

But before I sketch in my friends' fortunes, which give us a glimpse of life in the city changing for our generation, if ever so slowly and in different ways, we say farewell to Volodya Smirnov, the only one who had fought through the war. In the last letter I received from him, in the late sixties, written in his execrable handwriting, he wrote of a journey he had made to Chekhov's, Turgenev's, and Tolstoy's country estates, and to Tolstoy's grave,

> which has no headstone. Nothing at all! Just a little mound of grass and nothing more. No inscriptions . . . a tremor ran through my soul, and I felt so ashamed of my own miserable life. Does that ever happen to you, Mary? Or do people who study jurisprudence lack souls? As before, things look gloomy. No one will employ me. So you can imagine how I feel. But it's all nonsense really. I'm happy to sit and write. I'm writing what and how I please. And perhaps happiness lies in being a small boy again and doing what you want, and not what boring grown-up aunts and uncles tell you to do. Incidentally, Lenin showed good sense when he said, "Healthy ideas are the prejudices of the age." Do you agree?

I made, I think, only one further visit in the sixties—in 1965—when I flew into Leningrad as a tourist with Alastair, my future husband, then a graduate student studying in Moscow. We were met at the foot of the airline steps by a small man in a Robin Hood hat who quizzed us, said all was in order, and delivered us to the lounge for foreigners where a man smoking State Express 555 cigarettes engaged us in further conversation. But all was not in order: the Astoria Hotel was unprepared for our arrival. "Who," said the receptionist, when I handed over Alastair's passport, "is this?" "He's my friend," I said. "I hope he can stay with me." Everyone raised their eyes to inspect him. "What do you think, Valentina Valentinovna?" called the receptionist to her superior across the hall. "He's not that large," came the reply. "We can make up an extra bed on the couch in the room." The receptionist took his passport. "Should I pay something?" I asked. "No," she said. "We don't have a regulation that covers a case like this."

And, again, I cannot resist fast-forwarding to the receptionist at the Tretyakov Gallery in Moscow in the late nineties. *"Pensionerka?"* "Yes," I replied, "but not a Russian pensioner."

"I don't have such a category," she says, looking at her list. "What shall I do?" She thinks. "I'll have to consult the manager." She leaves her booth, locks the door, and disappears. The queue grows longer, shuffling its feet. She returns, unlocks the booth, and sits down. "The manager is having lunch," she says. Thinks. Sighs. "I'll give you a ticket as though you were an ordinary pensioner, but don't tell anyone."

And one more such story: I am at the airline office in Krasnoyarsk, in Siberia, buying a ticket for Moscow. *"Pensionerka?"* says the receptionist as I hand over my passport. But then, "I don't know whether foreigners are entitled to reductions, and I can't take a decision, you'll have to come back tomorrow, and go to window three." Next morning, at window three, I explain the situation to a young blonde women with purple nails. "No," she says, "no reductions for foreigners," and takes my passport to start the process; but then she pauses, picks up a phone, and I hear, "Well, she is, after all, quite elderly. . . . Yes, yes, she is quite normal. . . ." She replaces the receiver. "Kras Air," she says to me proudly, "has agreed to make an exception for you."

Somehow all those regulations prompt people to find a way round them. We'll see more of this in later chapters, but now back to the seventies and early eighties. In 1965 I had moved from Glasgow to a lectureship in politics at the University of York, and in 1966, now married and with a child, to Princeton, where Alastair had a visiting professorship. In 1968, back in England, we moved to the University of Essex, where Russia was one of the specialist areas, Alastair to the department of economics, and I to the department of government. In 1985, with Gorbachev in power, I moved to Oxford.

Friends from the Sixties

Of my hostel friends, only Galina remained in Leningrad. On graduating with a degree in history, she lost out in the competition for a graduate stipend to a fellow student whom the dean had recommended. As compensation she was given a place in the philosophy department, where she was offered "The Moral Code of the Builder of Communism" as a thesis topic. Within a couple of years she was back in the history faculty and, when appointed to a lectureship specializing in Byzantine history, the dean applied on her behalf for the issuing of a permanent Leningrad registration certificate, a *propiska*. Galina, the prettiest girl in the hostel, never married. That's all I shall say on that score. After fifteen years of renting a room in a communal apartment, she was allocated a one-room apartment in one of the new housing blocks the university had begun to build out at Peterhof, a suburb, but still a Leningrad "city" district. Zhivkov's geranium went with her. On my visits, I would go out to see her and walk in the park.

Her elderly parents had a two-room apartment in Tula, the city south of Moscow. In the early eighties (after her father's death), her mother exchanged this for one room in Leningrad. Now they had two one-room "Leningrad" apartments. These they exchanged for a two-room apartment on Vasilevsky Island whose occupants, a growing family, wanted to live separately. This was a relatively simple exchange, compared with some of those that you will learn about later. Here, suffice it to say that by the early eighties Galina was back on Vasilevsky Island, only a bus ride away from the university. Built by German prisoners of war after 1945 and known as a Stalin block, hers is a well-built five-story brick building whose apartments have high ceilings and spacious rooms. Here her mother joined her.

Galina had reluctantly joined the party, but we did not discuss politics. We never had. When she first left home for university her father said to her: "Remember, if anyone talks about politics, he is either a fool or an informer." We would visit Sofia Viktorovna Polyakova, the elderly classicist who had taught Galina Greek and who lived with her (large) dogs and two elderly women friends, one a well-known translator, Nadezhda Ryzhkova, in the three-room apartment where Sofia Viktorovna had grown up as a child and from where she had crossed the street to attend the elite "German" gymnasium in the twenties. Sofia Viktorovna grew quite irritated by the steady stream of "gifted young admirers," as she called them, who came to visit Nadezhda. This prompted her to admonish the two KGB operatives who, early one morning, rang at the bell with "not *more* gifted admirers of Nadezhda

Yanyuarovna. . . . At least have the decency to call at a reasonable hour!"
What they found, apart from torn-out pages of the proscribed journal
Kontinent in the lavatory, I do not know. Sofia Viktorovna was loathe to
explain to the operatives that the quality of its paper made it the best for
cleaning her dogs' behinds. I brought a new kind of retractable lead for
the dogs. Galina, now a Byzantine scholar and teacher, went in the early
eighties on a research visit to Hamburg, whose Byzantologists had links
with their Leningrad colleagues. We managed to speak on the phone—
between Colchester and Hamburg—and I sent her some money toward
buying a coat.

Vera, back from Sakhalin, now teaching in a technical school in
Tambov, wrote proudly of being accepted into the party and of receiving
a teaching award. She discharged herself from hospital, quite unwell,
to fly to Leningrad to see me for a day in 1982. Did I get enough to eat,
she enquired anxiously. I was still as thin as ever, and now I had three
children. None of my women friends had more than one child. Russian conditions—queuing, shortages, lack of services or help from a
husband—made it difficult enough for a working mother (and all my
friends worked) to manage with one child. Shopping by car from a supermarket and all the other things that made it possible for women of my
generation in Britain to combine a university job and family made the
contrast between our lives much sharper than it had been as students.
How lucky I was, they sighed, to be able to have more than one child.
This does not mean that it was easy to be a working mother in the UK.
Asked recently in an interview for the British Association of Slavic and
East European Scholars newsletter to describe "what challenges you
faced along the way, as a female academic," I replied: "In 1968, at an
interview for a lectureship at the Essex government department (still all
male), I was prepared for the question as to how, with two small children, I would cope. 'From living in Russia,' I said, 'I know how tough it
can be, from living in America, I know about washing machines and
fridge freezers, and we shall have an au pair girl.' It was tough with two,
and then three, children. It was difficult to be away on trips to Russia. I
could not have done it without Alastair, my husband, sharing the load,
and without colleagues at Essex helping out at times of crisis. By the
time I moved to Oxford (in 1985) the children were older, and St. Hilda's
was used to its women fellows having children."

In the seventies improvements had come in Leningrad—in clothing, consumer durables—but for those of my generation the main change was in housing. Under Khrushchev a building program was launched—to build five-story apartment blocks with prefabricated panels—and, in Leningrad, these appeared in the outer districts of the city. Then came brick-built cooperative blocks, whose apartments could be bought by those who could afford them, but with restrictions on the number of rooms, two or three, depending on the size of the family. It was these that elderly parents, with savings, might buy for their married children. Both El'mar's and Leva's parents did so. Both El'mar and Leva had by then remarried and would soon have young daughters. By the early eighties all my friends lived in individual apartments of one sort or another, whether in the center or in the northern city districts.

In 1982 El'mar and his school friends celebrated their fiftieth birthdays. They always celebrated their birthdays together—drinking, eating, and then singing to a guitar. They have drunk a lot of vodka together and sung a lot of songs. In the sixties it was Okudzhava, gypsy and war songs. By the eighties more of the old "romances" and civil war songs had come back in. Dark-haired Volodya, by 1982 a professor at the Institute of Technology, was the only one to have been abroad—to Cuba. Leva resorted to cutting out the most absurd photographs of ageing Politburo members to present to friends. On my visits the only dissident we discussed was Solzhenitsyn. Everyone had read his *Gulag Archipelago*. People knew of Sakharov but not what he had written. A frequent and depressing topic of conversation was Jewish emigration. Several of their friends had left for America or Canada. And sometimes talk turned to corruption.

Somehow El'mar continued to wander along a course of his own through the years, with detours into Freud, Jung, Weber, and Eastern religion, lecturing to students about his latest interests, shocking colleagues from time to time with his strange statements, always behind with his party dues and always late for appointments. To his surprise and dismay, in the mid-seventies he experienced difficulty in changing jobs and learned that his contacts with foreigners had placed a black mark against him in the eyes of the security forces. By 1980 he had a post in the philosophy department at the Institute of Culture, most of whose students went to on to work in museums, galleries, theaters, or the media.

His analysis of the present and future was gloomy. In response to an unofficial "underground" survey, he suggested that, although the economic and social situation had worsened in the past five years, there was little social tension. Few were puzzled by an electoral system that provided no choice; only a few felt themselves constrained because art, and discussion, was in general so poor. Intellectuals felt alienated from society and "at some deep level we know we are lying, deceiving ourselves, not doing that which we claim we are doing." But, he added, this had a long tradition in Russia. The system could last a long while—"a shortage of goods and the civil and moral courage of a few dissidents don't create a crisis"—but perhaps there would be changes by the end of the century. Marxism, as a theory, he wrote, was outdated and had failed to bring any positive results for Russia, but the intelligentsia had produced nothing with which to replace it. Possible changes for the worse? Falling behind as a great power and perhaps the breakaway of the Baltic republics, Central Asia, and possibly ethnic conflict. For the better? More private initiative, market relations, maybe liberalization, and cultural improvement. But, he argued, the ability of society to act had been destroyed by the killing of so many during the Stalin period; it was difficult to imagine any real leap forward until the biological scar had healed. What would an ideal society look like? Perhaps Herman Hesse's republic where abstract thought prevailed and there was a realm of freedom for the mind, for culture, and for intellectual decision-making.

El'mar had long been interested in pre-revolutionary Russian philosophers banned by the censor, and it was books by Berdayev and Shevtsov that I brought in my raincoat pocket. He had contacts with the Baptists and with the Orthodox seminary, not because he was turning to religion but simply because all different kinds of ideas intrigued him. Religion, however, was in as a topic of conversation by the early eighties—it would be nice, several said, to be able to believe—but none among my friends became religious. However, they were drinking more, as was the population as a whole. Odd incidents made me aware that subtle sea changes were occurring. I left a party late at night with a friend and took a taxi back to the center; we passed a woman and child, and the taxi slowed, but when the driver saw that the woman was dead drunk, he swore and left them standing in the darkness. We reached the center and stood, at two in the morning, watching the melting ice floes sweep down the dark river and talking. "Did I believe in God?" he asked me, and had I read Thomas Mann's *The Magic Mountain* because, if not, I would never understand Russia. No one, among either naïve or cynical friends, believed in God in the sixties. Extrasensory perception gained a following. The board game Monopoly began to enjoy a vogue, then Alexander Zinoviev, the most original and pessimistic thinker among the recent émigrés. I brought Elton John records for El'mar's daughter, and clothes, and medicine.

The only friend from the sixties who took action that immediately jeopardized his future was Leonid, the Romankov twin, who worked on automated systems in the Television Institute. He wrote to *Izvestiya*, a leading newspaper, protesting against Sakharov's exile, because "he felt he had to as a human being." In 1982 the KGB raided his apartment and took away feminist *samizdat* (underground) literature; he was immediately sacked from his job but friends and colleagues denied his having lent them any books. He got off with a warning and found a job in another institute. We continued to meet, but carefully.

Liuba, who as an applied physicist worked on polymers in the Phys-Technical Institute, was chosen to attend English classes five times a week so that she could represent the department when foreign delegations came. The task included taking them around the city. On one occasion, knowing that her colleague had already opted for the Hermitage, she proposed visiting a building in her street that had a Lenin plaque on the wall, the Lenin monument at the Finland Station, and the reconstructed hut on the Finnish gulf where Lenin had stayed. Keeping a very straight face, she watched the committee members trying to hide their dismay. Her knowledge of English and her research took her to foreign conferences—to Czechoslovakia in 1971—from which she returned to tell her colleagues that her greatest impression was that she had been treated with respect as a woman. In her laboratory, as the mother of a young child, she was treated patronizingly. At one point, offered a higher post in another laboratory, she approached her department head: "Liuba!" said Serafim Nikolaevich. "I'll be very sorry to lose you and this is a rare chance for you to get a senior research post. I can't offer you one and am unlikely to be able to—after all a nonparty woman—that's even worse than being a Jew." Being Liuba, she put loyalty first, and stayed.

"Worse than being a Jew"—surely this statement makes my readers flinch. I had been puzzled, and taken aback, on my first visits to Russia by the way people would refer to someone as being "Jewish" rather than "Russian." Yes, of course I knew that the Jews had been treated as a different people and victimized in many European societies, but—at least for my generation in the UK—you were first and foremost British or American or French, and being Jewish was an extra—like being Catholic or Protestant. It wasn't a category that had any importance in everyday living and, anyway, how would you know who was Jewish? In the school I went to there were Jewish girls, some of whom chose not to go to church on Sunday and went for walks instead, but others were confirmed Christians, and they were all as "English" (or British) as the rest of us. But in Russia, in their passports, their nationality was "Jew," not "Russian." And then, I learned, there were quotas for Jews for entry to higher education institutions. Despite this, Jewish scholars, artists, and musicians played a very significant role in the intellectual and artistic world, including among its celebrities. In the mid-seventies Jewish emigration—to Israel, to the United States—began, despite the obstacles. The persecution of religious believers (Christians, Jews, Muslims, Jehovah's Witnesses) continued.

I had no contacts or particular interest in religion, or Jewish emigration, but one incident is worth recounting. In the early eighties I found myself traveling to Leningrad on a British Academy grant together with a young British scholar who was going to look at rare Hebrew manuscripts in the public library. He spoke no Russian and was given an interpreter and guide. I felt slightly responsible and, although irritated by his pestering me with questions on whether or not x and y in the Hotel Moskva restaurant would be kosher, made suggestions as to how he might use his spare time creatively. Alas, he chose to sit on a park bench that had just been painted—he could not read the sign—and spend time buying a samovar in an antique shop. The evening before we left he came to ask me to take out a manuscript for him—given to him by someone at the synagogue. I refused. At the airport we were both subject to searches (the only time I have been), and my research notes were taken away for inspection. Meanwhile he was calling to me—"Mary, they are taking away my samovar as an antique! Help me!" Eventually I got my notes back and we boarded. I was still upset but as we flew off he turned to me with a smile. "See," he said, "if you want to get a manuscript out, buy an antique samovar." It makes me smile, now. At the time I wanted to smack him.

Marking Time

Most friends gradually moved away from the position they had held in the early sixties—seeing Stalin as the culprit who had halted society's move to socialism—and began to view Marx's and Lenin's ideas as responsible for the Soviet system, which they identified with "socialism." Now I found myself having to defend the principle of a national health service. Living in Britain, I could retain a belief in socialist ideals and see the benefits they had brought; for me the problems were the British government's dismantling of the public sector and tying access to education and health to the ability to pay. My Russian friends were living in a system that claimed to be socialist but was failing to meet even rudimentary needs.

As time passed, clothing and consumer durables began to lag behind again. Only Oleg, a doctor, had a car, which he drove extremely dangerously while excitedly arguing with his wife over the route they were taking. The streets were still mercifully empty, and the center remained almost unchanged. A new hotel had been built, the Leningrad, on the northern embankment of the Neva, near the famous battleship *Aurora*, and then the Moskva, a dark concrete monstrosity, appeared down by the Alexander Nevsky monastery. Foreign academics on research visits were put up in one of these. The Hotel Moskva was dreary. Finns who had come on weekend drinking bouts fell over in the corridors. Banners hung out of their tour bus windows proclaiming "Vodka—our glory."

And my visa limited me to Leningrad. Occasionally, very occasionally, like in a badly plastered wall, a crack appeared. I pestered the travel bureau in the Moskva. Could I not join a trip to Kizhi with its restored churches, outside Petrozavodsk, in Karelia, north of Leningrad? Finally, the woman gave in—she would issue me a train ticket to Petrozavodsk and a piece of paper for the Intourist hotel, but since I could speak Russian, I could look after myself. So, jubilant, I went. Not surprisingly, the Intourist hotel in Petrozavodsk was not expecting me and did not know what to do. The easiest course of action was to tell me where to catch a bus to get to the quay for a boat to Kizhi and to forget that I had appeared. Off I went. Kizhi will have to wait for a place in another book, but an incident at the Leningrad railway station has forever stuck in my mind. It was usual for the coach attendant to stand at the open door as the train slowly left the station. As we prepared for departure, a large man, not young, came running up the platform followed by a porter with two large suitcases on a trolley. "Quick, quick," the man gasped and, as the train started to move, grasped one suitcase and threw it into the coach, the train began to glide away, a little bit faster and faster and, with a gesture of desperation, he was left standing on the platform with his other case. The attendant calmly shut the door. Did he ever get his suitcase back?

Perhaps in part because the present had become so dull, by the late seventies I moved away from the study of contemporary politics and began to study the interwar city, the documents, the old tattered newspapers, the memoirs, and photographs. Now, on research visits, I was attached to the Institute of History, where discussions with a colleague had to take place either in the room where the secretary responsible for foreigners (KGB) had a desk or on a couch in the hall. I made one new friend, the historian Vitaly Startsev, who accompanied me out onto the street one day before inviting me to come and meet his family. Perhaps, partly subconsciously, I shut my eyes to the city of stagnation and emerged from the libraries to walk in the streets I had just been reading about, reliving the past. Politics and culture were at a standstill, with only the occasional appearance of new talent. But no new or exciting theater productions or art exhibitions during those years stick in my mind.

I always called on Pashkov, my supervisor from the sixties, who had moved from the Law Faculty to head a new center studying industrial relations. It was a curious outfit, consisting of a few rooms in the still half-ruined Bobrinsky Palace (built for Catherine the Great's illegitimate son) on Galernaya Street. Alexei Stepanovich had a large room, with a large desk. I would ask after members of the original department, we would spend about ten minutes on relations between Britain and the USSR, and then, with a sense of relief, he would ask after my family and personal life and we talked of everyday things. There was a button on the desk, which he would press with a fleshy finger. He would smile with pride when his well-dressed secretary appeared, bringing us coffee in smart little cups and biscuits. Perhaps my last visit was in 1985, when Gorbachev had come to power. This time his secretary brought not only the coffee but a tall box, a present for me. He began to pull it open, a pedestal appeared. "Oh dear," I thought. "Please, not Lenin." It was Pushkin, as he stands in the square in front of the Russian museum. I almost, but not quite, kissed Alexei Stepanovich.

At the time of the Afghan war, in 1980, when relations between the Soviet and British governments hit a new low, I was refused a visa. I was back by the early eighties, either as a tourist with my teenage children or making a research visit. Travel was cheap. I took groups of Essex students to Moscow and Leningrad on packages advertised by Intourist. In Leningrad we visited the grand flat where Kirov, the Communist Party leader murdered in Smolny in 1934, had lived; Vitaly Startsev told them what really happened when the crowds stormed the Winter Palace in 1917; and we went out to the Piskaryovskoe cemetery where the victims of the Siege lie buried. Quite what the students made of the visits I am not sure, but I doubt that any of them struck up friendships with Russian students in the way that we had in the fifties and sixties.

It had become more difficult to meet new colleagues too. Even El'mar clearly felt constrained in simply taking me along unannounced. In 1974 Vladimir Yadov, now the leading sociologist in Leningrad, was heading a section in a new Institute of Social and Economic Problems. Andrei Alexeev became the party organizer for this institute but within a year he was removed from the post for defending an Estonian sociologist who had been expelled from the party on political grounds. Yadov was in trouble by the early eighties: two Jewish members of the institute had emigrated, sociology was under a cloud, and it was difficult to do any interesting and critical research. On my visits I only met him at his home, as a friend.

Change Below the Surface

Had I been there for longer periods, I surely would have felt more of the subterranean changes that were taking place. Everyone knew of the poet Brodsky, already in trouble in 1963, sentenced in a public trial for anti-Soviet writings, released in 1965 after an international outcry, and forcibly deported in 1972 after refusing to take advantage of his Jewish nationality and emigrate to Israel. (There's a charming film, *A Room and a Half*, made in 2009, on Brodsky's life in Leningrad. Among other things, it shows life in a communal apartment.) But I only heard of the discussion group that met at Lev Gumilev's apartment from one of its participants after he had emigrated. Nikolai Gumilev, poet and member of the White Guard, husband of Anna Akhmatova, also a poet, was shot by the Bolsheviks in 1921. Akhmatova continued to write until her death in 1966. One of her most famous poems, *Requiem*, tells of her standing in a queue outside a prison to deliver a parcel to their son, Lev, who spent most of the years from 1938 to 1956 in prison camps. He then became an ethnographer, working in an academy institute, an idiosyncratic thinker with a circle of followers. There were other groups too. Jazz groups. And some individuals simply went, literally, underground, took jobs as yard sweepers, which included sleeping in the boiler room under a block of flats, and eked out an existence on the very basic pay, while writing "for the future." You could live on very little.

A few, both of my generation and younger, took actions that cost them dear. One night Yuly Rybakov, an artist, painted a forty-meter-long slogan, "You crucify freedom but you cannot handcuff the human soul," in huge letters on the wall of the St. Peter and Paul Fortress, visible, when morning came, from the other side of the Neva River. The KGB operatives found themselves in difficulties, the river unexpectedly rose, and they had to resort to requisitioning coffins from a nearby workshop and stacking them against the wall in order to hide it. Other exploits included painting "Listen to the Voice of America" on the windows of a shop selling radios and, during the night, painting "for a free politics" on the sides of trams in the tram depot, whose drivers, quite unaware, then drove them around the city next morning. When Rybakov returned from prison in 1982, disillusioned by his fellow prisoners' lack of interest in political freedom, he concentrated on supporting experimental art.

A group of younger people gathered at Arseny Roginsky's apartment in the mid-seventies. Roginsky, a forty-year-old historian, educated at Tartu University in Estonia, was sending *samizdat* abroad to the émigré press. Following searches and warnings, and then dismissal from his job as a schoolteacher in 1979, he was warned in 1981 either to take advantage of his Jewish nationality and emigrate or risk arrest. He chose arrest and spent the next four years in a prison camp. Disaffected younger scientists, writers, and artists met in the Café Saigon on Nevsky to smoke and talk. Much has been written since about the Leningrad "scene" at this time; here I am drawing upon memoirs or conversations many years later. Both actions of protest, and knowledge of them, remained the purview of small groups of people. You were careful with whom you shared knowledge. As I write I find myself wishing I could ask El'mar how many of these groups and individuals he knew then—some of them is my guess—but knowledge was shared carefully between people you trusted. And phones were tapped.

El'mar introduced me to Galina Starovoitova, then a young ethnographer who had written on St. Petersburg before and after the revolution. And we met to talk about the ethnic profile of the city. But when she simply failed to turn up for a further meeting in the academy library, it felt best not to pursue it. A critical report prepared by a leading economist, Tatyana Zaslavskaya, had recently been leaked to the west, and the KGB was trying to establish who, among the circle of those who had received it (one of whom was Starovoitova's husband), no longer had their copy. When we met again, nearly ten years later in Oxford, she had become a leading figure in the democratic movement, and we had more interesting things to talk about. Tragically she was murdered, shot on a staircase in St. Petersburg in 1998, a political killing.

Near the Troitsky Bridge stands the big constructivist block built in the 1930s to provide housing for those who had spent time in prison under tsarism. It has long corridors with the flats (each with a large kitchen and one other room, all identical) ranged along them like prison cells. By the 1980s among its residents was Yury Dinaburg, born in 1928, son of an engineer who was shot in 1937. Yury, already a student, was arrested in 1946 as a member of a small group advocating a Humanist Communist Order. He spent the next eight years in a prison camp for "politicals," shifting logs and learning from an elderly German professor, but on his release was "rehabilitated" on the grounds of an inappropriate sentence for his age and admitted to Leningrad University. El'mar took me to visit him. He was working as a tour guide at the Peter and Paul Fortress, an eccentric and original guide who puzzled and intrigued the visitors (erudite, but sometimes out of boredom he would add or subtract a few years from historical events, just to make a change). He lived with Lena, his second wife, then a slight thirty-year-old who had married him when she was twenty and devoted herself ever since to typing his unpublished manuscripts and weaving little baskets out of bark.

It would be wrong to imagine that for my generation, or indeed for any generation, Leningrad under Brezhnev was a lively city, either intellectually or in the arts. It wasn't. You could go skiing in the Palmyrs or to the south on archaeological expeditions (as did the Romankov twins), go on holiday in the Crimea (as did the Sokolovs), ski on the Finnish gulf or rent dachas in the Baltic states, but back in the city, and at work, many felt they were marking time. And by the early eighties the KGB were, shall we say, intrusive.

Andrei Alexeev and a Survey

Who had organized the unofficial survey to which El'mar had contributed in 1980? None other than Andrei Alexeev, the young journalist who had visited England in 1961. In the autumn of 1965 he had decided to change careers and become a sociologist. During the following ten years he read widely, including a range of forbidden literature. He did not question the rightness of October nor the ideals of socialism, but he came to doubt that the Communist Party was furthering them. He then arrived at the conviction that they could not be realized under a system of one-party rule. By the 1970s he worked out an intellectual and moral code for himself. Not only was an individual responsible for the world around him but, he now added: "Don't take on a task that is beyond you, but make sure that those which you do undertake, willingly or otherwise, you do better than anyone else could have done—whether it concerns work, love, friendship, a trivial task, revolution, or death." His list of axioms included:

> Award the same respect to others as to yourself.
> Answer a dishonorable blow with an honorable one.
> Don't stand in a queue for more than fifteen minutes; you can get by without.
> Don't engage in unnecessary physical movement.
> If someone steals your ideas, it means they were worth stealing; comfort yourself with that thought.

In 1979 he devised a questionnaire to explore the views of the Leningrad intelligentsia on the current and future situation in the USSR. He had to find people he could trust, and who would trust him that their replies would only exist in anonymous form. This resulted in forty-odd responses. The respondents were not, of course, a representative sample but they constituted an intellectual and cultural group of which Andrei felt himself a part, one that overlapped with my friends and acquaintances. I read the responses ten years later.

My views on the political situation had differed little from theirs, but they took a much gloomier view of the economic and social situation. Only the occasional individual offered an optimistic scenario. Almost all considered that no significant political or economic changes would come before the new century: while the economic system had raised the standard of living for the great majority of the population, it was now in deep trouble, incapable of further development; while providing "bread and sausage," its use of resources was irrational; it stifled any initiative and demoralized the labor force. Housing, health, transport were all suffering; even the supply of consumer goods was deteriorating. Only "home, amenities, and work" interested the majority of the population, and alcoholism was increasing. The need to get by, to bribe, to cheat in a society whose everyday rules contradicted the proclaimed ideals had produced an amoral people. The ruling elite reproduced itself, while a huge stratum of officials or bureaucrats maintained the status quo. The intelligentsia was demoralized, castrated by the dual standards by which all had to live and by the constraints on culture. Brave though the few dissidents were, politically they were unimportant. Such a system could not survive indefinitely but its very "contradictions" produced a society that was "hyperstable," a situation of "stable crisis," "inertia," "like a glacier spilling down a mountain." Change might come from an external threat (almost everyone referred to China); internally, only from change at the top. Few thought that this was a possibility; equally likely was a new leadership bent on reintroducing a more centralized, repressive order. However, one respondent concluded, with illogical optimism, "but consciousness will change and, one wonderful day, the self-seeking functionaries will notice with terror that people's eyes are turned in another direction." And, oddly enough, as we shall see in the next chapter, this is what happened in Leningrad in 1989.

If his respondents were demoralized, Andrei was not. The twin imperatives of doing whatever one is doing *properly* and of the individual's responsibility to society suggested a strategy for action. He would return to the factory bench and, as a sociologist, analyze and endeavor to improve the work process. And, it goes without saying, he would be an exemplary worker. Yadov supported the idea, party permission was given, and at the end of 1979 he joined the factory Lenpoligrafmash as an apprentice turner-adjuster.

He worked in the same shop for nine years, keeping a record in the form of letters that he sent to a group of close women friends. From reading them, although this is clearly not their author's intention, one begins to feel a certain pity for shop and factory management. They had the misfortune to allot Andrei a lathe that could not be relied upon to produce true items. He set about getting it in good working order. Management found itself bombarded with written requests, and each department tried to transfer responsibility to another. Andrei found a foreman from a nearby factory willing to try and mend it during his holiday; when management reneged on an agreement to pay him, he paid him out of his own pocket, fought with management over the issue, and raised it at a party meeting. He got permission for his cousin, an engineer, to come in and try to find the fault. Eventually it was established that the key worktop was slightly crooked. By this time half the technologists in the plant had spent time inspecting the lathe, deputy directors had paid a visit, the paperwork was enormous. It took six months to make it a proper working instrument but, fifteen years later, when others had been jettisoned, it was still operating smoothly.

In his letters he describes the daily struggle surrounding the lathe and, as the final discovery is made, he begins to write of "the General Line" being at fault. If that is bent, then everything will be distorted. He soon became highly critical of management. The term he uses is *razgildyai*, "a lack of interest, incompetence, and irresponsibility," qualities also present among the workforce, although many workers were willing to suggest improvements that management simply ignored. He still hoped that change could come through the party. In 1981 at party meetings he was arguing that only a quarter of his time was spent doing the job he was paid for. He was a thorn in the flesh of management. "It's not," he wrote in one of the letters, "that I want all the workers to start writing. . . . I simply want to show that it is possible for ordinary, unexceptional individuals to take action."

However, in the early eighties, following the death of the aging Brezhnev, and with Yury Andropov as leader, the Leningrad KGB began to target potential troublemakers. Andrei's apartment was subjected to a search in November 1983 and papers, books, letters, and diaries confiscated. The following morning he went to the public library, ordered the Criminal Code, and wrote an official complaint to the procuracy, listing the nine points of the law which the KGB search party had infringed. Not surprisingly the code name the KGB gave to the Alexeev case (each case had a code name) was "Asp."

He received a formal warning, under the terms of an unpublished decree of 1972, for illegally possessing and circulating politically dangerous literature (a text by A. Zinoviev, Orwell's *1984* in English, works by Mao-Tse Tung, an unpublished novel by Iskander, and eight documents "for official use only," including Zaslavskaya's memorandum). Although the KGB only managed to get hold of one survey response, and under questioning Andrei insisted that he had destroyed the others (partly true—he had burnt one set of the responses on top of a hill in the snow), he was accused of engaging in a tendentious unauthorized survey whose "questions were formulated in such a way as to produce negative assessments of Soviet society and the perspectives for its future development." Under the guise of "letters," he had written a slanderous account of work relations. During questioning, the written warning concluded, he gave dishonest answers and refused to offer any justification for his actions. The practice, in such cases, was for the accused to read and sign the indictment. Andrei, however, refused to sign unless he had a copy, and this was grudgingly agreed to: he copied the document out by hand, then signed both, and kept the copy.

His exemplary work record probably saved him his job. He was expelled from the Union of Journalists and in April 1984 he was expelled from the party. Two members of the shop meeting abstained in the vote; at factory level one member, who demanded that he read the letters and then protested that he saw nothing untrue in them, was excluded from the party commission. The Central Committee of the party confirmed Andrei's expulsion in September 1985.

*

Leningrad in 1985, its cityscape; the shops, markets, hotels, and restaurants; its universities, institutes, and schools; its cultural life and leisure activities, was still in many respects the city of the 1960s. There was still hardly a car in sight. There were no new restaurants or shops. Huge party slogans still decorated the squares for the celebrations. The *Morning Star* was the only English-language newspaper available. The markets had the same stalls, selling the same produce. The kiosks were selling tickets to the same ballets. There were no banks, just the post office where one could put money into an account. No telephone connection to the world outside. And even inside the country, people sent telegrams rather than telephoning to someone in another city or town.

New housing, it is true, had transformed the districts surrounding the city center and the metro had spread to keep pace. But the trains out to the countryside still had their wooden benches; the rest homes on the Finnish gulf, property of state-owned enterprises or institutions, and the little wooden dachas, had changed little since the 1960s. During the short summer when for a month the sun never sets, the city's populace set off, out of the city, to dacha country to grow fruit and vegetables, or to the rest homes and sanatoria on the Finnish gulf, part of Russia since

1945. And the imperial parks and palaces—Peterhof, Pushkin, Pavlosk— now partly rebuilt and with their ornamental gardens and wild stretches of woods or fields—were within easy reach. But this was still a city only visited by foreigners in tourist groups or on educational or cultural exchanges. No one any longer came on the *Baltika.* Aeroflot now flew from London to Leningrad, to the small Pulkovo airport. Friends would be there, waving excitedly as I came through the barriers, forbidden literature and letters in my raincoat pockets. We would walk down to the main road to catch a bus into the center. But its own citizens, except for a privileged few, could travel no further west than the Baltic states. Only Jews could emigrate, and only those who, with persistence, managed to thread their way through a thicket of bureaucratic obstacles.

However, with Gorbachev's accession to power in 1985 the glacier began to move, slowly at first, and then with ever-increasing speed.

5

Last Days of Leningrad

By the late eighties the city was shabby, literally falling to bits in places. There was no money. The palaces needed painting. Old apartment blocks stood empty, half-gutted; the drainpipes were broken, the roads pitted or dug up and left untouched. But the city had never been neat and tidy. On the contrary, it was always a jumble of grandeur and poverty, with a kind of carelessness about it that was part of its charm. It had been through bad times before—the civil war, Stalin's purges, and the Siege in World War Two—and pulled through. Now it was in for another rough time. But, by then, as its fabric decayed, the beautiful but silent city of the late Soviet period found its voice.

In 1985 Mikhail Gorbachev, energetic and a reformer, had become general secretary of the Communist Party and leader of the Soviet Union. He talked of *glasnost*, or openness, and *perestroika*, or restructuring. In 1986, when the famous nuclear scientist Andrei Sakharov returned from exile after a telephone call from Gorbachev, the television cameras were there at the railway station in Moscow to film his arrival. First cautiously, then at a faster pace, newspapers and television screens began to address long-forgotten or forbidden themes. If the early sixties, the Khrushchev period, were a time of change and a time of hope, the late eighties brought unbelievable changes. By 1990 the borders were opening and the ending of censorship had produced a cacophony of voices in the media and on the streets; property was privatized, buying and selling became legal, law and order began to break down, and all this was accompanied by new forms of poverty . . . and a new politics. But even in 1990, few if any of my Leningrad friends could have imagined that in the summer of 1991 Leningrad would have voted in competitive elections for a "democratic" mayor, Anatoly Sobchak, and for the renaming of the city as St. Petersburg. Still less that at midnight on December 31 the raising of the Russian flag over the Kremlin would mark the end of the Soviet Union.

The skeins of memory that link these years with today are much thicker and more tangled than the threads of the sixties—partly perhaps because they are newer but also because it was such an extraordinary time. If in 1961 I had stumbled through the snow with El'mar to hear the film director Grigory Chukrai talk about his films, which touched on long-forbidden themes, in 1990 I was negotiating the planks that covered deep pits in the road outside the Railway Workers' Palace of Culture to hear El'mar lecture on Berdayev's social philosophy. In 1961 people were skating on thin ice, it was risky to criticize the past. Khrushchev might do it as party secretary, but that did not authorize others to copy him, and there was a great weight of officialdom and social opinion ready to react against society's mavericks. In 1990 it was quite different. A generation of the committed and the fearful had gone and, more important, the crumbling of the party's power had suddenly dissolved any sense of authority. "Anything goes" was the new convention. There were political meetings and possibly the freest television in the world. I stood in the drizzling rain in Palace Square, listening to the speakers standing on two open lorries who were arguing for selling shares to workers. Speakers on open lorries in Palace Square? Maybe the last such occasion was 1927, when Trotsky and a handful of his supporters tried, unsuccessfully, to appeal to those in the November 7 parade. Now this was an everyday occurrence, but there was not much food in the shops. I brought food, and stayed with friends. Porridge, bread, and black coffee became the staples of a miserable diet.

However, in a café near the new Institute of Sociology, to which I was attached as a visiting scholar working on the new social and political movements, there was sometimes apricot juice and cognac, and among my new friends was one of its members, Andrei Alexeev.

The Institute of Sociology

The Institute of Sociology was headed by Boris Firsov, who upon graduating in electronics in 1954 had moved first into full-time work in the Komsomol, then, during those heady Khrushchev years, into party work, from where he was promoted to head the Leningrad TV channel. A born leader, with energy and imagination, he would have gone far had de-Stalinization continued, but by 1966 the new political climate and his handling of issues on television brought his dismissal. He moved into sociology, where he worked under Yadov until, in 1984, instructions from the regional party committee saw him dismissed from his post. But with Gorbachev in power, he was back in favor. By 1989 he was director of a new Academy of Sciences Institute of Sociology in Leningrad, while Yadov moved to Moscow to head the academy's institute in the capital. The young party activists of the Khrushchev period, now turning sixty, were heading the reform agenda in the social sciences.

The new institute attracted individuals of different generations but, with the exception of Andrei, those in the Sector on the Sociology of Social Movements were in their thirties or early forties. All participated, one way or another, in the new political campaigns. They saw their task as one of research and of furthering the democratic process in the city and in society. The ethos of engaging in reform, albeit far more radical reform, was in this sense similar to that in the labor law department thirty years earlier. Similar too were the reports on the sector's work, the joint projects and planned publications. The belief in collective work survived the ending of Communist Party rule. But the discussions were different. This was a group of people who now traveled to America, Britain, and Germany, who knew much of the western literature, and who could talk freely in public about the society in which they lived. Despite generational differences we shared many of the same interests, and spoke a common language. By now I had moved from Essex University to Oxford and was back studying the present: the political changes, not only in Leningrad but also in several regional cities, traveling to the Urals, to Arkhangelsk in the north, and to Krasnodar in the south.

Many who had been young under Khrushchev wanted to see political changes (but of what kind?), greater freedom in the media, the arts, and sciences, freedom to travel, and reforms to the faltering and stagnant economy. But Communist Party rule was deeply embedded in society, and there were no alternatives to hand. Most watched developments from the sidelines. They read the revelations on the Stalin era—all that was like being back in the Khrushchev period—and sat riveted before their television screens, but they did not engage in action.

Andrei, as might have been expected, was one of the few who did. His argument was quite simple: "We must not wait for changes, we must bring them about. Perestroika will only happen if people like you and me make it happen." His strategy, as before, was to insist that rules be observed. When in 1987 Yadov failed to be elected as chair of the Sociological Association, he challenged the validity of the vote on the grounds of lack of a quorum, and when the association unwisely accused him of libel, he won the court case. Given a written reprimand by his shop superintendent for being ten minutes late after the dinner break, he was back in court; he argued for elections of the factory director and of a Council of the Labor Collective. By this time fourteen fellow sociologists had written to the Leningrad party committee requesting a review of his expulsion from the party. The factory party committee was not in favor—his statements were "of a demagogic nature, adversely affecting relations between management and workers"; he had carried out unsanctioned sociological surveys, dragged the enterprise through the courts, wasting time and money . . . and "refused to accept any criticism or admit his faults before the party." But the tide was beginning to turn in his favor. Sixteen of his fellow workers sent a letter to the Central Committee stating that they had not been given the proper facts in 1984.

In September 1987 the newspaper *Literaturnaya gazeta* published an article in which he was described as a hero of our time. He was reinstated in the party, and his party record restored. A popular journal, *Ogonek*, devoted an article to him. The publicity, however, had begun to affect relations with his fellow workers, and he left the factory to return to work as a sociologist. In the autumn of 1987 he was a founding member of Perestroika, a discussion club that brought together a group of

Andrei Alexeev. (courtesy Zina Vakharlovskaya)

Leningrad intellectuals, some of whom subsequently rose to political prominence at national level.

In the summer of 1990 he left the party, disillusioned by the failure of the Party Congress to adopt a more democratic stance: reform would not come through the party. He did not stand himself but worked on behalf of individual democratic candidates in the 1989 and 1990 elections. Now in the newly created Institute of Sociology he set himself the task of creating an archive of printed materials: unofficial and official newspapers, journals, leaflets, and manuscripts relating to the new movements. He built it up with minimum resources, including his own salary. In 1990, when I first met him, in his worn jacket with its Solidarity badge, there was still room to move between the old steel safes and bookcases in the sector's room. By 1992 it had overflowed down the corridor and up the stairs.

El'mar and the Romankov Twins

Elmar's activities, as might be imagined, were of a different kind. He wrote a letter to the public library proposing the opening of the Closed Collection (of Censored Books), and took a group of Hari Krishna into the House of Scholars for a discussion evening. The House of Scholars, an association in one of the small palaces on the embankment set up by Maxim Gorky after the revolution to provide assistance to impoverished scholars, still functioned as a discussion club. El'mar was on the committee but was rebuked for his action. The Romankov twins took more direct political action by participating in a campaign in support of Sakharov's nomination as a candidate in the 1989 elections to a new Congress of People's Deputies, and with these elections suddenly the rules of the game changed.

In 1988 Gorbachev had proposed that in elections to a Congress of People's Deputies, where some but not all of the seats would be competitive, a candidate would need 50 percent support to be elected. Among those standing were high-ranking Communist Party secretaries, never doubting that, as was customary, they would be returned. In Leningrad the first party secretary, among others, failed to win a seat. When the results came out, a deathly silence was heard from Smolny, the party headquarters, and people looked at each other in disbelief. As a deputy put it to me, people found that they simply had to cross the party secretaries' names off the ballot sheet and they were gone, shadows.

By the summer of 1989 the political environment was changing fast and the future was quite unpredictable. How long would present opportunities last? Did Tiananmen Square lurk round the corner? Now, for the first time, El'mar could travel to the west and he, his wife Tamara, and their daughter came to England as our guests. They came by train, and then by boat from Holland to Harwich. Baltic independence was the topic we discussed endlessly, with El'mar now in support. They bought a large television set, unobtainable in Leningrad. Their return to Russia was marred by their being deported from Holland back to

Britain because their transit visas through Germany had expired, then finding that they were not entitled to reenter Britain, and that German transit visas could only be extended in the place of issue—which was Leningrad. Somehow, with the help of the police at Harwich, we got them allowed back into England—for twenty-four hours. "Why don't you do my signature?" said El'mar helpfully, at a tense moment in the German consulate in London, "and I'll do Tamara's?" "El'mar," I said, "we are talking about signatures." "So what?" he replied. "It's very boring only to do your own. In Russia we often do each other's."

Upon his return, he wrote: "We are just under impression of our journey to England till now. Myself was somewhat troubled with excitement and have tried after returning to 'reconstruct' my usual life mental condition with help of going to the forest and especially for berries. . . . P.S. i) Leva rang up just a minute ago. He bought a car, old one, worse than yours . . . and now he has lost every peace because he must get accumulator, other details, and no things in our shops now! ii) our political, ideological process goes very quickly, but there no changes in economy, and situation with power isn't clear. We hope for better times."

Over the next two years the economy grew worse, and the political system underwent a transformation. In March 1990 competitive elections saw a loose coalition of "democrats" under the banner "The People's Front" win a majority on the Leningrad City Council. Among them was Leonid Romankov, whose earlier encounters with the KGB had probably worked in his favor. He was one of the many "democratic" deputies whose political program stressed human rights, political freedom, and improving conditions in the city. A month later, as the council opened, I was staying in the Sokolov family apartment, back in the Botanical Garden, just as Jim, the British student, had done in 1958. I too had no special invitation, I had just bought a train ticket in Moscow and come. The difference was that, even if the KGB knew I was there, nobody any longer cared. Control over speech, publications, and political activity had evaporated: fear had disappeared.

The council's opening sessions were televised live, and straightaway we witnessed the new politics in action, disorganized, often chaotic (more than an hour was needed to reach agreement on who should take the chair for the day), with queues of deputies clamoring for the microphone. But before describing this new Leningrad politics, let's look— even if only cursorily—at what was happening to everyday life. In Part II, the daily struggle of the city's residents to find food, cope with privatization, and retain their jobs in the newly named St. Petersburg in 1992 occupy center stage. The situation as regards food was probably even worse in 1990–91, but the excitement generated by the media and political developments pushed everyday living, for the moment, into the background. Let's see what I can bring back.

Everything Breaks Down

In 1990, when British Airways started to fly to Leningrad, the red slogans that had adorned the old Pulkovo airport had been replaced by two advertisements, one for a new German beer cellar on Nevsky Prospect, the other for an Indian restaurant. No one worried any longer about being searched for literature. Anyway, I was bringing food, as much as I could carry. But the small airport had become a dangerous place. Foreign tourists promised rich pickings. The new British Airways office manager would meet a delayed late night flight, shepherd the anxious travelers into the two or three "safe" cars he had organized, and deliver them, in a dark city, to their hotels.

In September 1990, on a research visit to the Institute of Sociology, I found myself in the Morskaya Hotel, an ugly gray concrete building in the port at the end of Vasilevsky Island. It's not far from Galina's flat. In the early sixties when we left from there for Tilbury, that part of the island was all open spaces and little yellow houses. Now it's covered with high-rise apartment blocks. But the little eighteenth-century shipbuilding inlet, fringed with pine trees, was still there, tucked away and quite unspoiled. The dreariness of the hotel symbolized the degradation wrought by those years of stagnation. There was a large room with Space Invader games and a huge sailing timetable. There was a restaurant where, during the day, the waiters in their dinner jackets idly rearranged the pink table napkins and chatted; they only served in the evening and then only tourist groups with preassigned tickets; a "Gril-bar," which shut by seven, had a carbon-copy menu that bore no relation to its meager offerings. The buffet on my floor always had black coffee (but the cups were chipped and cracked) and bread, sometimes curd cheese, tomatoes, pale frankfurters or bits of chicken, and sometimes sweet cakes. A six-inch-wide strip of the imitation parquet flooring had buckled and made a ridge running across the floor, over which every other person tripped as they turned from the buffet holding plate and cup. No one showed any signs of mending it.

There were clothes moths in the cupboard, no plug for the sink (but that was usual in Soviet hotels), and a TV that could only get two channels. A sign proclaimed, in English, "7th floor: Off-beat Business Centre." I went in search of it and found two women cautiously tapping at word processors, but they told me they were closed. The next day they said they were open, and a young man, lounging in an armchair, smoking a cigarette and looking at the aspidistra, agreed to do a Xerox for me. It took him a quarter of an hour and much wasted paper while one of the women worked out the foreign currency rate and wrote out the receipts. My reaction was one of delight and despair. Delight because, after ten years of refusals by libraries, I could now photocopy an article; despair because "moving to the market" seemed totally unrealistic as far as that hotel was concerned. The only sign of change was that the elderly women who guarded the keys to the rooms had been replaced by young women in skintight jeans and heels. They broke off their interminable telephone conversations with women friends to write again to Axel or Heinrich in Hamburg, who had not replied to their last letters.

When one evening, for old times' sake, I invited friends from the sixties to the Astoria, there were only two parties in the restaurant—our party and a table of Russians from abroad treating their relatives. The service was appalling, three times we were asked how we were going to pay, the waiter brought the pies with the main course rather than with the soup, he muddled up the main courses, when we asked for a third bottle of wine he said only two were allowed, and the kitchen staff were going home. To try and make up, he brought us an extra empty plastic mineral water bottle (so useful for taking to the forest and other things) and then he had to run after us because he had given me the wrong part of the Visa receipt.

Henceforth I would avoid hotels and stay with friends or acquaintances wherever I went. The only problem was that meant they fed me, and there wasn't much food. An extra mouth to feed was a burden. The old system of distribution had broken down, the means of transport had failed. Container lorries stood at the border full of consumer durables, but the rolling stock needed repairing and there was a shortage of fuel. The fields around Leningrad were full of potatoes and carrots, but the party could no longer order factory directors to send their labor force out to bring them in, and the City Council could only issue appeals. So in September 1990, the only way to get carrots in for the winter—carrots lying in a field barely thirty miles from the city center—was to persuade mathematicians to go out with buckets and pick them up.

It was not surprising that talk of "rackets" and corruption in retail trade was so common. A television program made a specialty of discovering warehouses filled with rotting produce, of dealers slipping goods out of the state network to private traders. Everyone talked incessantly, anxiously, of the approaching "market." Nobody knew what this dark frightening thing looming on the horizon was, but all repeated the phrases—"markets are *necessary*," "a market is what societies ought to have"—as though by matter-of-fact talk the fear of the unknown could be exorcised. Outside the Primorskoye metro there was usually a clutch of lorries, up from the south, from which the traders sold their melons, tomatoes, and grapes. An old man waiting at the tram stop began to complain bitterly: "Did you see the prices? When were tomatoes ever 4 rubles a kilo? And all the traders are dark skinned. What is happening to Russia?" He grew ever more agitated, stamping up and down in his felt boots, as two old ladies started to tell him that he hadn't seen anything yet, "Once we move to the market . . ." "What market?" he asked angrily, but the old ladies stuck to their ground. "Everyone says we've got to have a market and then the prices will more than double."

Would the intellectuals be going out that winter to dig the peat bogs, I wondered, as they had in 1920? There was no doubt that the economy was in a mess. "The preparations have not been made for the winter" was a constant refrain, but the suggestion that in the past the city was somehow all buttoned up, no broken pipes, everything in readiness for the snow and ice was, according to my historian friend Vitaly Startsev, quite untrue. The city would muddle through, if it could get the fuel. The winter would take its toll and the population would be sicker and more weary, but nothing like civil war Petrograd let alone during the Siege. It was hardest on the old people, both materially and psychologically. The old ladies, Vera's great-aunts, whom we used to visit in their one-room apartment in 1961, had had a tough life: sent out in the twenties to work as young doctors in Central Asia, back in Leningrad working and barely surviving through the Siege, eating grass and twigs, and by the sixties drinking strong coffee, smoking strong cigarettes, playing endless games of cards at which they cheated, and reminiscing over lives that had their share of painful personal memories. For them, their past had had a future. The old man at the tram stop ("Was this what I fought through the war for? I'm eighty-six and I can't even buy a tomato") had nothing.

1991 was the hungriest year. Most of my friends lost weight. They got sick too. Making comparisons of the standard of living over time is difficult. My expectations had changed, as had those of my friends. Were things *worse* in 1990 than they were in the sixties? As far as clothes and footwear were concerned, they were immeasurably better. While it was far more difficult and expensive for the young to get hold of jeans, jackets, and trainers than their western counterparts, for a price they could be found. But the food situation had deteriorated. When in 1961 Vera had sent me out to the food store across the street, the list included potatoes, carrots, butter, a tin of peas, salami, Dutch cheese, mayonnaise, and sweets. That was for a special occasion. You could not count on getting those in 1990, definitely not in one shop. The cafeteria where in the 1960s we used to buy pork cutlets was down to chicken claws. The food in the public library and in the student cafeteria number nine had markedly deteriorated.

And time had moved on. In Britain we were eating much better than our parents had, while the middle-aged Leningraders were still queueing for milk and the array of milk products had shrunk. In the sixties, you will remember, by the end of the month the students in Mytny were drinking hot water with sugar, but at the beginning of the month we drank champagne and ate blackcurrant ice cream in the theater intervals. In 1961 I had brought chocolates back from the Mikoyan sweet factory. By 1990 there was no chocolate in the shops. Food was scarce, monotonous. The salami largely fat and cheese only a memory. The markets had a variety that they never had in the 1960s—Coxes apples, Williams pears—but who could afford them? Students had never been able to pay market prices but by the nineties even the professors could shop there only occasionally. In December 1990, when I flew into a dark city with a group of Oxford students to find that the foreign department at the Herzen Pedagogical Institute had made no provision to feed them, the only solution was to take the whole group to the Sokolovs—to consume part of their winter store of potatoes together with the salamis we had brought as gifts.

Media Freedom—Press and TV

Leningrad was still recognizably Leningrad, with its familiar streets and shops, crowded trolleybuses, waves of tired pedestrians searching for food after work, but now it was home to activities never before allowed. There was a strange discordance between the old familiar surroundings and the new world of public speech and action. While everyday life still stumbled along the well-trodden paths, the world of talk and the printed word was alive and crackling. Editors, journalists, TV and radio staff had offices, received salaries, and were freer to do what they liked than their counterparts anywhere else in the world. They were accountable to no one, not to an owner, a political master, nor to the market. The only constraint was the shortage of print and paper.

By 1990 a variety of papers and leaflets had appeared, often badly typed and Xeroxed two-sided offerings, either on the thick blotting paper churned out by a factory whose target was in tons or on near tissue paper. The anarchists (appropriately enough) were still producing very rough copy, and there were still all the odd fly-sheets produced by individuals as well monthly democratic and patriot papers. In April a makeshift stall outside a metro station was selling a variety of democratic publications and by September there were stalls on Nevsky Prospect. But more than half the tables were covered with sex manuals and astrology, and they were the most popular. The patriots were there in force one day, with their data on the Jews' dominance of Russia since 1917.

But none of the political groups were selling out. Compared with the publications of 1917 and early 1918 — also a time when there was a splintering of political opinion and a remarkably free press — the offerings in 1990 were meager, even including the regular dailies and the new weeklies. In April, with delight, I bought a copy of *The Black Banner*, an anarchist title that had disappeared after the revolution, and in September, traveling out to the forest, I bought another copy from the ragged long-haired anarchist who came down the train selling his papers. But the content was pathetic, and the middle-aged travelers who bought it used it as wrapping for their potato peelings and turned back to *Izvestiya*.

The extraordinary hodgepodge of ideas was best seen on the television screen. Alexander Nevzorov, the talented young producer of *600 Seconds*, which flashed the week's events before the viewer, lambasted the government and advocated monarchy as the best form of democracy. One of his short documentaries began with the famous statue of Peter the Great, now standing on a mound of live rats who, as they began to move, brought the statue down, a shot that was repeated at intervals with references to the "troubled times" that lay ahead of the city. We moved inside the Mariinsky Palace, seat of the City Council, a place that had become a distorted world of moving furniture, acrobats, flying papers, a skull whose grinning black teeth spelled "Power," a place where the cleaning ladies sadly dusted the furniture and talked disparagingly of today's council compared with the past, and where Anatoly Sobchak, the council leader, a dark silhouette against a window, criticized the deputies. It was brilliant television but hard to take. Either Nevzorov, the *enfant terrible* of the air, was only concerned with "scandalizing" his audience or his intention was to undermine the council. If the former, so much for his radicalism; if the latter, he was helping the conservatives in the party apparatus and possibly the patriots.

The Fifth Wheel, a much sharper Leningrad version of *Panorama*, offered a devastating series of interviews with mothers whose sons had died while doing their national service after brutal beatings by their fellow conscripts or officers, for which the military authorities refused to admit any responsibility. A meeting of some of the women with Yeltsin (wiping his eyes with a handkerchief at one point) was included. A deputy from the City Council commission on human rights read out a letter from a father threatening to pour gasoline over himself and his son and burn the two of them to death because of lack of support from a district council; another gave an account of prison conditions in the city.

In 1988 it had been unacceptable to raise a question mark over the benefits brought by the October revolution. By the autumn of 1990 the revolution was commonly referred to as a disaster, in a matter-of-fact way as though this was self-evident. Sobchak referred to Lenin's mistaken view that unqualified people could run a government. When Nevzorov, in *600 Seconds*, asked Ilya Glazunov, the artist, "Who, in your view, is the greatest criminal of the twentieth century?" we already knew his answer: "Without any doubt it was Lenin." Not one TV would blow its fuse. While there were those who were scandalized and deeply upset by this response to the 1917 revolution and the Soviet past, reactions were difficult to predict. The staunchest old party members might have become the most radical of critics, or they might not. The opinion polls revealed that the elderly were more anxious to retain the name Leningrad, and understandably: many had come to the city as poor rural youth seeking their fortunes and found it in the form of education and work, fought through the war or lived through the Siege, and quite simply were not prepared to describe those years as wasted. My friends tended to support the renaming of the city, but there were colleagues and acquaintances who were bitterly opposed.

After so long a period of one official truth (and one believed in by many), the rejection of the sacred truths had to be savage. Lenin, the kindly, caring, astute figure of millions of books and posters, became the vindictive, narrowminded murderer of intellectuals and priests. In 1990 a collection of quotes, carefully culled from his works to show a hatred of intellectuals, was popular reading. And, to run ahead a little, in 1992 a widely advertised film, *The Russia We Have Lost*, contrasted the shining final years of tsarist rule with the drunken beer queues in today's provincial towns. By 1993 writers had joined in. Soloukhin's study of Lenin as a psychotic personality sold out quickly. Stolypin, a conservative tsarist minister assassinated in 1911, was resurrected as a heroic statesman-like figure who had had the answers to Russia's backward agriculture. In 1990 the execution of the tsar was frequently discussed. Rumor had it that the son of the Bolshevik Chekist who shot the tsar was alive and lived in Leningrad. . . . In a film being made on the last days of the tsar, Malcolm McDowell, playing the part of the soldier who shot the tsar, struck a slightly jarring note when, in a TV interview, he said that he saw the role as one of a wholly committed, idealistic Bolshevik. I grew tired of being expected to feel particular sympathy for the tsar and his family. Were they any different from the countless other families who were victims of the revolution? And the tsar had more blood on his hands than most. I quarreled with El'mar over this.

There was a subtle campaign aimed at raising social tension, spreading despondency. The sensationalism of the crime reporting—the camera moving in on a murdered woman lying in a park with a knife in her back while the young policeman took clippings from her nails, the shots of a grotesque burnt body on the roof of the building accompanied by the journalist asking "suicide or, one has to ask, something more sinister?"— heightened the fear, particularly felt by women, that the city had become a wholly dangerous place. Of course it was true that the streets were not as safe as in the sixties, when women could expect nothing worse than the attentions of the odd drunk. El'mar was attacked at the entrance to their staircase and had his briefcase stolen (it had nothing but a typed article in it). The militia and the old women were far less interested in keeping order now and crime was up, but the obsession with crime and violence was also an emotional response to a situation where anxiety and uncertainty about the future was running high. Stories of doom, gloom, breakdown, and crisis permeated the air by the end of 1990. Meanwhile the television interspersed its coverage of gloom with (just imagine!) *advertisements*: for speedy English classes, for small silver-haired poodles, for kung fu lessons, for summer houses built to state requirements, and for a new cooperative, Planet, specializing in computers. Rewards for a stolen car or dog were offered.

It was not only television that had come alive. Artists and actors were striking out with new ventures. Andrei Alexeev introduced me to Nikolai Belyak, whose experimental theater company, Theatre of the Interior, was at the time renting two upstairs apartments in the eighteenth-century mansion that had belonged to the poet Derzhavin. These doubled as wardrobe and prop room, office, and performing studio. The surroundings are a crucial element in Belyak's productions. Among his aims at the time were the transformation of the mansion into a center of eighteenth-century culture and the staging of *Hamlet* in the entrance hall of the KGB building on Liteiny. That evening in 1990 he talked about his hopes to create a project called Culture in the Cosmos, in which cosmonauts would read poetry back to earth, linking earth and space with cultural waves. A huge vase of gray chrysanthemums adorned the old Russian stove, theater posters and his son's drawings decorated the walls, and he ground coffee beans as he talked.

I had had nothing to eat all day, nor had Andrei, but eating could be put off till the next day—or, if you were like Andrei, largely dispensed with. By 1991 he was surviving on bread, coffee, and strong cigarettes. It was too time wasting to scour for food and to stand in queues. One Sunday four of us went to see a performance in Derzhavin's House, but it had been unexpectedly canceled. We stood in the biting wind, wondering what to do. One of our party decided to join the half-hour queue at a nearby shop selling frankfurters. "Perhaps we can find a cup of coffee somewhere?" I said, foolishly, and caught the look of dismay on my friends' faces. There was nowhere in Leningrad in 1991 where you could buy a cup of coffee on a Sunday afternoon, apart from the hard-currency hotels, and nobody went there. But there were meetings galore.

Meetings Galore

In April 1990 I went with El'mar to a meeting, held in an apartment, of Free Russia, a group of perhaps twenty people, intellectuals, anxious to marry Russian national culture and traditions with a democratic order, to counter the voices of the party apparatus and of the extreme right. That was where I first heard someone say, "I've nothing against bringing back the tsar." Another individual, neat, well dressed in a three-piece suit, turned out to be a representative of the newly formed Cadet party visiting from Moscow. The Cadets, or Constitutional Democrats, were the most famous of the prerevolutionary liberal parties. St. Petersburg soon had its own small Cadet party led by Alexander Kozyrev, a physicist.

In September, at a meeting of democratic organizations in a Palace of Culture, where discussion of strategies for unity and action failed to produce agreement, I found myself transported back to a familiar world. The individual types in dark sweaters and jeans, the conflict between defending a group's principled position and yet working with others, the discussion swerving from organizational questions to fundamental issues were part of any left-wing meeting in Britain in the sixties and of the SDS gatherings in the States. There was a difference, though, and particularly compared with Britain, where the left-wing groups rested on clear ideological positions and drew upon a long intellectual and political history. The democratic organizations in Leningrad had nothing to draw upon: neither a political language nor an organizational history. Class, and socialism, was out. An aversion to the existing order does not constitute a political position, and a commitment to democracy is far too vague. A move to the market is not a slogan to capture the hearts and minds of a meeting. In the March elections they had, to a remarkable extent, combined forces under the umbrella of the People's Front, but by September a whole stratum of the leading activists had gone, fully occupied in their work as deputies. Grassroots political activity had faded away, and the new, now legal, political parties found they had few members.

On September 9 at a meeting called by some of the more right-wing organizations advocating a return to traditional values and the renaming of the city, several thousand gathered in Palace Square. There was no trouble, and police and soldiers were noticeably absent. Only one speaker tried to inject an anti-Semitic note, and the city's three main newspapers all gave the meeting front-page coverage. Even *Leningradskaya pravda*, the party's paper and the stuffiest of the three, showed a placard proclaiming "Enough of Lenin." But *Smena*, the now-radical Komsomol paper, showed us a young man struggling to fasten a sheet onto the palace's massive wrought iron gates, the gates that in Eisenstein's film *October* block entry until, in an unforgettable scene, a boy scales them, the gates are forced open, and the crowd pours through and up the grand staircase in search of the remaining members of the Provisional Government. It does not matter that Eisenstein's re-creation of the 1917 storming of the Winter Palace bears scant relation to the actual event. The gates, and all they stood for, were real enough and that scene had become iconic. And in September 1990 a young man was again grappling with them, and his banner read "October 1917—the road to Golgotha."

Symbolic association apart, why did I feel suddenly knocked off balance? It was surely the appearance of statements and behavior that, within living memory, were wholly absent from the public domain (and, for many, not part of the private domain either) and the speed at which they had become *ordinary* acceptable assertions.

Religion Makes a Comeback

There was a large and hungry literate public, but a wasteland of ideas linked to viable organizations. Not surprisingly, religion made a comeback. Visiting the places of worship in the city, I was struck by the evidence (lacking in so many spheres) of communities that had already begun to take action. The churches were shining, the floors clean (washed by the faithful old women), and a plaque to commemorate the sailors drowned in the submarine off Norway had joined the 1905 naval memorials in the Nikolsky cathedral. A guide talked at length to the tourists of the Bolshevik attack upon religion, of churches destroyed and priests executed, but many churches still stood, used for forty years as depots, storage facilities (the Lutheran church on Nevsky converted into a swimming pool), or even as cinemas. On Vasilevsky Island few were of any architectural interest. The finest is the Andreevsky cathedral, dating from the early eighteenth century when Peter the Great created the northern capital. Completed in its present graceful form by 1780, it stands at the crossroads of Bolshoi Prospect, opposite the market and the street of eighteenth-century residences that leads down to the waterfront. In 1938 the church was closed; in 1992 it was returned to the St. Petersburg Orthodox Diocese, reopened, and renovation started.

Gradually, over the next twenty years, churches would be rebuilt and reopened. In 1990 the Buddhists got back their temple on Stone Island, for a monthly rent, and were restoring it. The synagogue in 1990 was a hive of activity, now housing a kindergarten and a Jewish national school (ages seven to seventeen) with, at a rough guess, about seventy children as well as a cafeteria and a library. Would religion again become compulsory in schools? It seemed quite probable in 1990.

The reaching back into the past was very marked. At a time of crisis and uncertainty, the past may be all there is to hold on to. The conservatives in the party were clinging desperately to their Soviet past; those for whom this could no longer serve needed to find something else. Ethnic, cultural, religious attachments became straps in the metro, something to hang on to in a society where group identities were weakly defined and authority had been undermined. One Sunday I went with friends out to the country to pick mushrooms. The forest was green and damp, and we walked all day, slowly gathering mushrooms, without meeting anyone. But as we sat on some logs eating hard-boiled eggs and bread and cheese and drinking vodka, a tall young man with a beard, and his mother, came into the clearing. They asked for directions to a lake. One of us, a Slavophile, asked him, "Are you by any chance a monarchist? You look as though you might be of my persuasion." "Yes," the young man replied, and they continued on their way. There weren't any monarchists picking mushrooms in the sixties.

The Party Clings On

There was still a political battle underway. Although in retreat, the party continued to control key institutions and resources and the political future was quite unclear. The Smolny Institute was still the headquarters of the Leningrad Communist Party. In the early sixties tourists and schoolchildren went in to see Lenin's bedroom, but by the seventies (when it was simply known as "Smolny") the institute had become a forbidding place, with its guards, black official cars sweeping up the avenue, and a special road built just for the use of the first secretary. It was from here that the city was ruled: the feeling of power seeped out through the iron railings.

In September 1990 a journalist arranged an interview for me with Yury Belov, the party secretary responsible for ideology. In all my years studying Soviet politics, I had never got near a regional party secretary. Such powerful people were far too busy to meet with a western academic. But now Smolny was like a morgue. The hall was empty; the two old ladies in the spotless cloakroom were looking after a dozen coats. We whispered as we hurried up the empty red-carpeted staircase and found ourselves in a long deserted corridor. No one was coming in and out of the offices. There were no enterprise directors trembling in their shoes, no journal editors biting their nails. The long empty white corridor (where Kirov had been assassinated in 1934) stretched down to the office of the current first secretary, Boris Gidaspov. There was no one in the spacious anteroom to Belov's office except his secretary. Belov appeared and asked us to wait a few moments before inviting us in. He could, he said, only give me half an hour and placed a clock on the table in front of us. But was he really busy?

His credentials as one of the new, more "progressive" secretaries was confirmed by his sporting a beard. He had, however, little to offer as a program to a party demoralized and on the defensive. In late 1990 the choice for a party secretary was either to opt for the no longer credible *status ante quo* position or to talk of a role for the party in a multiparty system, "maintaining socialist ideals." His or her more important task was to fight to retain as much control as possible over the party's resources (money and buildings). In the spring of 1991 I received an approach: Would I be willing to discuss Lenin's ideas with him for a radio program? Yes, I replied, if we also spent half an hour discussing the political present. That held little charm for him. Time had moved on. The campaign for the Russian presidency was underway.

A meeting in support of Yeltsin had been organized by the Kirov Workers' Committee in the plant's Palace of Culture. (This was grander by far than the hall where, in 1961, I had celebrated the October revolution with its shop floor workers.) The huge hall was packed, sitting room only on the floor by the time I managed to squeak in. Solidarity and Russian banners dotted the hall, leading Leningrad Democrats and the chair of the Workers' Committee sat on the platform together with the director, and the audience gave Yeltsin a standing ovation. I, to my surprise, was quite won over. Although his speech lacked punch, within minutes he had established a rapport with the audience. He was direct, humorous. The hectoring headmaster's style—the trademark of Soviet politicians, Gorbachev included—was absent.

And now, thirty years on, I was back in the big industrial enterprises. The directors were still the powerful individuals they had been in the sixties but their clothes and concerns were rather different. They wore well-cut suits or a casual suede jacket, and their preoccupations were either extracting huge investments from the government in order to modernize the plant or acquiring ownership of the factory, which would give them the right to buy and sell and strike deals. They brushed aside questions of unemployment as unlikely. The reaction from the shop floor, where it existed, was a far cry from the Solidarity movement in Poland. In a few enterprises Councils of Labor Collectives or Workers' Committees competed with the official trade unions. Meetings of their representatives produced statements far more critical of management than anything voiced earlier, but the Kirov Workers' Committee and the other worker activists I met were the exception rather than the rule. The Kuzbass miners' representatives who came to seek support received little except sympathy.

While Smolny, the party headquarters, was a morgue, the Mariinsky Palace, seat of the City Council, hummed with life. The palace occupies one side of a square not far from Nevsky Prospect and dominated by St. Isaac's Cathedral, with its huge dome. The square is well worth a visit. The Manege, or classical Riding School, is there too, as are the hotels—the Astoria, now five-star, and the Angleterre—and visible down a side street is the main post office. The palace itself has a dull exterior but this hides splendid rooms beautifully decorated in Wedgwood colors, red-carpeted staircases, and a rabbit warren of winding corridors. It has a remarkable spiral staircase, so constructed that a horse can be ridden from the sixth floor to the ground floor. And the large council chamber, created in Soviet times, is tastefully done, with boxes for visitors to observe the proceedings. Unwittingly I usually chose for my vantage point one of the best, the one that previously had been reserved for the first party secretary. In the early nineties, the public could go in and out and attend sessions.

Here I offer just a glimpse of the council at work, of the four-hundred-odd deputies with no previous experience of democratic politics trying to tackle the appalling problems facing the city. "Everything should be privatized," argued Petr Filippov, a leading Democrat. "Schools, hospitals?" I queried. "Certainly." "And the university, and research institutes?" "Well, perhaps not quite everything." In 1990 these were just words. By 1991 privatization was on the agenda. A human rights commission decided to concentrate on the rights of children, on religious freedom, and prisons but was quickly overwhelmed with letters and appeals, many of which related to the lack of housing—and they were the most difficult to deal with. People could spend eighteen years in the queue for an apartment, living six to a room in a communal one, while party workers and justice officials moved to the top of the queue.

"Could one say that your commission was primarily concerned with defending social and economic rights?" I asked Yuly Ryabakov, its chair, many years later.

> Yes. Really our commission became a kind of emergency service. There was no medicine in the shops, and people were dying, while the medicine was in the warehouses, and you needed to pay bribes to get it. [. . .] It needed someone to go and to argue. [. . .] It was the same with food. Once I had to prevent a riot by smokers. Suddenly cigarettes disappeared from all the shops, and smokers are excitable people. I was going to a human rights meeting on Fontanka when my assistant came running to say that barricades were going up on Nevsky and there was going to be a fight in a tobacconist's shop. I ran there. The crowd was angry. [. . .] I call other deputies, some go off to some warehouse or other to get cigarettes, I stay there. [. . .] After a couple of hours they brought a lorry load and start to sell the cigarettes but during those two hours I had to calm the smokers down, and also the police who wanted to beat them up.

A deputy could choose either to keep his or her job and be paid by their place of work or resign from it and be paid by the council. Leonid Romankov chose to resign from his institute and was soon involved in the commission for culture. Most deputies spent all day in the council, and they were desperately overworked. However, there were perks. By virtue of being deputies, they (together with all who worked in the palace) could eat at the cafeteria. That was standard Soviet practice for any institution, and the higher the ranking of the institution, the better the food allocation. A deputy took me to lunch there, squeezing me past the dragon lady doorkeeper. It was a bad moment. The variety and quality of the food (nice salads, two kinds of good soup, fresh buns with cranberries, three hot courses to choose from) was way above anything I had seen in a cafeteria elsewhere. The tables were clean, the utensils were not bent, and there was fruit and salami to buy from the buffet. Everyone left with a brown paper bag: the secretaries, cloakroom attendants, the conservative and the democratic deputies. I was dismayed. Why hadn't the new council voted to exchange its food allocation with that of a hospital and old people's home? But then, in 1990–91, everyone was hungry.

The Communist Party Bows Out

But how were my friends, who were party members, responding to the party's predicament? Galina simply left. El'mar's participation in politics was that of an interested observer. He could not bring himself to identify with any of the new political groupings any more than he had been able to find a religion to believe in, and he had never been one for active participation in an organization. He was happier running a discussion series in the House of Scholars with speakers of very different persuasions. Why, he argued, should he leave the party now? He had never approved of the party: to leave would imply he was making some moral or political statement. Why didn't I come to the next party meeting in the Institute of Culture? He would explain to the secretary that I was a scholar studying Russian politics.

The meeting demonstrated the absence among rank and file membership of anything resembling a political position. As was usual at any meeting or lecture in the Soviet Union, it took place against the background of a low hum of conversation, the exchange of newspapers, knitting patterns, or photographs of visiting nephews. The ten or so written applications to leave the party (grounds included the incompatibility of teaching literature and belonging to a political party) went through without question. One elderly member pointed out that in any democratic country literature teachers could belong to political parties. "Is that true?" my neighbor whispered to me. It was all routine business. A suggestion that, given the economic and political situation, the members should have a discussion of the party's role produced not a flicker of interest. Elections for new buro members and secretary found very few willing to stand, and an appeal from the good-looking young secretary that he be released from further offices so that he could write his doctoral thesis was granted. Everybody voted for almost everything and, once the result of the competitive elections had been declared, everyone voted to confirm the choice. The sense was of an organization whose members were still there because they were not sure whether it was wise to leave or because none of the new parties appealed. There were some who, while highly critical, felt that to leave now would be cowardly and a few who did not wish to desert a party they had always believed in.

If the thirty-year-olds had entered the political arena, students were little interested in politics. Were there any meetings held in the student hostels in 1990 to discuss the situation in Eastern Europe or the Party Congress? I suspect not. There was a murmur of protest in the summer of 1989 over the compulsory military service sessions (which students had to do in lieu of conscription), but this faded when the Ministry of Defense quickly made concessions; complaints over having to spend September bringing in the potato harvest were resolved by offering the students pay for the work done. A few, a very few, participated in the new political organizations. In the words of one who many years later would become an activist: "At that time politics did not interest many students, including me. The country was changing before your eyes, and you were more concerned with your own fate than with that of the country. You saw how full of lies the system was, how the old system had exhausted itself, and a new system had not yet come into existence, and it was not clear whether in fact it would. Of course you had your doubts. You had to get involved in business, earn to keep yourself alive."

They had something in common with Thatcher's children, despite the differences in social environment and the political present: they owed nothing to society, they wanted (and felt they had a right to) a good life for themselves, and if Russia could not provide it then they would go west. But who could blame them? Years of isolation had made the west an obsession. Their university professors were falling over their shoelaces in the scramble to get invitations to Paris, New York, and London. And who could blame them? Parents worried over their children's future and actively encouraged them to leave.

The newly elected deputies of the Leningrad council were vanishing abroad to attend training sessions or to discuss business deals with western firms. Leonid showed me the program for the visit of a delegation from a very right-wing American foundation: high-level meetings with city leaders, "deluxe" accommodation for the directors and their accompanying wives. "What do you know of the foundation?" he asked. When I said, with a sigh, that I would never touch their money, he replied, softly, "The trouble is that we have no choice." I felt sick at heart. Those friends of my youth, who had retained their integrity, their commitment to intellectual and cultural values through all those years, now had to entertain the west's most right-wing emissaries: people who knew nothing of the city and its people and who prized free enterprise above all else. The reaction against a system that was working so badly was often extreme. Everything had been state owned and had gone wrong; if it was all private, it would work well.

Five years later I would leave academe to work for the Ford Foundation, one of America's richest foundations — and, yes, when I brought its president and trustees to St. Petersburg, they stayed in the Europa Hotel on Nevsky — but the Ford Foundation supported Russian organizations or institutions in the fields of human rights, arts and culture, the media, and higher education. In 1996 it would support a new graduate college, the European University at St. Petersburg, which Boris Firsov and colleagues from academy institutes had set up to train a new generation of historians and social scientists. But for the moment we are still in 1991 and Leningrad was still Leningrad.

*

Early in the morning of August 19, 1991, Vladimir Kostyshev, head of the Sector on Social Movements at the Institute of Sociology, rang his colleagues with the news. In Gorbachev's absence on holiday in the Crimea, his Politburo colleagues announced their decision to remove him from office and to take control themselves. Kostyshev had a dental appointment. All the waiting patients were sitting silent, apart from the receptionist. Shuffling the patients' cards, she said, "And a good thing too, now we'll have some order in the country." He left, first going to a bookshop to buy up books that might disappear for good, and then to the institute to meet with colleagues and decide on a plan of action. Saving their word processors and the Xerox machine was their first concern; the next was Andrei's archive. But how to move the heavy safes? Andrei was on holiday, as was the secretary, who had forgotten to leave the key. They telephoned a colleague already in the Mariinsky Palace to see if he could get a truck. In his search he went to the room where the commission on social and political organizations met. There sat a small group of sad-faced deputies, looking at piles of documents. "What are you doing?" he asked. They explained that they felt it their duty to destroy the files which contained the names of so many individuals; first they had thought of a bonfire in the courtyard but, fearing that the smoke would give them away, had tried to burn them in the men's room but had been stopped because of fire regulations. One suggestion was to eat them, but the piles were daunting. He left them to decide, but he couldn't get a truck.

It was August, always the month when bad decisions come from above. Many were out of town, including El'mar and family. Galina was in Moscow, staying with her sister. They took food and water out to the bewildered young soldiers in their tanks, which had begun to roll into the city, appealing to them not to fire. Andrei Alexeev was in a train traveling back to Leningrad from a nature reserve in the North Caucasus. The inhabitants of the compartment heard the radio announcement in silence. Andrei reckoned the best strategy was to sleep for the next twenty-four hours to conserve energy for whatever the future might hold. He arrived back on the evening of the twentieth, and shortly after midnight, when Sobchak called for all able-bodied men to come to the Mariinsky Palace, he went to sit in silent protest should the tanks come. That, he said, was when he realized he was free: he was no longer afraid of what might follow. Kostyshev and his younger colleagues were there too. In Moscow, where the action was, Yeltsin led the opposition from the White House, the seat of government, the crowds surrounding the tanks grew thicker and thicker, and by the twenty-first the putschists had lost their nerve and it was all over. Kostyshev went back to the dentist. Boris Firsov called a meeting at the institute and publicly announced his resignation from the party.

On September 6, with celebrations, huge crowds flocking down Nevsky and to Palace Square, the city was renamed St. Petersburg. Sobchak took over the Smolny Institute, left vacant after the party's dissolution, and moved the Office of the Mayor into the building. At least for the time being, he said. A year later I walked up the drive, still flanked by the two big busts of Marx and Engels, to find the car park full of cars, the guards gone, but Lenin still standing on his pedestal, overcoat flapping, pointing the way forward to a radiant future. The hall was busy again. But why was I there?

Part

2

St. Petersburg

A City Adrift, 1991 to 1994

6

The Political Background

On Christmas Eve, January 6, 1993, the city hosted a Businessmen's Christmas Ball in the Tauride Palace. The celebrations were shown on television. They began with a regimental band, in eighteenth-century costume, heading a procession of horse-drawn coaches to the blue and white Smolny cathedral. The guests, in expensive fur coats, stood in the huge cathedral and listened to a choir singing sacred music. Then came the bells and a blessing, and the regiment marched off down the road to the palace, now blazing with lights. Flunkeys stood at the door. The sponsors were Babylon shops and Smirnoff ("the purest vodka in the world"); the guests were the new businessmen and bankers who paid 100,000r (perhaps $200) a ticket and members of the world of culture who came for free.

The stage managers, also in eighteenth-century costume, read out proclamations, gave a waltz demonstration, and lounged over the upper balcony to create an atmosphere. Alexander Belyaev, the chair of the City Council, gave the first toast on behalf of the city (the mayor, Sobchak, must have been abroad), and led out, uncomfortably, a lady in an eighteenth-century ball dress for the first dance. Most of the guests were in their thirties and forties, with a practical look about them; some of the men were in dinner suits, most in dark suits, some of the women were elegant. But there were no trendsetters. Hardly surprising if, as an ex-party secretary said to me, many of them were ex-Communist Party and Komsomol officials, those practical people with connections, who had now turned their hands to banking and business. They sat at tables in the great ballroom, ate and drank, and watched a floor show (singers of varying quality) while above their heads, against the wall, hung the great banners—Babylon and Smirnoff. There was a fireworks display in the park.

Was this the return to St. Petersburg imagined by those who had flocked to Palace Square in September 1991?

The choice of the Tauride Palace, a beautiful eighteenth-century building set in a park in the center of the city, was not accidental. It holds an iconic place in the city's history. In 1917 it was taken over by the Petrograd Soviet of Soldiers and Workers' Deputies. It was here that the Constituent Assembly, the only assembly elected on the basis of universal suffrage, met in January 1918 and was then closed down by the Bolshevik sailors. After the revolution the palace first housed a Workers and Peasants University and then became the Party High School. By 1990 the school was moving with the times. Although still offering higher education courses to party and Soviet officials and to media employees, the school was planning to transform itself into an Institute of Political Science, open to all, and working to get its degrees accredited. The well-built forty-year-old head of the politics department there came to pick me up in a chauffeur-driven white Volga in September 1990. He exuded energy and confidence. Times had changed, so there were posters announcing a lecture by a British specialist on the Soviet Political System, and the lecture hall was packed with party and Soviet workers, mostly in their thirties, surely wondering what their future careers were going to be. I asked if I could see the hall where the Petrograd Soviet used to meet in 1917, the smoke-filled hall off the grand ballroom, crowded with soldiers and workers, the place where Lenin first claimed the party's readiness to take power. The seats were still arranged as in 1917, and suddenly the old photographs came to life. I felt quite disoriented. Seat of the revolution, Party High School, and now swiftly, almost without warning, home to Political Science? In September 1990 my host could point out to me the place where Lenin used to sit. In December, when I returned with a group of Oxford students, the guide talked of the hall's tsarist past but the revolution had dropped out of its history, and no one knew where Lenin might have sat.

After the failed August putsch of 1991 there were several claimants to the palace. The Party High School stayed put, now transformed into the Northwestern Civil Service Training Center, but found itself in competition for the palace with a new Interparliamentary Assembly of the Commonwealth of Independent States. There was squabbling, picketing by the students, but no decision was forthcoming. In early 1993 a group of democratic politicians, campaigning for a Constituent Assembly to determine the future of the country, decided to hold a conference in the Tauride Palace on January 17, the day the Constituent Assembly was dispersed in 1918. The announcements appeared in the papers but authorization from the chair of the Supreme Soviet in Moscow was required. It proved impossible to contact him by telephone. One of the conference organizers went to Moscow, spent two days sitting in the anteroom to his office, and received a refusal. At the last minute, therefore, and too late to publicize the change of venue, the Conference opened in the Mariinsky Palace, courtesy of the St. Petersburg City Council.

If the pre-conference arrangements were typical of the maneuvering that characterized politics in 1993 so too, sadly, was the conference itself. Sobchak, in a bright red pullover under his sports jacket, called for a minute's silence in memory of those demonstrators shot by the Bolsheviks seventy-five years ago and subjected the audience to a quite confusing piece of oratory. Many of the four hundred or so who attended the first day—activists, political observers, journalists from St. Petersburg, a few from Moscow, and a scattering from the provinces—wanted to speak on the question of a future constitutional order but not necessarily on a Constituent Assembly. Elena Bonner (Sakharov's widow) prefaced her comments by expressing her dismay at the way the city had changed since the Second World War: that morning, in the metro, someone had said to her, "Why doesn't your sort get off to Israel?" With the opening session over, however, many left and the discussion sections, which were to have drawn up proposals, largely collapsed. By next morning perhaps fifty people were left. People drifted in and out. But at two o'clock the members of the Organizing Committee suddenly appeared for the press conference. They expressed the hope that the conference would recommend the calling of a Constituent Assembly and set up a campaign committee. According to the press, the conference was a success. Old ways die hard, I thought despondently, even when the politicians are among those who fought against party rule and when the press is free.

I start with these events because they illustrate both the extraordinary changes that were taking place and the disarray, confusion, and quarrelling over political power that characterized the city's new life as St. Petersburg. Following the dissolution of the USSR, Russia was in need of a new constitution. In January 1993 this was still the subject of an increasingly fractious debate. Yeltsin and the Congress of People's Deputies were at loggerheads. In March 1993 Sobchak responded to Yeltsin's appeal to the people by calling a meeting in support of the president, 5:30 p.m. in Palace Square. It was one of the first spring days and, walking along the embankment and across the bridge, I was pleasantly surprised to see crowds moving in the same direction. I had thought few would come. But two to three thousand gathered, with a handful of the communists shouting opposition slogans. There were all sorts, including the young, and the atmosphere was good humored. Sobchak, who was at his best addressing a crowd, picked an anti-Soviet, anti-communist theme. It sounded dated but there was little that could serve as a positive new message. Artists, deputies, even a representative from the Kirov factory were among the speakers. It was quite encouraging. People were still prepared to turn out. But had Sobchak too been in doubt? I learned the next day that, just as in the old days, an instruction had gone around Smolny: all employees are to attend the meeting in Palace Square. But had they? I hope not.

One early evening in June, Galina and I were walking along Moika, a beautiful street lining the river, just off Palace Square. A militiaman stood guard at the entrance of one of its fine houses. A foreign consulate, I thought, as the white Volga drew up. But out jumped Sobchak and his bodyguards. "Is Ludmila home yet?" he asked the militiaman, as he made for the lift. So Sobchak had bought an apartment, opposite Pushkin's, on Moika. Politics, I thought, is getting more normal all the time.

There were flurries of activity but by the summer of 1993 politics had retreated to Smolny, the Mayor's Office, and to the Mariinsky Palace, home to the City Council. The democratic activists met for a reunion of the discussion club Perestroika but formed no plan of action: they had gone in different directions. Occasionally a small column of communists or Nevzorov's right-wing patriots marched down Nevsky. A hundred or so patriots might gather in Palace Square. They were the most active in selling their literature, often of a racist and anti-Semitic nature, taking over the pavements on Nevsky in front of Gostiny Dvor. The police had cleared most of the worst pornography but tended to leave the patriots alone. The monarchists might be heard in the House of Scholars arguing for the restoration of the tsar, or a conference of "revisionist historians" might claim the authenticity of the *Protocols of the Elders of Zion*. But while there were voices warning of a growing danger of a right-wing backlash against the city's minorities (Jews, Azerbaijanis, all those with "dark skins") support for the patriots was still very low. It was hardly higher, however, for the city's democratic politicians. For the ordinary citizen it was hard to see that the City Council or the Mayor's Office were doing anything to help them to sustain, let alone to improve, their lives. Few had found salvation in a new political creed or in orthodox religion. Spiritualism, the paranormal, and astrology were far more popular. After the main TV news an elderly gentleman with a flowing beard and a young woman (both in black gowns and mortarboards) took it in turns to give the horoscope for the following day.

By now I was traveling a great deal, comparing the changing political scene in half a dozen very different regions in Russia. I was in the city of Kazan, the capital of Tatarstan, in September 1993 when Yeltsin closed the quarrelling congress in Moscow. Congress leaders barricaded themselves in the White House, violence broke out on the streets as their supporters attempted to take over the TV Center, and Yeltsin brought in the tanks. The White House was briefly shelled, a few of its leaders were arrested, dozens died in the fighting before order was restored. Over the next few months a constitution was drafted that strengthened the president's position and created a parliament with far fewer seats than the old congress, and a second chamber, the Federation Council, with two elected representatives from each of the regions. In

December 1993 the new Constitution was passed in a popular vote and elections held for seats in the two chambers.

I was back in the city during the preparations and campaigning for the elections. The seats were hotly contested. Many who had entered the political arena in 1989 wished to continue a political career. In St. Petersburg where the "democrats" now belonged to different political parties, three or four could find themselves competing against each, easing the way for a "patriotic" candidate. How could it have been prevented? It's hard to see. At a meeting that brought together the four "democratic" candidates standing in the central city district, it became clear how unlikely it was that they would agree to support a single one among them. Only one stood down. As expected they split the vote and Nevzorov, the patriotic TV star, won. I acted as a vote counter at my local polling station, with accreditation from the Yabloko party, then went home to watch the results come in. Like many others, I watched with disbelief as the results from the east of the country began to roll in—with the patriotic LDP leading the field. Surrounded by jubilant supporters, its loose-cannon leader Zhirinovsky was doing a victory dance. The TV presenter became more and more uncertain of herself, and then the transmission was cut off.

In March 1994 elections were held for a new, smaller St. Petersburg City Assembly but the turnout was so poor, and again at a second round in April, that the city limped through without its assembly until November. Leonid Romankov kept his seat and spent the summer months drafting new legislation.

This was the political background to life in the city during the years 1991 to 1994. In the chapters that follow, everyday living occupies center stage. For the great majority of the population in the newly renamed St. Petersburg, politics was of far less concern than the move to the market. This dominated everything else. The casement window to the west was flung wide open. The early nineties wrought havoc in a city with long-established "ways of doing things." After so many years of isolation, the city was ill prepared for the introduction of the market, for the explosion of information, the waves of visitors and goods, and its own citizens' new experience of the outside world. Its buildings, institutions, and its people struggled with the fallout from the collapse of the state-owned economy.

How did people cope with privatization, rampant inflation, late payment or nonpayment of salaries, and rising crime? For some these times brought amazing opportunities which were realized, for others it brought impoverishment and insecurity. I knew none of the thirty- to forty-year-olds who attended the ball in the Tauride Palace, nor any of the shop floor workers whose enterprises ground to a halt. My account is very partial—its main focus the no-longer-young Leningrad intelligentsia of my generation. Others—of a younger generation, street children, secretaries, or artists—will appear and add a little more depth to the picture. But, dear reader, you should bear in mind—as I write about buying an apartment, housing repairs, getting a telephone line, shopping, and traveling—that not only was I a bird of passage, with habits and expectations formed in a very different environment; even more important, I was one among the very few in St. Petersburg in the early nineties (although their numbers were increasing) who had access to hard currency, to US dollars.

7

An Apartment and
a Telephone

W hen buying an apartment," said Galina in the spring of 1992,
"you must make sure it has a telephone connection, and then
there's the question of the door."

As I looked forward to spending two years' research leave based at
the Institute of Sociology, and with even cautious Russian friends in
favor, I began to think of buying an apartment. Visiting academics or
graduate students could use it when I was traveling or home in the summer, and I could sell it on to a friend. In May I happened to mention
this to a graduate student from St. Petersburg who was studying at
Oxford. To my surprise, he said that his father was a property dealer
(there was no such profession in the Yellow Pages, but then there weren't
any Yellow Pages) and gave me his telephone number. When I rang
Alexander Isaakevich next day, his first words were that he had a two-
room apartment with a telephone near the Vasilevsky metro, and I should
come to see it; I explained that I was in Oxford and asked him to contact Galina. The result was that within a week, and on the basis of two
phone calls, I had agreed to pay $15,000 plus $120 for the fridge. Vasilevsky Island was the district I wanted to live in and apartments there were
hard to come by.

Vasilevsky Island is one of the oldest districts of the city, bounded
by the wide Neva River to the south and the Finnish gulf to the west. At

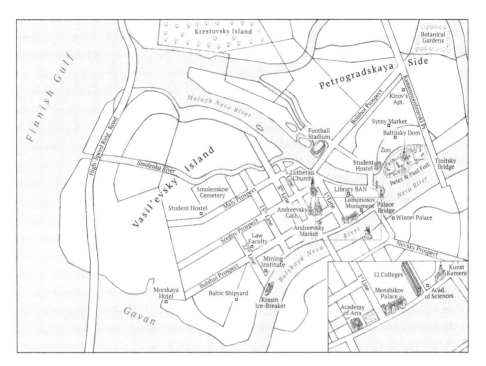

Vasilevsky Island and Petrogradskaya Side.

its western tip is the huge Baltic shipbuilding factory, with its cumbersome Orthodox church that serves as a warehouse. The old port is here, the ugly Morskaya Hotel, and the tourist liners. But follow the road past the factory and down to the embankment and there's the Naval Academy, the old icebreaker *Krasin*, and a frontage of buildings cleverly stepped to preserve the curve. Then comes the bridge of the Annunciation, now widened to sweep the traffic away from Vasilevsky and into the center of the city, toward St. Isaac's Square and the Mariinsky Palace where the City Council has its offices.

The island's grid of eighteenth- and nineteenth-century streets is neat and mathematical, with three main streets — the Bolshoi, Sredny, and Maly Prospects (the Great, Middle, and Little Prospects) — running east to west, crossed by wide streets, often tree lined, with tall apartment blocks, each street different in style and character, and simply called *liniya* (or line), and numbered. Sredny is the shopping street, food shops mostly, and always busy because it has the metro station and the trams. Maly Prospect is quieter, especially as it approaches the old port and passes a sprawling wilderness of silver birch trees in the Smolensk churchyard. In contrast, the Bolshoi Prospect, the grand street of the island, at dusk is one of the world's most beautiful streets, straight, spacious, with an avenue of assorted and untidy trees through which the street lights glimmer like fireflies. With its tree-lined grassy borders, it takes you from the port, past the old-fashioned fire station, past the ornate nineteenth-century maternity hospital, and on to the crossroads where the beautiful pink Andreevsky church stands across the road from the market.

Here one of the oldest streets, with its nineteenth-century pharmacy, runs down to the embankment and, once on the embankment, there's the Academy of Art, the Menshikov Palace, built for Peter the Great's councillor, then the university's green and white philological faculty, and the Twelve Colleges or Main University Building. Across the river St. Isaac's Cathedral dominates the view, there's the statue of Peter the Great on his rearing horse, the yellow Senate building and grand townhouses. Back on our side of the river, Lomonosov, father of Russian science, stands in the square by the university, then come the classically fronted Academy of Sciences, and the blue and white Kunst Kamera. Now we have reached the bridge, which takes us across the river to Palace Square, home of the Hermitage and the Admiralty, and to Nevsky Prospect.

An Apartment on Vasilevsky Island

The apartment in question was on 15th *liniya*, just off Sredny Prospect, almost in the middle of the island, but where there is still a feeling of openness and being near the sea. Over the following months, during which I was now the proud owner of a two-room apartment in a cooperative block, Galina's words came back to haunt me. The cooperative blocks built in the seventies—plain, six-story, pale bricks—have apartments with low ceilings, windows whose glass is too heavy for their frames, poor plumbing, and thin wooden doors. But I had parquet flooring, rooms full of sun, tall trees (ash, sycamore, the odd birch and rowan) outside my third-floor windows, and radiators that worked. Both the main room with its balcony and the kitchen looked into the courtyard where the toddlers played catch around the decrepit benches and the boys played football after school or organized snowball fights. Each room had double windows, and its little window for air in winter, and wide windowsills. Zhivkov's geranium was in place. But my telephone had been disconnected.

One of the hazards in any apartment block was the entrance with its door, which opens into the stairwell where the letterboxes line the wall and the postwoman delivers the newspapers. It can be dark, dirty, and reek of urine or stale potatoes. The rise in crime had brought the installation of doors that open by buzzing an individual apartment and getting a response. Unfortunately our buzzing system was faulty and the firm responsible was unable to commit its engineers to calling to repair it, but we had one of the cleanest stairwells in the city. We were a cooperative, with an elected chairwoman, and had a rota to clean the stairs and the lift. A very sleek black "cooperative" cat slept on the first-floor radiator, went in and out when he chose, and had established a right to having food put out for him.

Across the courtyard, in a third-floor apartment in an older building, a large dog used to sit or stand at his window for hours and, like me, watch life in the courtyard. Sometimes I waved to him. We were, I felt, fellow prisoners. He had nothing to do but wait until his owners returned from work. I was busy writing but my door buzzer did not work, my telephone connection had been cut off, and sometimes the lock on my front door stuck. I had no means of contact with the outside world—unless I went out, which of course I did. I would give the dog a wave from the courtyard; he looked sad. Perhaps he wagged his tail, but I couldn't tell.

But how had I paid for the apartment? A week after the phone calls, an English friend who herself had bought one on the outskirts for $3,000 in 1990, and who had gone with Galina to inspect the apartment on Vasilevsky Island, brought a scrap of paper with a name and a bank account number in Tel Aviv, and the request that I telex the money as soon as possible. I emptied my savings account, added an advance on a book, asked the National Provincial for a Home Improvement Loan for improvements we had recently done to the Oxford house, and, while the paperwork was being done, the principal of St. Hilda's lent me the money. I took an assortment of checks to my bank manager who agreed to telex the money immediately.

But—had I really bought an apartment? I had simply sent a large sum of money to unknown people in Tel Aviv on the basis of trust. Why Tel Aviv? By 1990 Jewish families, emigrating to Israel or America, had begun to sell their apartments for hard currency. The buyers were people with access to foreign currency by virtue of working abroad—in foreign trade or the merchant navy, diplomats, artists, athletes—now increasingly joined by those from the new commercial sector. All kinds of people started putting ads in the newspapers and quoting dollar prices that, by western standards, were very low but were very high in terms of Russian wages and salaries. Now I had bought one. But when I arrived in mid-June, it was still occupied by the family who were exchanging it for a three-room apartment across the street whose occupants were emigrating to Israel. They, in their turn, had "given" their two-room apartment to Alexander Isaakevich to arrange a sale and the sending of the money to Tel Aviv. The agreement worked, more or less, with the move delayed until early July, but the family took the curtain rails and light fittings and, worst of all, broke the agreement to leave the telephone connected.

But who owned it? Foreigners could not own property. I had hoped that we could put it in the name of a friend or of the child of a friend, who could register there. It was not that simple—not, I hasten to add, through any fault of Alexander Isaakevich, of whom more in a moment. First we must take a brief digression on the housing system in the late Soviet period and what happened with privatization.

In the Soviet period most of the housing stock in a city was owned by the municipality. Some enterprises and institutions had their own housing and, from the late sixties on, as we saw, the municipality built "cooperative" blocks in which people with money could "buy" an apartment. But regardless of who owned the housing stock, the critical piece of paper was a Leningrad residential permit, which gave one the right to live in the city, and to so many square meters of living space, or to be on the housing list. In Leningrad, in the central city districts, at the end of the eighties more than half the population were still living in communal apartments—a shared hall, a family per room, one lavatory and bathroom for the two to six families, and a large kitchen with several gas stoves. They made up the numbers on the housing list, awaiting reallocation to an apartment that would give them their rightful square-meter allowance. A single person or a couple might get a one-room apartment: an entrance hall, kitchen, bathroom and lavatory, and one living/sleeping room. Once you had an apartment and were registered as its occupant, however, you could exchange (i.e., buy and sell) as you wished: little strips of paper, with tear-off telephone numbers, were stuck up on fences and walls near metro stations and bus stops, giving details of the exchange or sale being sought. It was extremely complex and time consuming.

I have already described how Galina managed to move from Peterhof to a two-room apartment on Vasilevsky Island. Her neighbors, in the three-room apartment across the landing, consisted of a retired doctor, her married daughter, son-in-law, grandson, and younger daughter. They were looking for two two-room apartments in exchange and would pay cash for the extra room. Couples got divorced in order to get two separate rooms which they could then exchange for a two-room apartment; others made fictitious marriages so that one of them, for a price, could pass their room in a communal apartment on to the other before moving out. A lucky few had apartments grown spacious as grandparents, then parents, died and sisters or brothers moved out. After his parents' death, El'mar and his family moved back into the Botanical Garden, while his sister moved into their cooperative apartment. The Romankov apartment also housed fewer and fewer of the original family. Leonid, married and with a family, had moved out. The municipality had long given up putting those on the waiting list in an apartment where a single family lived.

Apartments had always been the most sought-after commodity in the city, hugely valuable to those who had them and, with privatization underway, now more of an asset than ever before. What did privatization mean in such a context? It was somewhat similar to the privatization of individual apartments in a local authority block in London (i.e., a tenant buys the apartment and becomes a leaseholder). In the summer of 1992 the local authorities in St. Petersburg invited any who wished to "privatize" to put their names down; it issued numbers in the queue, and began to work through the list. The rules were: so many square meters to be allocated per family member at a particular rate, any above this to be paid for at a higher rate; rates varied from block to block depending on whether, for example, it had a lift and central hot water. Once an apartment had been purchased, it could, henceforth, be sold, rented out, disposed of as the owner wished; payment to the local authority for services continued as before; the owner was responsible for repairs, for a property tax, and an inheritance tax was introduced. The purchase price was perhaps three times the average monthly wage—and many were anxious to buy—but in a communal apartment all its occupants needed to agree to buy or sell.

But to do any of this in 1992 you needed a residence permit and, as a foreigner, I was not entitled to one. The solution we reached—after days of discussion, telephoning, taking advice, and sleepless nights—was an agreement, composed by Alexander Isaakevich, which he and I signed and Galina witnessed, that stated I had "given" the apartment to him (and in the case of his death to his heir), and he would at any point make it over to me or to anyone I named; further I signed a witnessed statement as to what should happen in the case of my death, and both documents lay in a sealed envelope in the Institute of Sociology archive. Within a year, new legislation permitted foreigners to own apartments. In October 1993 I became the owner on the basis of a notarized document, heavily typed on top of existing typing (paper was short at the time), and in 1997 I sold it to a young colleague and friend.

In December 1992 the government passed a new law giving everyone the right to privatize their accommodation for a simple registration fee. The City Council announced it would repay those who had bought theirs but, given the rate of inflation, it was hardly an issue. The property speculators appeared, offering individual apartments out on the new housing estates to the inhabitants of communal apartments; desperate measures might be employed against a single unwilling family. (Some years later those still in communal apartments were given the right to buy their room and a share—say a quarter—of the kitchen, bathroom, and lavatory.) City center apartments could be restored to their pre-revolutionary elegance ("luxury ten-room apartment with water-front view," an advertisement might claim) and sold to the new business-men, foreigners, or successful artists. Rostropovich bought one on the embankment looking across to the Peter and Paul Fortress. Institutions, enterprises, and local authorities engaged in litigation over ownership of their properties. As with so much that was happening, the balance sheet tipped both ways: some got a deal they could not have hoped for a year before but the rich were getting richer while most people were getting poorer.

Membership in a cooperative cost about 500 rubles (or $4 in July 1992). The elected committee signed contracts for repair of the door buzzers, the lift, and with the plumbers and gasmen, and issued a monthly service charge bill. There was also a collective decision to pay 4or for the stairwell lighting.

My September 1992 communal services slip was itemized as follows (there were 100 kopeks to a ruble): major repairs, 26 rubles 8 kopeks; services, 93r 46k; radio outlet, 7r; TV aerial, 7r 50k; cold water, 8r 4k; hot water, 9r; heating, 24r 19k; door buzzer, 29r 44k; lift, 16r 49k; other 22r 43k—TOTAL, 243 rubles 63 kopeks.

With the dollar/ruble exchange rate now running at $1:350r, these charges—for anyone with access to dollars—were laughable. For a pensioner, on a basic monthly pension of 2,250 rubles, they were still manageable, but food prices were catapulting up, and no one could live on 500 rubles a week. It was customary to pay the plumbers and gas men extra for any job done. I also paid a standard rate per person for the gas cooker (1r 90k a month), read my electricity meter (24k per unit), filled in little forms and paid them at the nearest post office savings bank. We'll come back to prices, to skyrocketing inflation, and survival tactics in the following chapter, but here a word in advance. Ruble prices were rising in leaps and bounds, but not in the same way for different goods and services, while salaries for those employed in the state sector (and they were the great majority) were barely moving, if indeed they were paid on time. Those with access to dollars were in a privileged position.

While the US dollar/ruble exchange rate did not necessarily keep pace with the rise in ruble prices, it too rose dramatically (from $1:130r in July 1992 to $1:1,250r in December 1993; i.e., ten times). Dollars became the key currency. Prices for certain goods or services were sometimes simply quoted in dollars. Hence in writing of housing repairs and furniture (and I haven't forgotten the steel doors and the telephone) I'll mostly give the dollar prices, occasionally the ruble equivalent. (To put these into pounds sterling would add an unwelcome layer of complication. Suffice it to say that US dollar/£ rate was nearly 1:2 at the start, but for most of 1992–94 it wavered around 1:1.5.) We shall see how, simultaneously, the market was challenging old ways of doing things while breathing new life into traditional patterns of behavior.

Redecoration, Repairs

My apartment badly needed redecorating, plumbing, and electrical work—all that goes under the Russian term *remont*. There were ill-fitting cupboards, the taps dripped incessantly, little festoons of wires hung from the light fittings in the ceilings. Perhaps we could paint it white throughout? But Galina was unenthusiastic—the walls, she explained, are full of bumps—they must be wallpapered. Alexander Isaakevich was undaunted—he would take responsibility for *remont* and the acquisition of furniture.

Alexander Isaakevich was in his fifties, an engineer turned property dealer, emotional, a dab hand at drafting documents, deaf in one ear, with a button-up cardigan. He had many good qualities but promptness (unless it was a financial transaction) was not one of them. Furthermore, he seemed to find it very difficult to *spend* money, as opposed to accumulating it. His head was full of plans, or deals, that would either result in his acquiring dollars or my not indulging in what he considered unnecessary expenditure, or, best of all, plans which would achieve both these ends simultaneously but which often simply did not work. And, furthermore (this was in June), I should on no account travel south to the North Caucasus—it was far too dangerous—he would arrange for me to go instead to a lovely resort, not far from St. Petersburg, where food and lodging was provided in return for hard currency. However, I went to the Caucasus, to a nature reserve (of which more in chapter 9), and when I returned at the end of July nothing had been done. After a tiring day in which, visibly wincing, he handed over the money for three rolls of wallpaper and led me on a fruitless search for shops, long gone out of business, while insisting all the while that he had just the set of coat hooks and armchairs in his apartment that would suit me and surely I needed a dressing table with mirror, I turned in despair to Galina. We revised the strategy. She knew a young couple who would do the *remont*. Alexander Isaakevich would take responsibility for getting a few specified items of furniture.

When I returned from Oxford in September Alexander Isaakevich had done nothing at all except send Galina on two wild goose chases to look at broken secondhand kitchen cupboards; his one further contribution to *remont* had been to provide, for $10, a bronze door lock (made at the Arsenal munitions plant) with a faulty mechanism and to offer to provide me with very cheap garage locks that I could sell in England.

Although, by 1992, there was the occasional sign "Repair of Apartments," St. Petersburg was not a city where you could get quotes from builders, painters, or electricians for jobs to be done. You either did it yourself, buying the materials from a hardware shop (there were a few) if they were in stock, or, through acquaintances, you found someone who worked for a construction firm, had access to materials, and wanted to earn some extra money. My *remont* was done by a young electronics engineer and his wife, a doctor. They painted, papered, put tiles in bathroom and kitchen, redid the electric points, fixed new door handles, put down linoleum, varnished the wooden floors, and hung the kitchen cabinets—for $150 plus cost of materials. They managed to buy all the materials for the ruble equivalent of $88 and a bottle of vodka; and "a kitchen"—cupboards, a new sink, and taps—for the equivalent of $100 and $5 for delivery.

When I returned at the beginning of September with curtain material, paper lampshades, and ant powder, the *remont* was still underway and the only furniture was the new kitchen. There was no sign of the large postwar wooden wardrobe I had agreed to buy from a friend of Alexander Isaakevich's for $10. I rang him to say that I was going with Galina to the furniture store next morning and he agreed to join us there. The shop had one bed, solid, with a good mattress for roughly $25 and a "Sold" sign. The grumpy manager thought for a moment or two. "Would we guarantee to take it?" Then he removed the sign and said it was ours; he was tired, he explained, of answering questions about it. We looked at furniture and quickly decided on the heaviest, most expensive, comfortable, and ugly set imaginable: a sofa bed, two massive armchairs, and a pouffe, in brown and maroon with yellow flecks. Here we were talking of more than $200 — a university professor's salary for a year and a half. The manager wavered upon learning we did not have enough rubles but agreed to hold the furniture for us, as long as Galina remained as hostage while I went to the bank. I made it back in three-quarters of an hour to find Alexander Isaakevich, who had joined Galina, in a state of nerves: had I really managed to make my way through the gangs of southern bandits who hung around banks, he wanted to know, and was I sure I was not being followed by a tail? We counted out the piles of notes to the cashier and arranged with a delivery truck to bring the furniture straightaway (for $5); Alexander Isaakevich and I took the tram and, by the time we arrived, they were already there.

By September 20 the painting and decorating was finished and the floors were being varnished. It is customary to leave the gas cooker in place. Mine was old and dirty but working. Galina telephoned Vitya, a gas man with whom she retained contact because he was so reliable and, sure enough, Vitya was there with his little bag at the appointed time. He serviced the stove, checked all the outlets, declared it safe and in working order, and charged 30 rubles (the price of two loaves of bread); he agreed to come and do the pipe work, if we decided to move it, but that would cost 500r (or $1.50).

It was more difficult to get hold of the *santekhniki*, responsible for the plumbing and heating in the apartment block. I rang and fixed a day and time but, when it came, they were too busy with a broken pipe. On the third day they came — one was tall with dark glasses, a baseball cap, and trainers; the other was short and silent, in rubber boots up to his knees. They agreed to install the new sink for 1,500r ($4.50) and to check the lavatory cistern, and started work, turning to me from time to time for scissors or a screwdriver. The thread of the new hot water tap was damaged — "typical," said Sasha, the one in dark glasses. "What shall we do?" I asked, despairingly, well aware that there was no way we could return the faulty item and get another. "We'll think of something," he said. He did: the hot tap worked, but only by turning the wrong way. (Alas, I did not warn a British colleague who borrowed the apartment for a month the following summer—during which time the hot water is turned off—and who left the tap fully open; when the hot water came back on, it overflowed from the sink to the apartment below.)

Because equipment was sometimes faulty or parts were lacking, cobbling together was an important skill. Ingenuity was ever present. I wedged a sawn-off piece of curtain rod into the hole of a broom head to make a handle for it. The lavatory cistern had a bundle of corks tied up with string in place of a ballcock because someone had borrowed it; when he brought it back, he dropped it into the cistern "to use if need be." It will float there for eternity. The *santekhniki* claimed the cistern was fine and there was no way they could replace the broken lid because none were available, but then the short one in wellingtons said he had seen a notice on a wall offering one for sale for 30or ($1), went to get it, and they fixed it. To install the new sink meant removing tiles from the wall, which they did, with care, so that I could replace them: I would never manage, they said, to find the matching color white. I spent three hours scraping the grayish cement off the back and acquired a large bottle of tile glue. In theory grout (*gruntovka*) existed but when there is a *defisit* (which there was at that moment) people mix together alabaster and something else to use as a substitute; I never learned what it was because, it turned out, there was also a *defisit* of alabaster. Vitya came and moved the gas stove. A young former student of Galina's who was trying to find funding to support a new private school, where he taught history and Latin, came and checked the light fittings, put up a couple of shelves, and struggled with the curtain rails.

Steel Doors

I look back, wryly, at my naïve optimism of those first weeks. Surely I would be in my apartment by my birthday, September 25? Galina talked encouragingly of the progress we were making, sent me to look for curtain rails (I found them—metal with savage dragon teeth hooks that grip the top of the curtain—bought a 3 meter rail and fastenings for less than a reel of imported cotton), and then suggested that the next major item was a steel door. She had been trying for two years to get new locks for her doors. First Vasya, a carpenter, had come, turned the inner door round, did half the job, and then left with a promise to return within a week. He left some of his tools and a spare pair of trousers but never came back. Another, Viktor, came and measured up but then developed a bad back. Both her outer and inner door locks could jam, leaving her trapped in the little entrance hall, with keys stuck in all the locks. She had a huge iron hook to secure the outer door and at night propped a sloping piece of wood between the two doors. I explored the possibility of bringing Chubb dead locks from England but St. Petersburg doors are 2mm too thin. By September, however, she had learned of a new "firm" that made steel doors, for 15,000r ($75), and also good quality wooden furniture. Nowhere, new or secondhand, had I been able to find bookshelves or a plain, solid table to serve as a writing desk. Perhaps they would make them—for dollars? We went to investigate.

We found two young men in jeans and leather jackets sitting on an old sofa in a small office. A steel door was propped against the wall, and someone was drinking tea in an inner room. One of the young men took out his notepad, made notes of our order of two doors, agreed to send someone to measure up, and promised a two-week fitting. Then we mentioned a table—for dollars. Ears visibly pricked up, we moved into the inner room to discuss details with an elderly designer, and were promised a quote by the next day. It was steep: the equivalent of $350 for one door, the table, and bookcase. We went to argue it out with the boss, a tall, strapping engineer in his late thirties, who had not wanted to commit himself to a price for a door for Galina because hers was nonstandard but then proposed a deal of $400 and 14,000r for both doors and furniture; we got it down to $400 and 5,000r and top priority for the job. I paid $100 down. The next day Igor, smelling of drink, came to measure up my door; then we went together, with a brief detour for him to buy vodka, to measure Galina's. He then upset her by suggesting that our locks were very ordinary and, for safety's sake, we should change them now. So next day I went in search of reliable locks, but to no avail. Vavylon had sold out, the hardware shops had heavy standard locks, the Commercial Center had one huge garage lock on a shelf together with Tampax and Wash and Go shampoo.

The firm took three weeks to complete our order, which was not so bad, and we set out to inspect the results. We took a trolley, then walked down a muddy country-like lane by the waterfront until we came to the red brick entrance and large gates of a factory yard. Waiting by the turnstile was one of the young men, who got us past the doorkeeper and into the "military-industrial complex." Perhaps the factory produced something heavy, judging by the size of the huge trucks and the metal castings, but "conversion of the defense industry" meant that our private furniture firm now worked within it. First the young engineers had leased one shop, then set up a store and an office; they were working with a Finnish firm on designs, to get materials, and to export; they hired their own labor—perhaps fifty carpenters, designers, and locksmiths—and paid their workforce well. Once we had inspected the doors and tried the locks, approved the table and bookcase, agreed that delivery would be at one o'clock, and paid the balance, we went to see the workshop. They were working in pine, in oak, and producing garden furniture in teak, making bedroom suites, kitchen and dining room furniture for, as they put it, the "new bourgeoisie and millionaires." It was nice, and expensive.

They came on time, half a dozen of them, carried everything upstairs, put the table and bookcase together, and left fifteen-year-old Valery and his mate (a huge bruiser of a man with a cropped head) to install the door. Mine was only the second door Valery had installed. He somehow never got things right at school, so he had left and joined his father, who designed and made locks for the firm, in the hope that he would do better with his hands. They undid the wires of the doorbell and asked for some cotton so they could tie the wires of their electric drill to them to get a connection; they also borrowed scissors because they had forgotten a knife and asked for toothpaste to mark the lock fitting. We had to use Johnson's Baby Oil (I had no other) to oil the lock. They filled the corridor with smoke from the blowtorch and scorched the new linoleum. They worked from 1 p.m. till 7 p.m. and finally had to admit defeat: the lock would not work smoothly. Next day Valery's father came, took it apart, worked all morning, and finally I had an inner door of steel, cased in wood, with bolts that shot into place.

Valery and the big bruiser spent all day on Galina's door, again rigging up an electric power connection but one which, this time, blew the fuses. As they were finishing, her neighbors stopped on the stairs. "Well," they said, "with a door like that you will be the first target for all the thieves. Whatever made you waste money on it?" and swept out to the theater. And these were friendly neighbors. Galina burst into tears; Valery, on top of the ladder, gritted his teeth. "Shall I go after them and give them what for?" he asked.

A fortnight later a friend sent two women, decorators at her place of work, to fill in the gaps around the hinges and repaint the surrounds. They came during working hours because there was a power cut, and they had nothing to do. They filled the cracks with rags dipped in plaster, painted and varnished; 500r (or $1.50) for about six hours' work on the two doors, and I gave them bars of chocolate for their children. Next day my lock stuck completely. I telephoned Galina. Hers was fine, but water was dripping into her bathroom from the apartment above whose occupants were out at their dacha in the country. It took her two days, and a sleepless night emptying buckets of water, to sort it out. I spent the night there, and next day Valery's father came and freed the lock. A few days later while visiting Galina I found her doorbell was missing and there was a pool outside her door: someone had taken against her for installing an expensive door, had broken the bell and removed her notice (Please Knock!) three times; now he had pissed on the doorstep.

The Telephone

At last we come to the telephone. Here, for the reader, is a glimpse of the role played by that instrument in Soviet everyday life and how citizens and the state responded to each other in their attempts to gain access to or retain control over this priceless resource. It's history now. Perhaps, in the Russian context (and not only the Russian?), the mobile phone was the most revolutionary invention of the early twenty-first century.

A communal apartment would have one telephone in the entrance hall for all the occupants. A one-family apartment might have its own telephone line. A telephone was vital because everyday living took an enormous amount of organizing. The phones on the street and in institutions often did not work and 15 kopeck pieces were in short supply. Given that there were not enough lines to satisfy demand, getting a private line was a major undertaking—maybe a fifteen-year battle—and in such a situation money (bribes) and connections counted. In the sixties, a friend used to ask every taxi driver whether he knew of a way to get a telephone. Finally one said yes and gave her a telephone number; she rang and was told to find 300r (a year's student grant) and come on a certain day, at a certain time, to an address on the outskirts. She and her mother scraped and borrowed and set off together. There, in a half-empty apartment, sat a large man in a sheepskin coat; they counted out the money, he said that in three months they would have a telephone, and they left. For the next three months they looked at each other with dismay: how could they have been so foolish? But three months to the day, a piece of paper arrived: they had been given a line and the number was such and such. The stories are legion. Someone noticed two telephone engineers fixing a phone on the street outside his apartment. For a bottle of vodka they obligingly put a party line through the wall into his room and, ever after, he had a free phone.

Now my apartment had a line (and I continued to pay line rental); it just happened to have been disconnected. Alexander Isaakevich, however, refused to be too concerned: it could all be sorted out. He knew the vice rector of an institute who would help. That was in July. By mid-September he had managed to contact the vice rector who, it turned out, had met me on a previous occasion; he had spoken to an official in the Mayor's Office and sent him a letter requesting that as someone who brought benefit to the city by organizing a scholarship program for graduates I should be given a telephone. Everything, Alexander Isaakevich assured me, would be sorted out in a couple of weeks: sufficiently important people were involved. I began to hope. But then came the call from the telephone exchange: yes, the telephone could be reconnected for the going commercial rate: 150,000r ($500). Alexander Isaakevich flapped helplessly. I rang the vice rector who, initially unsure whether to back out or not, agreed to ring his contact in the Mayor's Office. At this point I turned for advice to a friend in the City Council whose wife had worked with the vice rector: she would find out from him how matters lay and tell him that the City Council would write in support if need be. A few days later I received a message that I should ring an official in the Mayor's Office, and a week later, after several phone calls, I walked up the crowded avenue that led to Smolny for a 3 p.m. appointment. I gave Lenin a cheerful wave.

My official, a fair-haired young man in his late twenties in a dark suit and carrying a clipboard, shepherded me into the corridor, stopping to go over some papers with another young man, and then, as we went up the now busy staircase, explained that he had arranged a meeting with the head of the communications department who was very tied up and that he himself only had "a small window" free in the middle of the afternoon: maybe we would have to wait. Although the office was busy, the Head of Communications, a dapper ex-communications engineer in his mid-fifties, agreed to see us almost immediately. I explained that I was here to do academic work for two years and also helped with academic exchanges; I was living in a private apartment but the phone had been cut off and a request, supported by the vice rector, that it be reconnected had brought a request for 150,000r. "When was the phone disconnected?" he asked, "and to whom does the apartment belong?" I explained that it belonged to Alexander Isaakevich, but that he was not registered there. He thought for moment, wrote down the details, and rang the head of the district telephone exchange—asked him to find out whether the number had been reallocated and to ring him back immediately. For the first time I heard the language of command used by a political superior, both then and a few minutes later when the district official rang back to report that the number had been reallocated to an invalid and that he had absolutely no free numbers whatsoever. The tone of the department head was good natured, even joking at times— "We haven't yet developed a system of residential permits for the English"—but on both occasions his voice abruptly changed, became hard, almost metallic—"All the same you will find a number, you will issue it, as an exception, as a temporary number on a two-year basis; we shall send the supporting letter to the Head of the Telephone Exchange, and you will make the ordinary charge for an expert, who acts as a consultant to the Mayor's Office"—and then he resumed the friendly tone of conversation between equals. He gave the young official his instructions—his department should prepare the document, stating that I was a consultant, and pass it to him; he would sign it, and then the young official should take it to Yashin, Head of the Telephone Exchange.

Out in the corridor the young official was pleased: it had gone well, Alexander Alexandrovich had written down all the details; he would do the document today but needed to check with the vice rector on the exact wording of the phrase "a consultant to the Mayor's Office." Feeling that I ought to earn such a title, I suggested that I could help with corrections of English texts produced, for foreign firms, by the Mayor's Office. How long, I asked, might the telephone take? A foolish question. He hesitated to say. I persisted. A week, do you think? "Well," he said, "there's all that paperwork involved, perhaps two weeks, but I can't answer for the telephone exchange."

I walked back through the Tauride Palace gardens, eating a currant bun (5r from a new "Scottish breads, Staff of Life" shop), but neither the colors of the autumn park nor the thought of the two kilos of buckwheat I had been lucky enough to buy raised my spirits. I had asked a favor from individuals operating a system in a way that I disapproved of, and thus condoned the practices themselves; I had set out win over the department head and smiled and thanked him, while being inwardly dismayed at the way he spoke to subordinates. Was this any better than offering a bribe? The other aspect that depressed me was to feel the atmosphere in Smolny—a hive of officialdom, the seat of power, dispensing rights and favors—so similar to the old party headquarters.

Two weeks later I telephoned the young official. He had not actually done anything because he still required a few details; I gave them to him. He suggested I ring the following Monday. Surprisingly, he was there, assured me that the letter was done, and we could expect an answer on Thursday. On Thursday he assured me it would be Friday; on Friday, silence. Then came the November holiday. Tuesday, silence. Wednesday, Thursday, silence. . . . But maybe, *maybe*, I comforted myself, the engineer who was to have come to mend the door buzzer would call in the evening? Nina Timofeevna, chair of our cooperative, had put in another request but, as she explained, it would all depend on whether he came into the office to pick up the request slip. Galina counseled patience.

November came and went, the door buzzer was fixed, but the hope of a telephone receded into the distance. The young official was elusive but, when caught unexpectedly in his office, always promised an answer would be forthcoming the following day. It never was. We changed the strategy, and the academic secretary of the Institute of Sociology rang him on my behalf. It was the same story. Alexander Isaakevich insisted that until I said the magic words "I shall be very grateful to you" (i.e., the offer of a bribe), we would get nowhere. The young official insisted that he had delivered the letter to Yashin, Head of the Telephone Exchange, but Yashin's deputy confirmed that no letter had arrived. Finally, at the end of the month, the young official reported that Yashin had said that he did not want to make exceptions, and we should request for a line on a commercial basis. At least something was clear.

Newspapers had recently reported that the new rate for a telephone line was 97,000r (or $220 at existing exchange rates, a university teacher's salary for two years). Alexander Isaakevich went off to the district office. I was hopeful and prepared to pay. However, in the middle of December a letter came stating that the number was to be reallocated to the next WWII veteran on the waiting list. Alexander Isaakevich was enraged and talked of going to court; I felt bad about the war veteran but everyone said that was a fiction. I went to Moscow, leaving matters in the hands of an acquaintance who knew a number for telephone engineers who, for a price (around 6,000r), could usually get a number allocated. But when I returned, the news was bad: my district exchange was small and numbers in great demand; the pressure, it seemed, would have to come from on high. I left for England for Christmas disheartened.

But on my return after the New Year, to my amazement and delight, friends who were living in the flat showed me a card stating that the telephone was going to be reconnected the following day. I couldn't believe it. Alexander Isaakevich came, collected $100, and went off to get the agreement. He had managed it after all. The vice rector had gone to see Yashin; what was said, I don't know, but George Soros had just given $1 million to Russian science, including telecommunications, and the original request had mentioned my connections with the Soros Foundation. Yashin had authorized the request, and for the price of 20,000r (perhaps $50). Galina and I spent a morning in the telephone exchange, sitting in a queue. As our turn approached, a woman turned to us. "Could I go before you?" she asked "I need to get to the cemetery to visit a grave." "No," said Galina, usually the kindest of people. "Whoever is in it will wait for you." We signed the deal with the district officials who were not pleased that it was being done so cheaply. Some of the $100 went on a bottle of Yves Rocher scent (for whom?), and we agreed I should invite the vice rector to dinner.

The telephone came to life but it was faulty. I could ring out, but it didn't ring for incoming calls. The next day I went to look for a telephone. The shop on Sredny Prospect that sold guitars had a snazzy red pushbutton phone in the window, but the assistant was selling the last one as I went in. I headed for the Technical Literature bookshop, just off Nevsky, which I was told had some German phones but there were only very expensive ones from Bangkok (the more exotic the foreign phone the less well it worked); Gostiny Dvor did not have any; Passazh had two huge Polish telephones, the size of small tanks, expensive and no guarantees; Melodiya, the music shop, had a Phillips car phone. I gave up and headed for home but, as a last chance, called in at the hardware shop on First Line—and there was a lilac-colored Russian telephone for 2,000r ($5), complete with its passport (electrical goods have passports; i.e., a document with a stamp and the sales assistant's signature). It did not have a plug, but I thought I could use the old one. No such luck. My new phone had two wires, and the old one had four. I turned to a neighbor for help, and he attached my new phone wires to the old ones. There is a *deficit* of plugs. It worked. Suddenly everything became manageable. It was an uncomfortable lesson though—because I had used connections to get the telephone line and, by the end, had ceased to feel a qualm.

8

The Market Wreaks Havoc

How did the market—at first stealthily, then brazenly—change ways of life in the city, and what we can call "the Soviet shopping experience"? And who were the winners and the losers? Trying to make sense of my collection of receipts and notes and the changing relative prices in those years, I went to Andrei Alexeev. He had always kept receipts and train and theater tickets. "Are they in the archive," I asked. "Can I check how much our train tickets to Krasnodar cost in 1992?" "No," he said, "if you are writing a memoir, it should be of what you remember. You are not writing a scientific analysis." I was quite disgruntled. Surely I should try to check my figures? And surely my account was. . . . But then I started to think, yes, that's a task for a future historian. So, I am grateful that he has made my task easier. If I can't provide a "scientific analysis," I can offer a series of snapshots.

In November 1992, standing at the dairy counter, looking at prices, an old woman turned to me. "Can you help me out, I'm a pensioner, and I'm six rubles short for eggs?" In early September eggs were 27r for ten, now they were up to 90r or 100r. Not having an egg container, I had to carry mine, carefully, in a plastic bag. Walking home along Bolshoi Prospect, I was stopped several times and asked, "Where did you get eggs, and how much were they?" A woman sitting next to me in the metro asked, "Can you tell me where in the city one can buy cheap sour cream?" I found myself swallowing back the gramophoned reply, "You won't find cheap sour cream anywhere, everything's become expensive nowadays." "I don't know," I said feebly and resigned myself to hearing about her struggle to prepare for her son's birthday.

Pensioners on the basic pension of 2,250r a month were the worst off. They would not be paying more than 30or for rent and services but they weren't eating well for 50or a week. Potatoes and onions and cabbage were within reach (30r a kilo) but any decent meat (500–80or a kilo), sugar (16or a kilo), or biscuits (10or) were luxury goods. It wasn't just prices that were the problem in 1992. The real problem was the availability of goods. If you saw a staple (sugar, cooking oil, flour, rice, buckwheat, salt), you immediately bought no less than two kilos. Once you had stood in the queue for twenty minutes, already late for work, the rationale of buying two kilos rather than one became strikingly obvious. And the staple might not be seen again for the next two months. In November sugar reappeared but cooking oil and salt had not been seen since mid-September.

In 1992 and the early months of 1993 the shortage of goods and their rocketing prices dominated people's lives. It could take an hour to make one basic purchase. By the summer of 1993, with careful planning, I could make three. Smart new food shops had opened whose customers arrived in cars. One such, on Vasilevsky Island, was called Antante (every schoolchild grew up knowing of the iniquitous Entente Cordiale). It sold imported food, alcohol, and fruit and had a battery of shop assistants who stood checking for theft. Its prices were very high but people were buying. Some just came to look, others to buy one lemon for a sick child, or an impoverished intellectual might be seen purchasing 250 grams of salami to take to a relative in the hospital, but there were young couples filling baskets of goods. As I stood at the cash desk— with two bottles of Moldavian wine for 2,40or ($2 each), a packet of digestive biscuits, one of Leibnitz biscuits, a packet of frozen chicken livers, and some sliced pork for a total of 11,00or (or $10)—I realized that I was no longer the richest person in the queue. The new class had arrived.

By the end of 1993 what mattered was whether your wage or salary was rising and whether it was being paid on time. And access to dollars was critically important to keep abreast of rising prices or to purchase the new sought-after goods that were appearing. More and more it was true that if you had money you could find what you wanted. But not always. Electric light bulbs might disappear for a month or two. Spare car parts were notoriously difficult, I was told. But, as I wrote in October 1993, "Living is different from a year ago." In 1992 I had spent days trying to find china plates, pots, and bowls—any household things. I had spent a day fruitlessly looking for door locks. Now I could be pretty sure of finding what I wanted in a morning. Maybe I had been lucky with the doormat (someone had taken mine while I was away) but the ironmonger's had blossomed—now it had a large wallpaper section (imported from Spain).

By the autumn of 1994 when I left for home, everyday living was still fraught with uncertainty and for many, particularly the elderly with few resources, very hard. But nothing was quite like the extraordinary years of 1992 and 1993.

Autumn/Winter 1992–1993

In the autumn of 1992 a theater ticket cost less than an egg. An air ticket halfway across Russia cost the same (450r) as three scoops from the new Baskin-Robbins ice cream parlor on Nevsky. A bottle of vodka cost the same as an imported spool of cotton thread; a week's basic pension could buy you a fine-writer ballpoint pen. Some of these, it is true, were imported goods. But hardware goods seemed absurdly cheap in relation to food (a shower curtain for the price of a kilo of potatoes, a doormat the same as a kilo of tomatoes), and books were still very cheap—good quality volumes at 35r or 50r (less than a lemon)—as were theater and concert tickets. Travel was still extraordinarily cheap: an airfare to Arkhangelsk for the cost of 500g of salami?

There were a few elementary rules that governed shopping. First, never leave home without a sturdy shopping bag inside which you had put three smaller plastic bags. (If you suddenly saw butter, or rice, or eggs, you would need the bags for the assistant to use; if you were hoping for sour cream, take a jam jar with a screw top.) Second, buy two kilos rather than one of any staple. Third, before joining a queue, ask.

Queueing for sugar, I asked the old lady in front of me if I needed a special token. "Of course," she said. "Do you qualify as a Group 1 or Group 2 invalid?" Fourth, if there were milk products but no queue, the milk would be sour. Finally, if you saw any item (a mirror, an extension cord, a doormat) that you needed, buy it there and then: the chances of it still being there the next day were slight.

One day I was in high spirits. I called in at the ironmongers and they had meat grinders ($1.50) and plastic lids for jam jars, both large and small size (2r each). "What a happy day it is," said the elderly man who joined me at the counter, "even small jam jar tops." Now the day before I had spotted that they had little saucers for jam, and got my cash slip for six (less than a dollar) but then came the frustration: the two large men in front of me had bought three tea sets (8,000r or roughly $22 each). The assistant (and there was only one) had to check each piece of china to make sure it was sound and then repack the lot. Still, never mind, not only had I got a meat grinder and the jam jar tops but also theater tickets for Bulgakov's *Day of the Turbines*—for 8r each. I splashed out and bought a lemon for 56r.

Outside the metro stations and down the main streets, kiosks appeared selling T-shirts, running shoes, tins of peas, sunglasses, cheap jewelry, and cigarettes, all jumbled together. Individuals hawked cigarettes at street corners, kittens and puppies in the underpass on Nevsky Prospect. Children tried to sell newspapers in metro passages, and beggars and cripples sat against the walls with their battered caps in front of them. Currency dealers appeared in every guise. The availability of all kinds of alcohol, and the general slackening of police or social control, meant that the drunks appeared on the streets. One weaved his way past me, saying, "I may be a drunk but I can play the piano too." They were mostly men, staggering quietly along the pavement, but you might meet a woman singing raucously as she skipped along, tipping a beer bottle back.

The markets had changed little since the sixties, except they were better stocked, full of flowers as well as fruit and vegetables (tomatoes, aubergines, cucumbers, grapes; apples and pears in September; apples, grapes, and pomegranates were still there in November, as well as the basic potatoes, carrots, onions, garlic, and cabbage). The fruit sellers were mostly from the south, from Georgia or Central Asia, as they always had been, while Russian peasants brought the vegetables, meat, curds, and honey. Meat prices were double those in the shops but the quality and availability much better: beef and pork, equally expensive, a little veal, big rabbits, scrawny chickens, little suckling pigs, salt pork . . . but at phenomenal prices. Few could afford to buy in the markets.

But it was the time required to make purchases that was still the real killer in 1992. Home in Oxford for Christmas, my husband Alastair and I went food shopping. Standing in Sainsbury's car park, looking at a shopping trolley that contained food for a family for a fortnight, I nearly wept. It had only taken an hour to purchase the lot. The luxury Christmas items left me cold. It was the shelves of household goods, mops, cleaning materials, bathroom mirrors, and tin openers that held my attention. Monday hammered home the same message. By 4 p.m. I had had my eyes tested and ordered new spectacles, been to the dry cleaners, and to the bank; I had been to St. Hilda's, gone through my mail, spent an hour going over work with colleagues, and had lunch. In St. Petersburg I would have been pleased to have achieved just one of these, and even that would have taken a day's planning. Then to the Youth Hostel Shop with a pair of boots that Andrei Alexeev had bought on a visit in 1991 and which were beginning to crack in two places. I did not have the receipt nor the five years' guarantee (had the firm counted on the boots being worn *every day* to trudge over hard pavements, I wondered?) but the assistant immediately agreed to send them back to the factory, either for repair or for the issuing of a credit slip. But would we get them back by January 4, when I was due to leave? Might not Christmas and New Year mean the factory was shut for a week? She telephoned to find out and was told to give me a replacement pair there and then. The size was not in stock. No problem. She telephoned around, and the Cambridge branch agreed to put a pair in the post that afternoon. I left feeling stunned. The whole matter had been resolved in such an efficient, matter-of-fact, and pleasant way, as though this was the *normal* way to behave, but from a Russian perspective it was extraordinary.

I had left Galina sick with pneumonia. Fortunately her neighbors were looking after her, and she had managed to acquire medicine. Everyone had to pay for medicine in Soviet times but the prices were miniscule;

now they had gone sky high and in St. Petersburg one pharmacy was selling for hard currency only. If you could not afford the medicine, that was it. The elegant pharmacy, near the Andreevsky Market on Vasilevsky Island, with its original late-nineteenth-century interior, potted palms, and china pestles and mortars, was selling American aspirin—100 tablets for 903r (nearly two weeks' basic pension). A course of antibiotics could cost 8,000r (two months' salary for Galina). True, the system still worked, up to a point. Sergei, a young historian in her department, awoke one night with a terrible stomach pain. The doctor came and then the ambulance, and within hours he was being operated on for a perforated ulcer. But it was not a time to be sick. In the summer Galina had developed an abscess under a tooth. It took a week to diagnose because the dental clinic, with no x-ray film, would only do x-rays for those who could provide an old piece of film. She had no painkillers. When they finally pulled the tooth, without anesthetic, she lost consciousness.

"What's new?" I asked the friend who met me at the airport when I returned after Christmas. "They are introducing a system of medical insurance," he told me. "The employer will deduct 5 percent from the wage packet to cover it." "But what will it mean in terms of medical care?" I asked. "As far as I understand," he said, "it won't mean anything different; you'll just get treated as before." So what did it mean? The original party hospital, the "Sverdlovka," the best in town, offered a scheme in 1992 under which, by signing a contract with them for 2,500r, an individual was entitled to use their services at slightly more favorable rates. Under such a contract medical treatment, in hospital, for a fortnight (not inclusive of surgery) cost 15,000r (Galina's salary for four months). Diphtheria arrived with winter (845 cases by January 1, up four times on 1992) and then a flu epidemic. A mass vaccination campaign got underway, but not for pensioners. A sensible policy given limited supplies of vaccine, but a little hurtful.

In mid-February I left for Moscow, on the fast overnight Thursday train, at a cost of 400r. The Institute of Sociology had issued me with a *spravka* (document) that entitled me to pay for train and air tickets in rubles and this meant (given the exchange rate now at $1:450r) that a ticket to Moscow cost between 50 cents and $1 (depending upon type of train), bedlinen and tea was 100r and 17r. The train from Moscow to

Perm in the Urals (a twenty-four-hour journey) cost $1.50, Perm to Yekaterinburg (overnight) less than a dollar. In March I flew from Yekaterinburg to Tomsk in Siberia, a two-hour flight, for $10, and from Tomsk back to St. Petersburg for $30. In May when I left from Moscow with a friend for a month in the Far North, I had $200 in my jeans pocket to cover our costs.

Spring/Summer of 1993

By January 1993 most of the state shops (the big department stores, the food shops, hardware and electrical goods, the stationery and the book shops, and the state chain of newspaper kiosks) had been privatized. The consequences for sales or service were barely noticeable. This was hardly surprising. The shops still got most of their goods from the state wholesale network, which delivered in bulk (if one food shop on the island had rice, you could be pretty sure the others would too); the assistants had always survived on poor wages by pilfering and paying little attention to the customers—and nothing had changed here. They were hardly in competition for customers. Hardware shops traditionally were shut on Mondays; they still all were. In most shops you still queued twice: first at the cash desk to pay and get a slip, then at the counter to collect the goods. Sometimes you still queued three times: first to have the cheese weighed, then to go and pay, then back again to collect it. Then you joined the queue for cabbage.

What had changed by the spring of 1993 (and spring in St. Petersburg comes in April) was that the old state shops now offered a sometimes bizarre assortment of western goods at very high prices, as well as their basic stock. The little bakery across the street had Italian liqueurs, Amoretto (for a fortnight's basic pension), and Wrigley's chewing gum. Gostiny Dvor, the big department store on Nevsky, had a Littlewoods section (for hard currency) and sections selling Smirnoff vodka, Martini vermouth, all kinds of dubious western alcohol, fruit juice, biscuits from Denmark and Syria, bars of chocolate from unknown firms, and poor quality Brazilian instant coffee, all at exorbitant prices in relation to Russian wages and salaries.

New private shops appeared in basements selling the oddest assortments of goods: leather jackets, a telephone or two, some instant coffee, and Pepsi Cola. Every one of them was a "salon." At first, mistakenly, I thought that St. Petersburg was now awash with private hairdressers. Not so, I realized after finding myself in a salon selling electrical tools and kettles and seeing a sign for a "Salon—Building Materials" and another "Salon—Books and Car Spare Parts." Even the tram drivers had been infected: "Move down the salon, please," one barked over the intercom.

New "western" restaurants and bars (including a new John Bull Pub off Nevsky that was said to be very authentic inside) appeared, bearing no resemblance to the old Intourist hotels or the cooperative (private) restaurants that had first appeared in the cellars. They were smart, well designed, and sold foreign draft beer, cappuccino coffee, and burgers. And, as I have already described, by the late summer of 1993 new food shops were offering a wide variety of goods.

An Audi, driven by a curly haired young man, pulled to the curb opposite the Antante; three businessmen in camelhair coats and smart leather shoes, standing by a chauffeur-driven car, turned out to be not Finns but Russians. In the Neva Star hard currency shop in the Hotel Moskva, where the clientele used to be almost exclusively Finns buying alcohol, two little boys chased round the chocolate counter, paused to finger the sweets, and asked their father in his leather jacket and jeans for Mars bars. But they didn't care when he said no; they had all the chocolate they wanted anyway. Even the grubby greengrocers across the street from my flat had had an amazing facelift by the autumn of 1993— smart, light glass counters with fruit and vegetables (kiwis and peaches), meat and cheese (a tin of corned beef for 1,000r, or $1), and alcohol and chocolate (a bottle of wine also 1,000r, cognac 3,000r).

However, for the majority of the population, and especially for the pensioners, the everyday search for affordable food was still exhausting. Food prices continued to escalate. Berlin in the 1920s came to mind—I had often wondered what the hyperinflation had felt like. Perhaps July to December of 1992 was the worst, when prices of basic foodstuffs (rye bread, milk, butter, and cheese) could double in a month. Over the two years between September 1992 and September 1994 a loaf of rye bread went from 13r to 500r, a kilo of cheese from 170r to 6,000r, potatoes from 25r to 900r. A basket of goods (bread, butter, cheese, potatoes, eggs, tomatoes) that had cost 600r in October 1992 was costing 3,800 by October 1993, perhaps 11,000r by September 1994. (In dollar terms: $1.75 in October 1992, $3.50 in October 1993, $6 in September 1994.) Train tickets, metro tickets, and telephone charges began to rise sharply in 1993. By 1994 a train ticket to Moscow had risen from less than $1 to $3.50 (7,000r) but communal services charges and theater tickets had remained low. Veterans of the Siege, but not ordinary pensioners, received free city transport.

In November 1992 a professor's salary was 4,000r; by November 1993 Galina was getting (if paid on time) on the order of 60,000r, or fifteen times her earlier salary. My colleagues in the Institute of Sociology remained on miserable salaries. Was Galina better off than a year ago? It did not feel like that—in part, perhaps, because of the change in relative prices, but in part because the array of goods had qualitatively changed. In the autumn of 1992 I tried living on 4,000r a month ("Quite perverse," said Andrei Alexeev, which I thought was rather hard coming from someone who believed in putting theory into practice) and managed it—including buying meat—until I needed to buy birthday gifts. Then my budget collapsed. Could I live on 60,000r in November 1993? Yes, if I ate the same as I did a year earlier, made no long-distance phone calls, and took no train trips to Moscow, and bought no gifts; if I bought just food, newspapers, travel card, some drink, and paid the service charges. But now the shops were full of things to buy—food products, wine, chocolate, soap, shampoo, washing powder, foreign foods, fruit—and, if unable to afford them, people could feel poorer. I found myself adjusting. Whereas in the spring I found it very difficult to buy foreign or expensive foods that cost the equivalent of the basic pension, the availability and the presence of a whole clientele now doing exactly that was turning me back into behaving like a western consumer.

But how were St. Petersburg citizens coping? Those on the basic pension without family support were the hardest hit. There were some municipal schemes to provide free meals and to distribute humanitarian aid, but many were unprotected, saw their savings wiped out, and were left with no hope of paying for a burial. The intellectuals, on their state salaries and particularly those who could not turn their hands and minds to business ventures, were struggling. And not only because they had little money. "Look," said Galina, standing with me in a shop offering some highly priced goods, "there's *nothing* on the shelves." What she meant was that there was nothing she could afford. An older generation found it very difficult to come to terms with this. In the Soviet period, if something was on the shelves, most people could afford it: the problem was that there might not be much of it. The notion of a whole range of goods or shops catering to a clientele who lived in a different world was very alien to the ordinary consumer. Everyone had known that the party elite and the ballerinas lived differently, but their shops had not been on view. Now such goods and shops were everywhere.

We'll come back to this after our visit to the Far North, but first a few glimpses of city life, both the changes and continuity.

A Changing City and Old Conventions

One of the charms of St. Petersburg is the presence of nineteenth-century red brick factories scattered across the city, surrounded by residential blocks that grew up around them, and the ship-building plants, the cranes and wharves that line the Neva, even in the center. It used to be that the sky, particularly on a clear frosty day, was decorated with straight white plumes from factory chimneys, but by the early nineties, as fuel became scarce and factories struggled, the sky was cloudless.

Compared with any major European city, compared even with Moscow, St. Petersburg still had little traffic: trucks hurtled over the potholes, there were trams, trolleybuses and buses, and dilapidated cars. Foreign cars were still a rarity. Private yellow vans, the *marshrutki*, with sliding doors and windows and sometimes inexperienced drivers, began to provide an alternative bus service. A dozen or more passengers would squeeze onboard and make a risky journey. But by the summer of 1993 St. Petersburg had BMWs on the streets, Littlewoods off Nevsky, and the price of the metro had gone from five kopecks to fifteen rubles. The scaffolding that had masked the Church of the Savior on Blood for thirty years had come down. Advertisements had appeared, some in

English. At the end of Vasilevsky Island, near the port, stood a huge billboard: "Two thirds of the globe is covered by water, *The Economist* covers the other third." Large advertisements for Marlboro cigarettes appeared in the metro. The mayor ordered them to be removed, but he had no control over the metro. Traveling up the escalator, I listened with disbelief to a placid voice announcing the availability of roulette wheels at competitive prices from a firm based in the Ksezhinskaya Palace. The grand townhouse had been a Bolshevik headquarters in 1917, then the Museum of the Revolution, and it now had a red neon strip in the metro advertising "Everything for a casino—blackjack, roulette."

Procter and Gamble flooded the TV networks with their advertisements for Oil of Olay (for the price of an airfare to Siberia and back), Old Spice, and Wash and Go. Lux, Camay, and Omo arrived (the latter at ten times the price of Russian washing powder with its unnerving ability to turn whites *gray*, slowly regaining whiteness while drying). Only the most outrageously expensive goods were now being advertised— holidays to the Bahamas or India, paper-shredding machines, and automobiles. Or, inexplicably, stock exchanges and holding companies. Galina and I watched a blank screen, quite baffled, as a voice said, "Our firm decided to make our advertisement simple"—pause—"very simple"—pause—"the firm Seldon." And then "Seldon" flashed onto the screen. We never learned what the firm had to offer.

By 1993 the market was beginning to upset relationships, status hierarchies, and conventions. But it was far too early to say that money and the market had displaced older ways of doing things. Hoarding was ingrained, a way of coping with unexpected shortages—and not only for those who had lived through the Siege. In a shortage economy—too many people chasing too few goods—networks of friends and acquaintances are an essential part of existence. While friends and relatives were important, some relationships in the Soviet period were based purely on expediency: coaching children for university entrance or offering medical or legal advice were "goods" to be exchanged for lifts in a car, farm produce, or being given hairdressing appointments at convenient times. This way of operating—by barter and connections—persisted long into the nineties both because it was customary and because an environment of scarce (or expensive) goods encouraged it.

Secretaries now spent hours on the phone establishing where sugar or aspirin was to be had and arranging how to get a child across town to grandmother. Not surprisingly, such conversations took priority over dealing with a client. Most Russians were very loathe to fix any appointment beyond the following day. Who knew what might need to be done the day after tomorrow? The notion of writing a letter and fixing something well in advance was even more alien. This meant that any arrangement usually required more than one phone call and might quite well be changed at the last minute. Secretaries often had no idea of their boss's whereabouts or future timetable; it was the rare individual, in any line of work, who had a diary. Appointments and plans that were thought to be firm turned out to have been nothing of the sort.

While objective factors in the everyday environment in the early nineties encouraged the tendency to live from day to day, cultural traditions were also at work. Many Russians had little sense of a structured day. Those with regular hours of work were, of course, required to observe them, but the notion of a day given structure by habits of eating and drinking was largely absent. "In Oxford," my Russian colleagues reported when they returned from a visit, "everyone has lunch at one o'clock." In Leningrad or St. Petersburg there weren't lunch hours. It was never clear when someone might or might not be in the office. Shops shut for lunch, some at one, some at two, some at three. You ate when you were hungry or when food was put before you, and you slept when you felt like it or when there was nothing better to do. I marveled at the ability of many to sleep in huge quantities or hardly at all; to eat three meals in as many hours or to go twelve hours without food. All those *plans* of the Soviet period—and the fulfilling of targets and reporting on planned achievements—were they all a desperate attempt to create some kind of structured environment?

The talk was all of unemployment, but there was little sign of a new work ethos among the countless women who served as secretaries in government or new commercial ventures. The usual scene was this: in the anteroom to a government official, a deputy or a director, a secretary sits behind a desk on which there is a telephone. It is unlikely that she will have a typewriter, let alone a word processor. The radio plays softly in the background. She is on the telephone to her son, mother, or one of her friends, with the conversation revolving around somebody's health or domestic arrangements for the day. In some business offices the television is permanently on, to relieve the boredom. Sometimes an administrator exerts his authority and orders not just one but two secretaries to take down notes of a discussion with clients—and neither of them, one might add, is doing this in shorthand.

How did western business clients react? Has anyone written a memoir? The Astoria, the hotel we've visited more than once, now boasted a business center where a smartly dressed young woman sat behind her desk and watched an enormous color television. I asked whether it was possible to ring New York direct from there and blanched when she quoted the rate: $75 a minute. "You could try the Hotel Europa," she said. "There they charge $10 a minute."

It was not that everyone sat around doing nothing. Some people were working to crowded schedules. It was rather that so much conspired to make productivity low. And the rules on what was thought of as fair play were changing. There wasn't a workable law on corruption, officials did not have to declare their business interests, traders were doctoring the spirits they sold, counterfeit notes appeared (a Korean counterfeiter, in a television interview, insisted he was doing it so that even the poor should have enough money). Yadov, the sociologist, sent out by his wife to exchange some dollars, was cheated by a trader who had folded the ruble notes in such a way that it looked as though there were five times as many; so as not to upset his wife, he did the same when he got home.

Talk and trading went on inside the public baths. Two friends took up a suggestion to go on an expedition to buy cheap spirit (raw alcohol): they should be outside a metro station on the outskirts, with their empty bottles, by six o'clock one morning. There they were met by big Edik with a small van in which they headed out, through the darkness, for a military encampment; the guards opened the gates for Edik, and then they were inside, on army territory. In one of the compounds they passed more guards, came to locked doors which Edik opened using a code, and found themselves in a warehouse with a huge vat and its guards. They filled their bottles, reckoned up, and then big Edik led them out, past the guards—one of whom saluted—and back onto civilian territory. A deal had clearly been done with the army commander.

Everyone talked of the markets being controlled by the southern mafia, and nasty shootouts occurred. One day a larger than usual crowd of Georgians, milling around the stalls outside the metro station, caught my attention; then two cars arrived, followed by a sleek limousine in whose rear seat sat a very smooth but solid individual, idly chatting to an attentive aide. The little cavalcade stopped, doors opened, half a dozen stepped out, the boss and those waiting for him disappeared into a building. Had he come to collect the month's money from the traders or to sort out a dispute? The police had recently arrested a leading figure in organized crime (and shown the preliminary questioning of him at the police station on TV). He gave his address as a well-known hotel but we were then shown one of his houses, a grand affair on one of the islands; he couldn't remember the name of the friend whose Volvo he was driving when arrested.

For some of the young, the unraveling city offered unheard-of opportunities, but it was also now home to the street children. In 1993 it was reckoned that at least ten thousand homeless children were living rough in the cellars, the railway stations, and the airport. Some had run away from drunken parents, some had been abandoned, others absconded from children's homes where they had been beaten and abused; most were from the city and surrounding region but some had come from further afield. With an age range from four or five to eighteen, they formed little gangs, often had dogs, and lived by stealing, begging, collecting empty bottles and claiming the deposit, and by prostitution. They all smoked, some sniffed petrol and glue. Some of the adolescents had a mental age of five or six; they had head and body lice and, eating whatever they could get hold of, suffered from chronic gastroenteritis.

Two enterprising women had persuaded the deputy mayor to allocate them rooms in an empty hostel on a new housing estate as a home for children. I went with El'mar, who knew the women, to visit the home. It was cold and snow was falling. It felt almost country-like: the air felt cleaner, lighter, people were not hurrying but stopping to talk, pottering around.

There were forty-five children, mostly girls, living in the three reno-
vated apartments. The young girls could be taken for boys: their voices
were hoarse and rough from smoking, their mannerisms tough, a defense against the world they lived in. They all still smoked and that was
allowed—on the stairwell. They needed endless care and lots of attention; they needed one-to-one tuition. Some of the children had been
found in cellars, some just turned up; several were quite disturbed. Tiny
five-year-old Petya, found in rags in a cellar, unable to talk when he
came, was sitting watching television hugging a doll to himself. The
older children were worse off. They only had one jigsaw—"Made in
England," a thatched cottage with roses climbing up the walls—and a
checkers game. Most of the equipment came from the Swedish charity
named after the children's writer Astrid Lindgren, and the home was
called Astrid House. The municipality paid a daily allowance for food,
to be bought at wholesale prices from a base that supplied children's
homes and hospitals, but medicine was a problem.

The home was an open one, the only constraint was that the children
must be in by nine o'clock. One evening they set their dogs on a mentally retarded man who happened to walk by. The staff locked them out
for the night, saying that people who behaved like that were not wel-
come. The children were bewildered; they built a little fire to try and
keep warm, and stood against the building all night. They were concerned that they had upset the staff, but they were not really clear what
the fuss was about. Gradually they got rid of the dogs. The staff's aims
were to help them to understand how to live an ordinary life and to find
them foster parents. In order to comply with the law, to safeguard the
children, and to encourage a family to take a child, the foster parents
were registered as "employees" of the home and entitled to receive the
food allocation for the child from the wholesale store. But the future for
the older girls looked bleak. What has become of these children today, I
wonder?

Distances in St. Petersburg are long, pavements are hard, shops and
offices were unexpectedly shut. It was not safe to walk home late along
deserted streets and through dark courtyards. Crime had risen sharply
over the past two years, but was it more dangerous than London or New
York? Who knows? A colleague was hit on the head with an iron bar

when he happened to pass by a street fight. Yury, now a well-kept sixty-year-old, carried a knife. Accosted by two young men, they called "Stop" to him in prison slang. When he did not and one punched him in the mouth, Yury knifed him in the stomach. "They've killed me," cried the young man, while his accomplice ran away. On a crowded bus one evening a Russian called a southerner "a black face" when he jostled him and the two men went for each other's throats and tried to head-butt each other. They could not do each other much damage because the bus was packed tight, but I felt sick. Tempers were short and fists flew easily. There was tension, tiredness, and irritability in the air.

But now we leave the northern capital and make two journeys, far afield, before returning to discover how friends, old and new, were faring in the unsettled city that was St. Petersburg.

9

From the Caucasus to the Far North

It was July 1992. The flat was not yet livable. Andrei Alexeev was about to leave for the North Caucasus Nature Reserve, a territory of forests, alpine pastures, and snowcapped mountains in the far south of Russia. Here Zina, a childhood friend, had been living since the early eighties. Together with her husband Kuzmich, a head teacher of a Leningrad school, they had moved to the nature reserve, where he and a small group of foresters waged a battle against the poachers and hunters. Zina received a miserly salary for taking weather readings every Wednesday at three o'clock and reporting on the flora in the forest. In 1990 Kuzmich had died of a heart attack. However, as Kuzmich's widow, Zina retained her right to the house and issued open invitations to relatives and friends to come for the summer. Andrei went in the summer of 1991. Now he and Zina were partners, and Zina was visiting St. Petersburg. Why didn't I go with them to the nature reserve?

Krasnodar: A Nature Reserve

We left in a party of six from the Moscow railway station: three adults, three children, and fifteen pieces of luggage. Rucksacks had disappeared from the shops but Zina had borrowed a sewing pattern. Somehow she had acquired maroon and white material, as well as zips, and had sewn one for herself and one for Andrei. He was ill, running a temperature, worn out with running the archive and editing a new weekly paper. We had bags and a bucket full of food for the three-day journey. The train was one where the corridor is also lined with berths (the cheapest way of traveling). We swapped tickets with other passengers so as to get at least four together and thus had our own table for eating. Sheets for the bunks, a towel each, and boiling water twice a day for making tea were provided. Each of us had an enamel mug and a teaspoon—crucial items for train travel—and we had two bottles for the hot water.

We left at five in the afternoon on a Saturday and traveled south, first through pretty Russian countryside with its wooden villages, large ponds and rivers, down through Tula, Kursk, and Belgorod into the Ukraine, through the slag heaps and rickety mines of the Donbass, until by early Monday morning we were traveling through the sunflower fields and past the little painted houses of the Kuban. The fields were sadly uncared for and full of weeds. We did a lot of eating—fried chicken, cucumber, meat rissoles and tomatoes, bread, cold potatoes, and a huge bag of home-baked biscuits—and drank a lot of tea. Andrei and Zina slept a great deal while I played cards with the children: Zina's nephew and niece, Sergei, aged twelve, and seven-year-old Dasha, and the daughter of a friend, Nastya, aged fourteen. They read *The Lion, the Witch and the Wardrobe*, recently translated into Russian.

We left the train at Belorechensk, an old Cossack settlement with its small houses and leafy side streets, and set off for the bus. There was a queue, and confusion. However, clutching our fifteen pieces of luggage, we scrambled in the back and, after some shouting from the front about the need to have tickets, the bus lurched off along the ten-mile road to Maikop, the regional capital. We stood, squashed together in the heat. At Maikop, from where the buses run to Guzeripl, we counted our bags again, then took a crowded trolleybus to the bus station. But now we learned that heavy rain had washed the road away and the buses were traveling only twenty of the forty-odd miles. We had nothing to gain by waiting and got tickets; Zina and I went to the market and bought the only meat that was left—a freshly skinned coypou (like a small beaver) and some salt pork fat—and a bucket of cherries. There would not be any meat in Guzeripl.

The bus took us out of Maikop, past an army encampment of tents, and through villages where pigs and cows and chickens wandered across the road. At one point there was a half-hour delay when the driver suddenly decided we should pay for at least some of our fifteen pieces of luggage, and Andrei demanded to see the rules. The passengers divided into two fairly equal camps, the argument went back and forth until, eventually, an agreement was reached. The bus continued, swinging up an unfenced ravine on a dirt-track road to its last stop. We stood in the light rain and looked at the fifteen bags. There were twenty miles to go. Could we walk it? I gave everyone a Rowntrees fruit pastille to keep our spirits up. We were lucky. Half an hour later a truck, open at the back, came by. It contained a young filly that was being delivered to its new owner up the valley, and two men were standing in the back to keep an eye on the frightened horse. They agreed to take us. We climbed into the back of the dirty lorry, sat on our bags, tried to avoid the horse droppings and the filly's hooves, and bumped, swayed, and lurched up the mountain road, across the muddy morass where it had been washed away, across a narrow bridge that had no sides, and into the village, where we delivered the horse. Then the driver took us the rest of the way. We had made it.

Perhaps a hundred people lived in Guzeripl. The houses are spread out, wooden, with high slanting roofs, some shingled in fir. There is a wide, fast-flowing river in a ravine, a fine waterfall, and near it a little electric power station. The dark green hills surrounding the valley rise to perhaps 1,000 meters, covered with fir, pine, and beech. The only work was for the nature reserve or the trade union hiking center, but in 1992 that was shut. No one had come in 1991. A bread truck brought the tin-shaped loaves three times a week, delivered them to the shop at 1:30, which then opened at 3 to sell them. The post lady, who had the only telephone, brought letters and newspapers to the bread queue to hand them out. The shop had biscuits, some sweets, a jar of preserved aubergines, and six tins of fish. There were two men's caps, some light slippers, a few socks, a child's dress, some scent, a comb, and two electric light bulbs. One day there was rice, another there was frozen fish, and one day the sugar ration arrived, 2 kilos a month. The village hall showed a film once a week.

Andrei Alexeev in the North Caucasus Nature Reserve.

Mostly women came to collect the bread. With their broad weather-beaten faces and steel teeth, their printed cotton dresses and rubber boots, some still with their white head scarves, they could feature in a photograph taken any time during the Soviet period. But one day, as we were leaving with our fourteen loaves of bread, a white-haired, sprightly old man clad all in black with bare feet, a flowing beard, and bright eyes appeared in the doorway. "Who," I asked in amazement, "is that?" "That's Diogenes," Zina said. "He arrived several years ago and settled down to philosophize; he's a good stove mender too. At first the women pestered him, disapproving of his odd ways, now they've got used to him. But his philosophical theme was 'a multiparty system' and one day the police came from Maikop and took his typewriter away."

For most of the next month there were twelve of us in Zina's roomy wooden house, sometimes more. Andrei's first wife, his daughter, and grandchildren had arrived shortly before us. He read them *The Hobbit* in the evening before we listened to the news from Radio Liberty on a large and scratchy radio. Short-term visitors slept on the floor. Somehow we all got round the kitchen table. There was electricity but water had to be brought from the well, and there was no sewage disposal. We ate at irregular times, taking turns to cook and wash up. We had porridge, salad greens and garlic, mushrooms we picked in abundance, new potatoes when they were ready, and bread. We bought fresh milk and sour milk from a neighbor. We had tea with sugar until the sugar ran out. The children sat in the berry patch, like little rabbits, and ate the currants and strawberries. Then they climbed the cherry tree and ate all the cherries. I had brought chocolate and chocolate biscuits. These we kept for the birthdays. On Nastya's birthday we ate the coypou, and for Dasha's we killed the one-eyed cock. He was big with black, dark green, and white feathers. I sat on the bench and tried to remember how to pluck a chicken. Dasha sat beside me and mourned his passing: "He was so beautiful, he was so good; he never pecked, and he would give you his claw to hold; oh, how beautiful he was, oh how sad I am that he is dead; the other cock is so bad tempered, but he was so good, and so beautiful." Against the background of this funeral dirge, I pulled his feathers out.

The forest is untouched, home only to its animals: the deer, wolves, wild boar, and bears. There are huge pines that reach to the sky, firs, and beech trees with a more mottled trunk than the English beech. Hanging from their branches is the wispy gray-green moss that grows when the air is clean. Fallen trees covered with green moss as thick as a carpet lay where they have fallen in the deep leaf mold. Rhododendron cover the steep banks of the icy, fast-flowing rivers that have gouged deep valleys out of the hills. Tiny wild strawberries and blackberry bushes line the path that leads up to the mountain pastures, and yellow, red, and brown mushrooms grow under the fir trees. Apart from the bird calls and the occasional thud of a falling tree that reverberates across a valley there is no sound in the forest. The animals keep their distance. Only people who work for the nature reserve and their guests are its visitors. When we were there, the foresters were all hay-making down in the valley.

Sometimes we went on short expeditions, then four of us went on a proper expedition—Zina, Andrei, twelve-year-old Sergei, and I—up through the forest to the high pastures and mountain huts at 2,000

Andrei, Mary, and Zina in the North Caucasus Nature Reserve.

meters above sea level. We took sleeping bags and capes made of polythene sheeting, bread, porridge, and macaroni, three tins of meat, garlic and salt pork fat, tea, coffee, a tin of tomato paste, and chocolate, and walked for six days. There are foresters' huts built at strategic points, with trestle beds, a stove, kettle, and a supply of dry firewood. A few bags of dry provisions — salt, macaroni — are always left hanging on the wall out of the reach of the mice who scamper over the sleeping visitors during the night.

The alpine meadows are waist high in grass and flowers — wild iris, geranium, daisies, even lilies — and higher up, where the grass is short, carpets of white rhododendron give way to heather, gentians, and tiny rock flowers. All around, in a huge circle, stretching as far as the eye can see, are the snowcapped peaks. We saw herds of deer and curly horned mountain goats, we disturbed two wild boar and a bison. Our boots filled with water, from walking through waist-high wet grass as much as from fording streams, and one evening we got lost in the mist and pouring rain on a mountain ridge. Another night we spent in the forest in a thunderstorm. Andrei and Sergei made a makeshift shelter with branches and polythene sheeting; I slept soundly in a hollow made by the roots of a thick pine tree. As the food ran out, we slowly made it back across the alpine pastures and down to the village, through the forest that was growing darker and darker. Odd white mushrooms stood out against the leaf mold, and the fireflies appeared, flitting, dancing over the forest pools until, gradually, all the light disappeared.

One of the short-term visitors was Vilen Ochakovsky, a friend of Andrei's from the Ukraine. In 1987 Andrei had received a letter addressed to A. N. Alexeev, Lathe-operator, Sociologist, Human Being, Lenpoligrafmash, Leningrad. It was from Vilen, a miner in the Aleksandrovsky coalfields. He wrote "Dear Andrei! We are of the same age and brothers in GOOD FORTUNE . . . which others may describe as misfortune . . . we both took up the fight from 1924 [Lenin's death] and I too went to the factory bench . . ." Andrei invited him to Leningrad and they became good friends. Andrei was a man of few words. Vilen finds it difficult to stop talking. Andrei was slow and deliberate in all he did. Vilen is endlessly on the move and impetuous. He had barely arrived when, stripped to the waist and in his jogging trousers, he had taken over the preparation of supper, adding to the soup nettles from the garden and spices from his rucksack. Within half an hour of our meeting, he was arguing that I should go to Yakutia and to Mirny, the diamond capital of Siberia, to see a very different Russia. By next morning he had written the outline of a journey, Operation Diamond.

Operation Diamond

In May 1993 Vilen, his son Fidel, and I were in the taiga, two hundred miles northwest of Mirny. From the top of a rocky and moss-covered scarp, rising behind the small headland that marks the junction of two rivers, the gray-green taiga—thousands of miles of larch, pine, and silver birch forest, undulating hills, and huge winding rivers—stretches as far as the eye can see. This is permafrost country. The subsoil never thaws, and the Vilyui is still bringing the ice floes down at the end of May. By then, however, the long dark winter nights have given way to endless day. The sun still shines at midnight, and the temperature can rise and fall by 30 degrees centigrade in the space of a few hours. Apart from the bears, elk, reindeer, wolves, and sables as well as the birds—the white-headed eagle, the cuckoo, and the woodpecker who damages his brain with his drilling—the taiga's only inhabitants are a handful of foresters and teams of geologists and drillers dropped from time to time by helicopter. Alexander Anikeev, a grizzled ex-construction superintendent and a friend of Vilen's, was the forester in charge of a stretch of territory perhaps half the size of England. He had built himself stout wooden huts and bathhouses at various strategic points up and down the rivers, including one at the junction of the Lakharchana and Vilyui.

We were on the banks of the Vilyui, the river was rising relentlessly, and the erratic radio contact alerted us to the fact that there would be no helicopter for several days. Anikeev set a marker and began to shift barrels up the bank. I helped to bail out the icehouse but Vilen was at his happiest when I sat with my pad on my knees. "When I see you working," he would say, "I feel I am participating in the international world of science." It was difficult, under the circumstances, to concentrate on science, but perhaps I could write of our adventures.

A few weeks earlier Vilen and I had left Moscow for the airport with rucksacks, a *spravka* from the St. Petersburg Institute of Sociology that entitled me to buy tickets in rubles, and another from Yadov, now director of the Institute of Sociology in Moscow, confirming that we were engaged in a research project. We had rubles to buy plane tickets to Irkutsk, the first leg of the journey to Mirny. Alas, the flights were fully booked. Vilen was in dismay. I took a walk round the booking hall and knocked on a door labeled "Administration." I struck lucky. A bored-looking man was sitting behind a desk. I explained our predicament and begged for his help. He brightened up—after all, it was not every day that an Englishwoman came to him to appeal for help—made a phone call, and ten minutes later, at window number three, we were sold two tickets on the next flight to Irkutsk. I had $100 in small denominations, folded up in a pocket in my jeans; I gave Vilen the other hundred. This should cover the cost of our month's trip, and henceforth Vilen took charge of our finances—buying tickets, giving a helicopter pilot or truck driver a few dollars, buying food, or contributing dollars to the family budget of the friends we stayed with. We still had a few dollars left when we arrived back in St. Petersburg in June.

Gennadi and Vilen on Lake Baikal.

We took off on a warm summer evening and flew through a short night, reaching Irkutsk in the morning with the temperature just above freezing. Gennady Khoroshikh was there to meet us, a tall man, dome-headed, with blue eyes and an untidy beard. Vilen kissed him through the railings, and we went out into the airport forecourt—in 1993 an un-attractive place with beer stalls, drunks, dilapidated taxis, and new businessmen with smart cars and bodyguards. Irkutsk, on the edge of Lake Baikal, feels like a trading point: a place where routes cross, where people from very different cultures have arrived and stayed. Gennady, a school-teacher, part writer, part political activist, was one of the founding members of the tiny Christian-Democratic Union of Irkutsk and would later become chair of the city's human rights commission. He lived with his wife and daughter in a single-story wooden house built at the end of a tramline by his father in the 1950s. The lanes between the little wooden houses are earth. There was electricity, but no water or sewage. During the winter months the water truck delivered churns; during the summer water ran from the garden pipe. For the next two days we talked about politics past and present; took a bus down to Lake Baikal to see a poet, who was out; and then Vilen and I boarded a small plane flying north.

But before I write of our adventures in the taiga, Vilen's story cries out to be told. Not because he is representative of our generation—far from it—but because from him you will get a striking picture of a rebel, a talented rebel, and of what it cost him. It was all happening far from Leningrad, but still part of the same country.

Vilen's Saga

Although I referred to Vilen as an ex-miner, that's only partly true. There's no way he can be classified. He was born in 1937 in a Ukrainian town, not far from Odessa. His parents were Jewish but this only reflected itself in his mother's wish that he marry a Jewish girl and hold a respectable job. His father, an electrician, remained a staunch Stalinist until his death in the late seventies. He named his second son Vilen, in memory of Vladimir Ilich Lenin. He was incorruptible, refusing bribes of food even in the hungriest years and for this, but for little else, Vilen respected him. It was, however, probably from him that Vilen inherited his passionate faith in communist ideals and a stubborn integrity. It was a combination, spiced with an irresistible urge to take the mickey out of those in authority, that was to cost him dear. Short but broad shouldered, black haired and blue eyed, a born organizer, endlessly seeking an outlet for his energy, before the revolution Vilen would have been a Bolshevik. In 1953, however, his ambition was to work for Soviet intelligence and unmask imperialist spies. His school-leaving application was rejected and instead he trained as an electrician. Then came the army and, to his great delight, he was allocated to radio intelligence, where he was taught English and monitored American aircraft reports.

During his army days he began an activity that he would subsequently pursue wherever he was: the writing of an accessible and satirical wall newspaper. Writing to him comes as easily as talking, particularly "journalism in verse." Within weeks of taking up employment anywhere, he would find two or three people who could draw and write and a newspaper would appear. If, as in the army, there were individuals in command who welcomed the venture, the paper might last several months; on other occasions its life would be shorter. In the army it was other activities that got him into trouble. "How can you describe yourself as a political instructor, with a party education," he asked the hapless political officer, lecturing to a hall of recruits, "when all of us sitting here are bored out of our minds with hearing from you the same things we heard at school? If you want us to listen to you, you must say something interesting, surely you were taught that at the higher party school? No one is reading the newspaper or arm wrestling at this moment because I am saying something interesting." "Class dismissed," shrieked the enraged officer. "Private Ochakovsky to report to my office in five minutes." Vilen was sentenced to ten days solitary confinement on a charge of "organizing an unauthorized meeting."

Somehow he completed his military service with a mixture of glowing testimonials, sporting achievements, and disciplinary censures. It was during these three years that he reached certain conclusions about the society in which he lived, and he held to them for the next thirty years. Political disagreements with his father led to blows, literally. The occasion was Khrushchev's Secret Speech denouncing Stalin in 1956. Vilen charged his father with cowardice: "How could you serve those wild animals, Stalin, Yezhov, Beria? How could you remain silent when they shot innocent 'enemies of the people' without trial? . . . You knew your local comrades who had studied together with you in the twenties weren't enemies? . . . Why are you silent now? Are you waiting for the next instruction? . . . I am ashamed, I am ashamed to have been born then, to have believed in Stalin like a naïve fool. Do you remember how we wept together when Stalin died and I, weeping, wrote a poem 'On the death of a mountain eagle'?"

"Shut your mouth, you shit," his father responded. "If I had not kept quiet then, you would not have been born. And anyway you're too green to understand such things."

"Better to be green than gray. And where's your Bolshevik discipline, comrade party organizer? The Party Congress has criticized the personality cult of Stalin and you, chicken-head, still have a little Stalin in your Marxist-Leninist head."

Enraged, his father resorted to his fists, but Vilen now had four years of fencing and boxing behind him and within moments his father was on the floor, and his mother had come running from the kitchen waving a towel like a referee.

The Communist Party, his army experience taught him, contained far too many ignorant, brutal little Stalins. His dream, in 1958, was to purge Lenin's party of all its dross. This was possible, he believed, because honorable and committed communists existed: he met them among the officers. Lenin was his hero and his inspiration. With a friend he developed a theory: "In the struggle with brutes, whether military, civilian, party or Komsomol, any methods are morally justified except for murder, rape, robbery and racketeering." The task was to educate and to inspire others.

Upon leaving the army, he applied to the Odessa police training school, received an outstanding grade for his essay "The USSR—The Cornerstone of Peace" and was accepted . . . but within two years he was expelled. Among the police officers the majority, to his utter dismay, had scant respect for the law and awarded top marks in "practical work" to those who pulled in, and roughed up, innocent citizens on charges of "hooliganism." He wrote an article with the title "A School for Tyrants," sent it to the national police newspaper, *Sovetskaya militsiya*, and confidently waited for its publication. Instead a colonel from the Ministry of Internal Affairs arrived. Vilen refused to speak to him because, he argued, this was a purely journalistic matter. Harried by the commanding officers, he added this information to the article and sent it to *Komsomolskaya pravda*, the youth newspaper. This time a journalist arrived but only to explain, patiently, that the paper would not publish critical material at a time when the party was anxious to support the police as an institution. By now Vilen was feeling desperately isolated. There were cadets who agreed with him, but no one was prepared to support him openly. His expulsion was the subject of an open Komsomol meeting. Here he had a moment of triumph. He persuaded two friends to demand that the newspaper article be read out so that all would be aware of its slanderous content, and the party secretary chairing the meeting found himself compelled to agree. Vilen read out his (truly libelous) description of certain leading individuals in the academy to the packed hall, which responded with roars of laughter, stamping of feet, and applause. The party secretary closed the meeting hurriedly, and Vilen received notice of his expulsion the same day. It had, however, been typed and signed the day before.

He was twenty-three, without a job, and convinced that it was for his generation to build a socialist society, untainted by Stalinism. He had acquired an elementary legal training and knowledge of the means of self-defense, both of which would come in useful. And he had come to the conclusion that it was pointless to act alone: collective action was the only way to defeat the powerful.

Yakutalmaz, Lensk, and Mirny

A few years earlier diamonds had been discovered in Yakutia, the northern territory four times the size of France, with a population of half a million. Two big state companies were set up—Yakutalmaz to quarry and process the diamonds and the Hydroelectric Company to build a power station—but everything, except timber, had to be brought in. A hundred and fifty miles south of the diamond find, on the flat northern bank of the huge Lena River, stood a small settlement of wooden houses and fishing boats, Mukhtuya. Renamed Lensk in 1963, it became the transit point for all goods for the north. Coal, kerosene, building materials, food, all had to be transported north, and labor was needed for this, just as it was needed to quarry the diamonds, build the hydroelectric station, and build a road. Both the state companies set up a supply base in Mukhtuya (Lensk) and sent their scouts out to recruit whomever they could, including people from Odessa. Thus it was that in the summer of 1960 Vilen signed a contract to work as a docker in Mukhtuya and found himself sharing a railway compartment with three other young Ukrainians also heading for the settlement. The train journey took the best part of a week, then came five days in a diesel-powered paddle steamer, one of a new fleet of passenger boats built in a faintly Edwardian style by the Hungarians.

From the air the River Lena, with its smooth straight edges, looks like a wide ribbon lying in loops on a forested plain. In the early sixties

Lensk—with its mess of little wooden houses, dirt backyards, new weatherboard barracks, tents, a cinema, canteen number one, and the single-story wooden houses for the Party and Komsomol committees—stood separate from what was called "the Base" where everyone worked: the port, the warehouses, the truck depots. In 1960 the four—Vilen, Edik, Oleg, and "Enemy" (so nicknamed by Vilen because of his scandalous statement that were he a pilot his first wish would be to bomb the Kremlin)—became friends. They shared a room in the hostel, and in the port their brigade carried off all the awards for exemplary work. In no time at all Vilen had been elected as the Komsomol organizer and organized a meeting, which overflowed into the street, to demand the wages their contracts had specified. But shortly afterwards, and hardly accidentally, the brigade found itself made redundant—they were laid off. Edik and Enemy left but Oleg got work in the motor repair plant, married the woman foreman from the dock, and remained in Lensk until his death in 1992.

The population in these frontier towns is heavily Russian and Ukrainian but many include also a mixture of very different nationalities: Bashkir, Greek, Pole, Chuvash. Many came from far away, lured by the high wages in the Far North; others moved on from exile in Siberia. There has always been a good proportion of ex-criminals in the unskilled labor force of the Far North. The recruiters took anyone they could get. Heavily tattooed hands are the sign of a long-term offender. You needed to be able to defend yourself if you worked on the docks. When Vilen and his friends arrived, Vasya, a mean but not physically strong ex-convict, was ruling the hostel and objected to the brigade's refusal to accept his authority. He came at Vilen with a knife one evening when he was listening to the radiola in the entrance hall but had not reckoned on Vilen's police training. "Come on then, Vasya," Vilen urged, beckoning him forward, waiting, crouched "Come closer." Vasya came, then suddenly threw the knife on the floor and ran, disappearing for good.

After a short spell as a road worker, Vilen was recruited as agitator and organizer by the local Komsomol committee. The next six months were some of the happiest of his life. He was writing for the local newspaper, had set up a fencing club, put on a satirical musical evening in the cinema (which incurred official disapproval), and, best of all, he traveled up and down the river to the little settlements and towns and installed like-minded young activists as secretaries in their Komsomol organizations. His days, however, were numbered. The dockers at the Base staged a strike. Tempers were running high. The party organizer, who responded with threats and foul language to their demands, received a box on the ear from a half-blind angry young docker. Vilen tried, unsuccessfully, to get a report of the strike published in the local paper and took up the young docker's defense when the party organizer brought a court case against him. He fought for the right to defend him up to the Supreme Court of the Yakut republic, but to no avail. The accused got a three-year prison sentence, and Vilen lost his Komsomol job.

In the autumn of 1961 a friend warned him that the KGB was beginning to take an interest in him and he should move away. The chairman of the sports committee in Mirny urged him to come north: jobs were available as loaders at the supply depot, jobs that were well paid and left you time to think. And so he went. While working as a loader Vilen organized a football club for boys and helped build the first wooden stadium; then he organized a summer football camp in Central Asia for children from all over Yakutia, wrote the sports column for the local paper, and read his poems to a literary circle. He did not try to reorganize the Komsomol any longer but his football club was a cooperative venture, called Kids Playing Football. Despite its national success, the club incurred official disapproval for its unorthodox and "unsocialist" rules.

One year the organizers of the Pioneer Camp asked him if he would spend the summer working as a section leader; the supply depot gave him leave, he agreed, and took the lower salary. Children in his section elected a president and a secretary and made decisions by majority voting; he was adviser to the president. His section was the best behaved in the camp but his relations with the other section leaders could be strained. When a cosmonaut came to Mirny on an official visit, Vilen took the matter to his children, who authorized him to arrange matters. He struck a deal with the local bus company—a bus would make an unauthorized stop at the camp to pick up his children. On the day, in their smartest Pioneer uniforms, clutching bunches of mauve gentians they had picked in the forest, his children sped out, boarded the bus, and were away. They had a wonderful day. They were the only children in town, they all met the cosmonaut, and the town authorities were delighted that they had come. Back in camp, the others were furious and became even angrier when Vilen argued that it was nothing to do with him. In his section decisions were taken democratically, and the vote had been properly taken.

For fifteen years Vilen worked as a loader, and then driver, at the supply depot. Because he drank little and had a good work record, the management chose him for responsible assignments—driving up north to collect a sack of three hundred reindeer tongues for a banquet for the district party secretaries or down to Irkutsk to collect the four sets of imported bedroom furniture ordered by local party officials. He knew all the shop managers, including "the colonel," a forbidding woman who wore a peaked astrakhan hat and managed shop number one, where the party elite received goods at the back entrance. He rarely used the opportunities offered by the job to get scarce goods on the side. Now married and with a son, Fidel, his wife complained that everyone but they had a carpet. One day, however, he recognized the poet Yevgeny Yevtushenko in the cafeteria (where there was no alcohol), and he approached the colonel. His opening—"One of the most famous Soviet poets has arrived in town, Yevtushenko, and I have nothing to offer him"—was cut short. "How many do you need? Six bottles of vodka. Take them. What else do you need? Herrings, sardines?" In May 1993 we went to pick up a sack of potatoes to take to the taiga. The colonel was still there, as impassive as ever: upon seeing Vilen, she simply barked out an order—"The sack of potatoes"—and took the money.

During his years in Mirny, Vilen did not seek out elected office, which would lead to direct confrontation with the authorities. Once, upon returning from an assignment, he learned that he had been elected as trade union organizer. "But that's not me at all," he said in dismay. "Call a meeting for tomorrow, with the first agenda item my resignation." All were there, including the director of the base. Vilen thanked the meeting for the honor but suggested he was not an appropriate candidate for the post. "But why, Vilen Yakovlevich?" asked the director. "You are known as a good worker, respected, literate." "The problem," said Vilen, "is the following. You are an incompetent and poor director, please forgive me for speaking the truth, and if I am the union chairman, it will be my duty to the collective to demand your removal, and this will be extremely unpleasant for all concerned; as just an ordinary union member, I don't have to do this, and I would rather not." This kind of repartee, at which Vilen excels, always gave him a following in the workplace. His workmates reveled in his ability to take the mickey out of the bosses or simply to outwit them in argument. "Go on, Vilya," the whispers would start. "Get up and give it to them." Later, in the mines, when the need arose to elect praesidia to chair meetings, he could be sure of election and his mates would urge him, "Get the chair next to the mine director so that we can see the expression on his face when he finds you next to him." "Vilya," the miners would say, "can out-talk anyone, even those bigwigs from Moscow." This did not mean, however, that he could count on support in a conflict with management and, knowing this, he made it plain that he was only prepared to fight if he had backing.

Radio Liberty was Vilen's main source of news of developments in and outside the USSR. Vilen's son Fidel remembers his walking up and down the apartment, holding the radio to his ear, trying to pick up what he could from the crackling and frequently jammed reception. He had little access to forbidden literature or, in the seventies, to dissident writing. He knew Sakharov's name but not what he wrote. Solzhenitsyn was a different matter and when, in 1973, Gennady Khoroshikh arrived from Irkutsk, with a letter he had written in support of Solzhenitsyn, Vilen added his name and took it to Moscow to ask Yevtushenko to send it abroad. Yevtushenko agreed, but only after cutting off their names with a pair of scissors.

From Arrest to Rehabilitation

In 1976 Vilen and family had moved to Gorky, originally Nizhni Novgorod, the city on the Volga. They now had a daughter too, Zhanna, named after Joan of Arc. Fidel had a place in the prestigious ice hockey school, and Vilen took a job as a delivery driver at the Togliatti motor works. Now he could fulfil an ambition to drive the length and breadth of the USSR. By the time Sakharov was exiled to Gorky, the family had moved on, back to the Ukraine, to a town called Aleksandria, and Vilen had taken a job as a coal-face miner and started a wall-newspaper. Although, as the seventies turned into the eighties, the political future seemed ever bleaker, Vilen never lost his optimism that, one day, someone would cleanse the party of all the scoundrels. He renamed the KPSS (Communist Party of the USSR) the Crimino-Political System of Socialism but he was convinced that it could be reborn to lead the country forward. Propaganda and a printing press is what we need, he argued. At the time of the Moscow Olympics in 1980, he wrote a satirical verse that began, "Our contemporary Ghengis-Khan conquered Afghanistan, put down the rebellious Czechs, and reduced the Russians to poverty. He's a party emperor, a famous writer with a print run bigger than Dumas, only his books are made of shit. The people are waiting for his demise, just as a child awaits a birthday." He signed it Spartak (Union of Truthseekers, an Anti-Bureaucratic Revolutionary society of Anti-Brezhnev Kommunards), made five hundred copies, and scattered them in Moscow and Donetsk. But he soon decided it was pointless. There seemed to be only two courses of action: to organize the miners and to write a satirical novel. "Perhaps," he only half-joked with Gennady, "I ought to experience the worst the system can do—psychiatric treatment. After all, I've had ten years more freedom than I ever expected."

The coal field, two hundred miles away from the big Donets deposits, was itself not large. By the autumn of 1982 he had organized a mine committee and had a half-written manuscript. Consciously or not, he was seeking a confrontation. He could not resist playing a joke on the party secretary. He took a volume of Lenin's works, put it in a brown paper cover, wrote on the front "A. Sakharov, *Peace and Coexistence*, New York," and handed it in a bag to the woman who gave out the lamps to the miners at the start of the shift, telling her that a friend would be coming to pick it up. He knew she would look in the bag and then give it to the party secretary—which she did. He was called up from the face to speak to the superintendent—and sensed that this was it. They had sent six to arrest him on the charge of possessing anti-Soviet material and moved straight to search the apartment. "Have they lost something here?" asked his little daughter in bewilderment. And then, helpfully, "Papa keeps his colored pencils at the dacha." The cavalcade of police cars headed for the dacha, where the officers found the manuscript and other papers, and dug up the garden.

Vilen was held for six months awaiting trial. His prison experience was painless because he is tough and physically strong: criminals leave him alone. A medical commission found him mentally normal but the case was then passed to the Odessa psychiatric hospital where a commission, headed by Dr. D. Maier, produced a diagnosis of schizophrenia. "I have read your writings," Maier said to him, "and they constitute a direct attack on the foundations of communism." No trial was necessary; he was simply sentenced—in his absence—to compulsory medical treatment in the Dnepropetrovsk psychiatric hospital. He spent two years there. They were two years of hell. He never lost his ability to joke (writing to Gennady that he was in a Seaside Resort State Hospital—KGB) and family visitors were allowed, but he thought he was there for life and that he might indeed go out of his mind. There were fifteen to a room, mostly criminals who had bought their way out of a prison sentence. They were fed vitamin tablets, a few were truly sick, and there was no more than one political. Buggery and sadism prevailed. The only survival strategy for a political was to admit to being ill and ask to be cured; an insistence on one's sanity brought even more brutal treatment. Even so, there were occasions when Vilen lost consciousness from dosages: insulin treatment, Triftazin, Haloperidol. They were fed on gruel. There was a small meat cutlet on November 7 and May Day.

Perestroika and his own personality saved him. In the spring of 1986 he was transferred to an ordinary mental hospital. In November he was allowed to return home and draw sick pay, pending further investigation. He wrote letters to the Central Committee, the procuracy, the KGB; friends and colleagues wrote in support. He also wrote to Gorbachev, whom he saw as the leader who could at last re-create a Leninist party and whom he advised to set in train a renewal of party membership, but of a different, democratic kind. All who worked in a plant or institution should be asked to vote, in a secret ballot, for those party members they considered worthy of membership. The result, Vilen argued, would be that a handful of good communists would remain and they would create a party of a new kind. He had hopes that, maybe, at last, he would be admitted to the party. "All those years," he said, "I saw all kinds of people being admitted, but no one ever asked me, and you couldn't put yourself forward. It was hurtful. I was sure I had a contribution to make. In 1989 I approached the party secretary and said to him, 'What if I got a job as a lavatory cleaner, you can't have many of that category as members, couldn't you perhaps find room for me then?' but he just said 'Vilya, you are absurd . . .'"

In June 1988 the Serbsky Institute annulled the diagnosis of schizophrenia, and on Victory Day in May 1990 the Supreme Court of Ukraine awarded full political rehabilitation and back pay for his forced absence from work. By this time he was back in the mine, but now working above ground as a despatcher in a little shack. In June 1989 one of the sections struck, refusing to come back above ground until their demands for pay and better conditions of work were met. The management turned to Vilen, asked him to speak to the strikers, while threatening to send the "accident team" down "to sort matters out." Vilen knew that meant bloodshed. He asked the strikers to send two representatives above ground to begin negotiations and to trust him that he would not betray them; they reluctantly agreed. At the meeting to discuss their demands, Vilen insisted that the general director leave "because no one trusts you here and your presence makes matters worse" and a decision was taken to await the arrival of Moscow representatives. They agreed to the miners' demands and a general meeting was called to ratify the agreement.

Here Vilen argued unsuccessfully for a different strategy: the miners should continue with token ten-minute strikes, while meeting their production targets; the off-shift team should picket the official buildings, demanding the removal of the Party and Soviet administration; a permanent strike committee should demand the resignation of the director and elect a new one. "Vilya," came the call, "don't pour kerosene on the fire." The agreement was voted for and work resumed. A week later the Kuzbass struck, and then the Donbass, and a year later when none of the conditions in the agreement had been fulfilled, the Aleksandria miners struck again. This time they elected a strike committee with Vilen as its chair but, even with a strike committee, there was little support for any real action. He resigned and took his miner's pension. Other political activities were now claiming his attention—Memorial, the organization to defend the victims of political repression, and Rukh, the Ukrainian independence movement.

Lensk and Mirny in 1993

In May 1993 the ice below Lensk had melted, leaving scattered lumps floating downstream and a white fringe along the banks, but above the town the ice was still packed solid and the boats and barges were icebound. The town still had a frontier feel about it. The roads were unpaved packed sand, rutted and bumpy, dotted with bird cherry trees, and the occasional silver birch. Log piles, odd scrap metal, Japanese cars, and Laika dogs were everywhere. Ugly concrete blocks of flats, crumbling and cracked on the outside, heavy square shops, metal tinbox garages, and little wooden shacks made up the town.

It was still a transit point, wholly dependent upon supplies coming in from outside, and run by the two companies. The Lena shipping company was still using the same fleet of Hungarian paddle steamers, still in good condition, but now their trade was all the other way: people were leaving Lensk, not coming to it. Those who were leaving for good flew out, their household goods following on the container-laden barges. They were going home to European Russia, the Ukraine, or Kazakhstan, to the places where they were born and where their relatives still lived. The paddle steamers, now with floating car decks welded onto their bows, carried those who were traveling west and south, with their families and their dogs, for their three-month holiday. There was more river traffic than in the sixties, but the scattered settlements with their sawmills looked very much as they did to the young recruits in 1960. We stayed with Oleg's daughter, Natasha, in one of the concrete blocks on Proletarian Street. With the exception of Moscow and St. Petersburg, few towns in Russia made changes to their street names in the 1990s. In Lensk the party committee may have gone but the big companies ran the little town as they always did. Natasha, who taught Russian literature in the secondary school, inherited beautiful oval eyes from her Buryat mother; her husband is the son of Ukrainian and Yakut parents.

As we walked along the dusty street to look for the hostel (now an untidy yard of charred timber), we met an elderly pensioner in a brown suit. Vilen greeted him with joy: he had, he said, so hoped to meet him, perhaps he remembered him, Ochakovsky, and the strike of 1960? Ivan Petrovich smiled wary acknowledgment. "This is an English friend," said Vilen, "but don't worry, she doesn't work for British intelligence. It seems a long time ago, doesn't it, that all that happened but I have no hard feelings. I have often remembered your comment — 'Ochakovsky's a talented political organizer but his ideas are half-cracked' — particularly when they clapped the diagnosis of schizophrenia on me. Did you read the interesting article in *Komsomolskaya Pravda* in January 1991, which mentioned the strike, and referred to me as an incurable Marxist?" After further pleasantries, we parted. Vilen crowed with delight. "That," he said, "was the party organizer, the brute who got the young docker three years; I twisted the knife all right. But at the same time, I really do forgive them, and they hate that even more."

By 1993 Lensk and Mirny were linked by a packed pebble-and-earth road that heads over the hills, through the pine and larch forests. For seven months of the year the road is beaten snow. Occasional plaques mark the places where truck drivers have met their death on the ice. There are a few tiny settlements, homes of the road workers — a tangle of wooden shacks, wires, TV aerials — and one larger settlement, Dawn, where, in 1993, a spick-and-span canteen sported the sign "May our great motherland, The Union of Soviet Socialist Republics, ever flourish and grow stronger." They served the best food I've eaten anywhere in Russia. We traveled the 150 miles in the cabin of a Kamaz truck, driven by Vadim, a cheerful truck driver, born into a Russian, Polish, and Buryat family, who was delivering a load of cement to a settlement further north. He came to Lensk as a boy of fifteen. An adolescent when Stalin died, he joined the party in the 1960s. While believing that Stalin had ruined the system, and that his successors, the "partocrats," had done little to reform it, he had never questioned the rightness of party rule. He and his fellow workers at the Base welcomed the attempted putsch in August 1991; Yeltsin, also a "partocrat" who had ruined the country, did not get their support in the 1993 referendum.

Mirny from a distance has a surrealist, science fiction appearance. Artificial hills of light blue Kimberlite support a town of shining white building blocks. But, nearer, everything changes. The dusty road reveals a town built next to the huge diamond quarry, ringed by blue and brown slag heaps, and caught in a dirt trap. The concrete apartment blocks of the 1970s and 1980s, standing on oil-filled piles to prevent the extreme temperature changes shattering the foundations, were cracked and shabby in 1993. They stood cheek by jowl with little wooden shacks, "temporary" accommodation of the late fifties, and with blue and green weatherboard hostels. Only two or three of the main streets were paved. Leningrad Prospect, built by a brigade from Leningrad in the early sixties, led to the town square, still dominated in 1993 by a huge, gleaming metal head of Lenin rising out of a flowerbed. To the left was the hotel, to the right the town council, and behind it the Palace of Culture. The most important building, however, was and surely still is the headquarters of Yakutalmaz, the diamond company that owns the town. Its spacious vestibule, ringed by a first-floor balcony and climbing plants, still had its large statue of Lenin, backed by a huge drape of artificial glass diamonds. There was no sign of privatization here. It's a company town, after all, where Yakutalmaz not only owns the Supply Base but also pays for the schools, the hospital, a professional mini-football team, and subsidizes the local newspaper.

We made our way over the planks that lie in the mud, climbed over the wooden stiles that cover the big central heating pipes which feed the houses from the central boilers (the ground is too frozen for them to lie under the surface), to the blue weatherboarded hostel where Vilen's son, Fidel, had a room. Fidel, named after Castro, is a professional footballer, a slight young man with a sweet smile. He was lying on his wooden bed reading Nietzsche.

The Taiga

We left for the taiga—Vilen, Fidel, and I, with our backpacks, a sack of potatoes, twenty loaves of bread, three cabbages, and dried fruit—first getting a lift to Chernishevsky, a settlement that grew up round the construction of a hydroelectric dam in the 1960s, and from where helicopters fly north. All through the seven-month winter it's dark from three in the afternoon till eleven next morning, but in the short hot summer it's light all night. In the sixties there were only tents and "temporary homes." By 1993 the wooden temporary homes were part of the landscape, they had electricity and some had sanitation. The settlement sprawled up and down the sides of a valley—a mass of wires, aerials, wooden houses, and ugly new concrete apartment blocks. The managers lived in a row of pleasant blue-green weatherboard villas on the side of the hill. There was a well-built small wooden hotel with a view of the dam, and the first indoor swimming pool built in Yakutia. But the restaurant and two canteens where everyone ate had closed in 1992. Some food was rationed—meat, condensed milk, flour—and the rations were ample, but there was no trace of fruit or vegetables. Those with heavy conditions of work received an extra allocation of dried milk and dried eggs.

Everyone worked for the hydroelectric plant or for the geology station, but in 1993 there was not enough work nor the money to pay the labor force. Half the workforce was on unpaid holiday by May, including Grisha, son of Vilen's friend from his Komsomol days. People hurried out to their dachas—it was planting time—or went hunting. There were no union or informal protests in this company town. By June some had been taken on again, but pay was in the form of tokens to be exchanged at the company stores. Grisha was a mining engineer, in charge of a stone quarry and a team of four men. There had been no demand for the stones for the past year, and not enough work to fill the day. He sat and looked over the wide river and read, worrying how he was going to feed his family.

It had been difficult to establish radio contact with Vilen's friend Anikeev out in the taiga. Grisha, however, knew one of the pilots from school, and he agreed to take us. We scrambled aboard an old military helicopter, laden with timber and with four oil drillers heading north for their two-week shift. Before we had left the ground the first bottle of vodka was opened, the tin mug went around, we tore off hunks of bread and ate pickled cabbage with our fingers. They smoked, flicking the ash on to the pile of timber or out of the open porthole. The sun was reflected in the wet ground, mirror-like, beneath us in the forest, not yet greening, the rivers wound and looped, and the low gray-blue hills stretched away as far as the eye could see. The helicopter alighted in a clearing "at Anikeev's place," we got out, and it clattered away.

We were clearly in the right place: there was the burnt-out bathhouse and signs of last year's fire. Anikeev had built a new hut—one low room with a stove, three wooden beds lining the walls, two small windows, a table and shelves. A bathhouse adjoined, and there was a lean-to porch, cluttered with pots, pans, buckets, furs, skins, sacks of provisions, barrels. There was a good log pile, half a dozen axes, and a fireplace. There was a small wooden smoke hut, an icehouse for meat still frozen shut, and another with a hollowed-out tree stump for a lavatory; a lean-to shed contained tools. The whole place was littered with old petrol drums, canisters, tins, empty vodka bottles, torn polythene, animal traps, nets and sacking. The inside of the hut was not a lot better. We could only guess that Anikeev and his seven-year-old grandson had gone upriver to one of the other huts or had gone fishing.

Three days later they arrived, with two Laika dogs, in a little motorboat. They were indeed living in another hut and had come to check this outpost. Anikeev took charge: we would make a bucket of elk stew and get the bathhouse heated up, then we would go to lay nets. Early next morning two drillers arrived, traveling upriver; they brought a reindeer they had just shot, and we had deer rib and deer heart stew, vermicelli, cabbage salad, and tea for breakfast. Then they moved on, upriver. We were busy with jobs, in a leisurely way, in the following days. The ice passed. When the ice is in full flood, the river is covered with a tinkling mass of broken crystal and clumps of diamonds, moving sometimes swiftly, sometimes slowly. The last of the ice floes drifted past, and then the Vilyui began to rise. Anikeev was unperturbed: the Vilyui usually only rises high once in fifty years and last year had been such a year. We went fishing. The motorboat failed and needed a day's work on the engine. There was cleaning up to be done, smoking fish, and making Lot's tombstone.

Lot was Anikeev's assistant, a cheerful Yakut whose settlement had disappeared when the hydroelectric station was built in the sixties and who had no relatives. His belongings consisted of his dog, whom he also called Lot, and a small suitcase which contained a few clothes, boxes of matches, bullets, and his papers, including a diary he carefully kept. He enjoyed shocking Russians by drinking a mug of reindeer blood and scooping out fish intestines and swallowing them in one gulp. "When the time comes," he had said to Anikeev, "bury me on the top of the scarp, but put a heavy stone on top so that a bear can't dig me up." We had made him a tombstone, and on the anniversary of his death, Fidel and little Sasha had set it in place, and fired a last salute over the river valley. But Lot himself did not lie underneath. Although Anikeev had taught him to swim, and he almost always wore a life jacket, one day the previous May the boat hit a sunken log and tipped on its end. He had no jacket and he panicked. He let go of the boat and of an alder, and clung to timber being carried downstream by the fast-flowing Lakharchana. Anikeev could not reach him, and he was swept away in the ice-cold water.

The evening sun was still shining when Vilen suggested we climb to the top of the scarp to visit the tombstone. We climbed up the rocky scarp, where the boulders lie in cushions of bright green and rust-colored moss, and the yellow gentians stick up in clumps. The taiga hills stretched away, dark and purplish, not yet greening. A woodpecker broke the air with his drilling, and a cuckoo called repeatedly. We came down to find the water was still rising. By the next afternoon we were all at work trying to save the ice house, moving items up the bank, clearing the lower shelves of the sheds, tying things down. We went downriver to another hut and found the water up to the windows, the bedding floating to the ceiling. That night Vilen decided he and Fidel would keep watch. At five in the morning Fidel announced that the water was now washing in from the sides of the headland and we would shortly be on an island: sheds and icehouse had long been flooded. Anikeev emerged in his underpants, surveyed the scene, and went back to his bathhouse bed— but two hours later he agreed it was time to leave. We had two boats but the motor did not work in one, and the other was erratic. Vilen and Fidel, in life jackets, each with a paddle, took their places in the motor-less boat and were pushed out into the current. It carried them swiftly away. Anikeev, Little Sasha, and I, with the valuable goods, followed in the other. Little Sasha gripped the empty bottle into which we had put a letter from the two us asking whoever found it to notify him in Mirny or me in Oxford. Once in midriver, he hurled it into the water. We forgot the dogs.

We kept the other boat in sight. There's always a danger of a hidden last piece of ice or a tree trunk. The water is icy cold and the current strong; once we reached the new encampment, we sent the drillers to bring the other boat in. A few hours later a fellow driller who had set off on his own hailed us from a little rubber dinghy: his boat had turned over in rough water the previous day and sunk, but he had managed to save the dinghy and paddle, himself and his dog. The following day Anikeev returned for the dogs. Our collective was complete. Anikeev had built himself a large wooden hut here, further up the bank. The five of us slept on wooden benches ranged along the walls. A big churn of homemade alcohol stood, fermenting at my feet, next to the stove, and the three drillers slept on deerskins on the floor. We caught huge pike and many other fish; Vilen cooked fish and meat stew three times a day; the drillers built a bathhouse and a smokehouse; Fidel carved a huge totem pole out of a tree trunk; I sat and wrote, then went exploring with Little Sasha, armed with his wooden rifle and accompanied by the dogs, in case we met a bear. "Are you good at climbing trees?" he asked. "Not very," I replied, looking at the spindly trees, and not wishing to remind him that bears climb trees. "Nor am I," he said. We stopped, while he thought. "Well," he said, "if we meet a bear, I'll take aim and you run for home as fast as you can."

I don't remember how we retraced our steps back to Lensk. But from there we took a boat downriver to the old town of Kirensk. We had a quantity of smoked fish, and I had a large reindeer horn. Then a train (or was it a bus?) took us back to Irkutsk. On our last day we walked with Gennady through the central park, an overgrown, leafy place. The elderly were sitting on benches in the sun. The little girls, in gauzy summer dresses and with big white bows in their hair, were hopping and skipping along. Cotton candy sellers were selling green and pink floss, but without sticks. We came upon a children's railway, winding in and out of the trees. It needed a coat of paint but, unlike some of the other rusty rides, it was working. With a jolt I thought of what was probably the first book I read about Russia, *Palaces on Monday*, a Puffin published in 1944, a story of two American children who traveled

Anikeev, Vilen, Mary, and a driller at Anikeev's place on the Vilyui River.

to Russia to join their father, an unemployed engineer who had emigrated in search of work. Their adventures, which ended in a Pioneer
camp on the Black Sea, included visiting a miniature railway built and
operated by children. At the age of seven I was not sure whether this
strange country, whose name was in capital letters—USSR—was real or
some kind of imaginary future place.

"The park is a pleasant place," said Gennady, "but it's built on bones.
This was the Jerusalem cemetery which, in the fifties, they turned into a
park and the church into a Palace of Culture. We ought to respect the
dead and return it to them." The damage, Vilen and I argued, was done,
but there should be a shrine. We left the park through the big arch,
shabby, partly crumbling, topped with the familiar letters: TsPKiO—
Central Park of Culture and Rest. To the right stood the Palace of
Culture, to the left the graves of the partisans and Soviet heroes who
had been buried outside the old cemetery. Rusty rides in a desecrated
graveyard. Was this what all those early hopes had come to? We stood

and argued the point for half an hour in a hot and dusty street. "We must think of the future," said Gennady, as we reached the empty Gagarin embankment. "When our party comes to power this will be a place of cafés, benches in the sun, a place to which all will come and talk in many languages." I suspect that now it is, but not quite as he had imagined it.

Although Vilen wears a yellow and blue Ukrainian cross around his neck, in 1993 his black hair was swept back off his forehead by a broad black headband. He put it on the day the Ukrainians voted in Kravchuk, the party functionary, as president and he vowed to take it off when his fellow countrymen got rid of the old party elite and abandoned the politics of nationalism. In 1989 he was writing, "If a miracle occurs and my odyssey is told, I want to be properly understood. I am not a dissident. I never thought, still less ever said, that socialism was to blame for the mess we find ourselves in. No, what existed was not socialism, it was not Soviet power. The tragedy of our generation lies in the fact that the bearers of 'good' were always in an absolute minority, and it ought to be the other way round. It's that active minority who are helping Gorbachev today with that which he began. When people start to weep, complaining that this or that is not right, I say to them, but look at what he has inherited! He needs help!" A year later, however, he had lost hope that Gorbachev would re-create the party, and by 1992 he no longer believed that Lenin's ideas, in particular a belief in state ownership, were the answer. That did not, however, mean that he saw anything good about the political situation in the now independent Ukraine. He considers himself Ukrainian and loves the Ukrainian language and literature, but he has no sympathy with demands for "Ukraine for the Ukrainians" and the excluding of any others from citizenship and office. He is too much an internationalist for that and distressed by the breakup of the old USSR into separate nationalist states. His stance was not a popular one in 1993, nor is it today. But before we come to that, we must return to St. Petersburg.

10

Survival Strategies

In June 1993 Vilen and I flew back to Moscow, then took the train to St. Petersburg. Andrei was there to meet us. Vilen was staying with him, while I, clutching my reindeer antler, headed home to Vasilevsky Island and invited my friends from the sixties to come and eat smoked fish.

Friends from the Sixties

How were they coping? Although some would deny it, they were probably eating better than a year earlier because now cheese, salami, and sweets were available and from time to time they could buy a little. The family income was almost entirely spent on food. The time-honored tradition of celebrating El'mar's birthday on November 6 with his school friends at the apartment in the Botanical Garden had been observed in 1992 but, despite it being his sixtieth, the celebration was sadly muted. Tamara could not provide the food she usually did, I paid for the wine, friends brought vodka or spirit acquired through work or other channels. For the first time in his life El'mar was having to put his mind to ways of earning money. Tamara, working in a research laboratory, had only a modest salary and their daughter, Katya, was a student. None of this had mattered in the old days. They had flown to the Crimea each summer and rented a room by the sea for a month, and sometimes El'mar took another holiday too. The idea of being able to afford a trip to England was now unthinkable. In 1993, despite drawing a substantial pension as a survivor of the Siege in addition to his salary and taking on extra work, a holiday in the Crimea was simply off the agenda.

But the potential for foreign travel was now there for those who could afford it or had access to a travel grant. It was as exciting as traveling to and fro across Russia was for me. We invited Galina to join us for a holiday—where would she like to go? She chose Italy—and one day in August she came through the barriers at Rome airport. Did we both cry from happiness? I think so. Then we set off for Sienna and the Tuscan countryside. Alastair and she visited the local café while I sat by the pool and, as she said, wrote like a war correspondent. Vitaly Startsev, my historian friend, came to Oxford and to work in the Grand Masonic Lodge in London; Andrei came with a group of archivists and spent time in the Bodleian; Vilen arrived, on a bus from Ukraine, and insisted on tidying up the basement of our house in Oxford. But none of El'mar's group of friends had the means to travel abroad and, in the new century, only Leva was able to take advantage of tourist trips to European cities.

However, in 1992 institutions that "owned" land outside the city had begun to distribute (free) plots of land to their members and, through the House of Scholars, the Sokolovs got a plot of land, two hours journey by metro, train and foot. Taking the train out of town to the Finnish gulf, or to the forests and lakes, used to cost less than a ruble; now it bit into the budget. It hadn't, however, affected the weekend exodus because a plot of land meant one could grow vegetables, and collecting berries and mushrooms in the forests had become more and more important. Car ownership was increasing (gasoline, still expensive, had now become available without queuing till three in the morning) but it was a risky business. It wasn't just the rutted roads (with their holes left by the stolen manhole covers and drain lids) or accidents or the cost of repairs but the cost of insurance (30,000r or six months' salary for university professor) that few could afford. A car might disappear overnight from the street, and that was that. Among El'mar's school friends, Oleg was the only one to have had a car in the eighties; now Leva had bought one.

El'mar and Tamara had decided to build a summer house on their plot of land. I went one day to help. We took the electric train an hour out of town to the station known as 65 km., walked three kilometers through the woods to the sandy lane where the dachas begin. Some are very grand—big, two-storied, with ornate carving—others are little and solid, the shapes and sizes depending on what the owners can afford. In the summer of 1992 the building of simple one-story wooden dachas were advertised for 60,000r (a year's salary) but El'mar and Tamara did not have that kind of money, hence the summer house. They started by collecting wooden crates, breaking them up, and bringing the wood out by train; then they bought second-grade, unfinished pine planks from the local timber firm and paid extra to have them delivered. They got a piece of asbestos sheeting from somewhere for the roof. El'mar collected cardboard that he stored in my flat. Both Galina and I offered them our old doors, now replaced by steel, and they were taking my old kitchen sink. All this presented problems. El'mar suggested that he and Tamara take my door home on the tram, but Tamara was more realistic. Leva agreed to come and collect the doors but could not promise a date, and Galina was anxious to see the last of hers—propped in the hall, it reminded her of the lid of her father's coffin, which in its time had stood there.

That Sunday in September it was warm and sunny. Tamara and I stripped bark off the planks with sharp knives while El'mar nailed them to the posts, driven into the ground. We did the third wall. The plan was get the walls done and the floor down before winter, a place big enough for two or three people to sleep on the floor. The earth is wonderful: black, peaty, with hardly a stone. They had cleared a large patch since May, planted vegetables, and got a good crop of potatoes and salad greens. But someone was stealing the potatoes from the plots: probably those who lived nearby took a few of a weekday evening.

El'mar was less enchanted by digging the soil than a year ago. For him, the freethinker, the disappearance of a world where he did not have to think about money, food, and material security was unnerving and disconcerting. Tamara had always organized the household; he had been free to do what he liked. Now came the realization that material things mattered. Hermann Hesse's republic could no longer serve as an ideal.

"What are the changes for the better?" I asked him. "Only freedom of thought," he said. "I used to think I thought freely but now I see that I didn't. The trouble is that it has come too late for me. I won't write an original book now." I am not convinced that his way of thinking did ever change. He once said that he always enjoyed meeting people from the west, their eyes were bright and alive. Surely they, with their access to ideas, would say really new and interesting things. But he always ended up being disappointed. His ideas were always as freewheeling as those of any western colleague, and he always parted company with conventional thinkers of the day. It was worse for those who were convinced that only censorship had prevented them from being recognized as writers or artists and now found it was talent that they lacked.

Walking back to the train that Sunday evening, El'mar spotted a peaty river, stripped off his clothes, and jumped into the cold water: in order to refresh his body and mind, he said. He then put his clothes back on again. Oddly enough, clothes seem to do a perfectly good job at drying a body.

In October the metro was full of elderly men with rucksacks on their backs, sometimes carrying large covered buckets or with little trolleys with sacks of vegetables on them. They had been out to the forests for cranberries or rowanberries, or to the fields to pick up the cabbages and carrots left after the pickers had departed. Some of the spritely pensioners were very organized: 10kg of cranberries on Monday, 15kg of cabbage on Wednesday. They were laying down supplies for the winter. Rowanberries are very tart, said to be full of vitamins, and they add a good flavor and pretty color to vodka.

Leva was now married to Gabriele, a Latvian, who had come to Leningrad to study physiotherapy and stayed. They had bought a one-room wooden house in a hamlet near Pskov, a day's drive away from St. Petersburg, in the countryside where Pushkin's country house still stands. In the summer of 1993 we three set out in the old car, uninsured, piled high with luggage and two cats who, because they travel badly, are given the run of the car. They meowed incessantly and licked the upholstery and my jeans to calm their stomachs. We made it out of the city without mishap, avoiding the gaping manholes, and were on the narrow highway to Luga, Pskov, and the Baltic states.

The hamlet of nine houses straggling along a grassy lane is one of many that lay within a huge state farm, stretching over the hills, taking in forests and rivers. The nearby hamlets, some of no more than three or four houses, are called Porridge, Horsefly, and Toad, linked by sandy lanes or a path through the woods. The houses were razed to the ground by the Germans in 1941 and the women lived in the forests, returning to rebuild them once the war was over. They have electricity and water from the well. There used to be a bus twice a day to the little town seven miles away; by 1993 it was only once. There was a village shop two miles away, the chairwoman of the village council had a telephone in her house up the hill, and on Friday the traveling shop came. The old women put on their white headscarves and set out, an hour or two early, some bent nearly double over their sticks, to sit in the shade and gossip while waiting for the van. They used to be able to buy salami out of their pension and have enough left to buy a bottle of vodka for the old man, they grumbled; now they could not possibly afford salami. There were only two elderly men left among the villagers. In the summer, as was usual in Soviet times, the grandchildren, nephews, and nieces arrived to spend the long holiday in the country. Everyone collected berries and mushrooms and a traveling theater came to put on a concert for the children.

Storks were nesting on top of a water tower near the state farm cowshed. A young cowherd rode a horse all day, herding the cows across the open fields, and a shepherd watched the sheep. The old men took turns sitting in the ditch and keeping an eye on the three private cows owned by the villagers, while the women worked on their plots of vegetables and gathered the hay. The state farm's fields of blue flax, maize, and barley were less well cared for. In 1993 there was no sign of privatization here. We walked through the fields and waded through the river to visit Pushkin's house. It was hot on the way back and Leva took off his shirt, only to be severely upbraided by one of the elderly women villagers for indecency.

I came back by bus, with a stop in Luga, where I bought an ice cream like everyone else, and thought back to that fateful visit in 1962 and to my thwarted request to visit the Pskov countryside in 1963. What a nonsense the restrictions had been, what wasted years. But recent

El'mar and Leva in Pskov countryside.

changes had brought minuses as well as pluses. Gabriele's brother, harried under Soviet rule for dissident activity, had spent time behind bars. Now he was free. But Gabriele had to choose between Latvian and Russian citizenship when Latvia became independent. Living in St. Petersburg, she opted for Russian. Pskov region borders on Latvia and her parents' house was an hour away from the hamlet—but now the border was closed. That meant that, in 1993, in order to visit her dying father, she had to pay a month's salary for a visa.

Personality, a work interest to sustain them, a salary paid on time, the ability to get a research grant or payment for a publication, the family environment, all played a part for those of my generation employed by the numerous research institutes or universities. Members of research institutes had very few commitments except to engage in research. Some did very little. Those in the humanities worked from home because they did not have a desk or a room in the institute, and often the working day was short. There were always domestic jobs to be done too, although the vast bulk of these were done by women.

With perestroika came a rush of new life into the arts and social sciences, followed by a financial crisis for science as a whole. Demoralization was worst in the natural and applied sciences, as money for equipment disappeared, young scientists left for the west where their skills were in demand, and institutes were told to make themselves commercially viable. Some went under, most did not and were still paying salaries (even if two months late and below the average wage). Grants from western foundations, governments, or from the EU for research projects or visits to the west were lifelines. I paid a young colleague £100 a month to act as a research assistant, and this kept his family afloat. University teachers or those in the teacher training colleges took on outside jobs, taking on two or three posts — lecturing for new private courses, teaching in school, acting as business consultants — and the research scientists from the academy institutes now doubled up as journalists, lecturers, or receptionists. The hotel staff became the most highly educated in the world: doctors of biological science carried the bags, physicists doubled as doormen, while classical specialists manned the travel bureau. But this was far truer of a younger generation than it was for those in their fifties or reaching sixty.

The Romankov twins, Liuba and Leonid, were weathering the changing times. Leonid, a full-time deputy on the City Council, working in the commission on culture and the artistic heritage of the city, was much happier working on cultural projects than he had been as a scientist. As a deputy he had a reasonable salary and access to the perks (the cafeteria), while opportunities to travel, including to America, opened up. The twins reestablished contact with a relative who had stayed in Germany after the war. And in 1987 when, with permission from Gorbachev, Rudolf Nureyev flew into Moscow on his way to Ufa to visit his dying mother, Liuba was there to meet him. As he came through she called and waved, and together they made their way out through the crowd of photographers. In 1989 Nureyev danced for the last time in

Liuba and Leonid Romankov. (courtesy of Leonid Romankov)

Leningrad and spent time in the Romankov family flat; in 1991 Liuba and her husband visited him on his island off Capri. By 1992, when Liuba and Leonid visited him in hospital in Paris, he was dying from AIDS.

Liuba, a physicist like her father, was still a powerhouse of energy: never home before ten at night, organizing or attending international conferences, making presentations in her very good English. By 1994 she had been to Montreal, Germany, and Holland. But salaries in research institutes in no way kept pace with inflation. In the laboratory they drank tea, but without any tea in it. And the young looked for other work. "A husband who works in Phys-tech is not a husband," the women said, and Liuba's thirty-year-old son left the institute to find a job in the car sales business. Now a grandmother, Liuba kept trim by running up (or down) escalators and had recently tried skateboarding but unfortunately broke her elbow.

This was shortly before a visit to St. Petersburg by Prince Charles. The British Consul asked me for suggestions of Russians who spoke good English to be invited to a small informal dinner at one of the new restaurants on the edge of the city. Liuba was among those I suggested and together we took the tram. Was it an interesting evening for Prince Charles? I can't tell, but Liuba, with her arm in a sling, sat next to him and recited a humorous poem she had composed in English in the prince's honor. Perhaps this made an impression.

Liuba is one of a group of women friends who, as young mothers struggling to cope with work and children, had come together in the sixties to support each other. They called themselves the Red Knitting Needles, because some of them would bring their knitting to their monthly evening meeting in one of their apartments. They were still meeting in the 1990s, now to discuss topics that interested them, exchanging news and useful information. But, as they always had, they kept off politics. It could have revealed very different and incompatible views. By the time I met them they were engaged in different pursuits—Liuba still a physicist, another a chemist, two other close friends were making modern designer lampshades, another worked in publishing, one in the art world—and they were surviving by using different strategies, from research grants and commissions to renting out a room (bed and breakfast) to visitors from the west or with support from their children.

Liuba and Leonid celebrated their birthday in November 1993 in the party room and sauna at the Hydroelectric Institute's sports hall. It was snowy and cold. A group of us went ahead with the food—bread, cheese, salami, butter, cold fish that Liuba had been cooking at three in the morning, casseroles of chicken and rice wrapped in blankets to keep them warm, little mushroom doughnuts, horseradish, cranberries, chopped parsley—and some of the drink—beer and coke to have in the sauna, cranberry liqueur, German and Hungarian wine, vodka. We lit the big wood fire to warm the room and went to the sauna in shifts. Friends came bringing cakes, fruit, drinks, and guitars, went off to the sauna or played pool or just drank and talked. I met a couple I had not seen for thirty years. Their only son, born in the mid-sixties, went to prison for grievous bodily harm in a drunken fight and shortly after his release died from a damaged liver. We all sat down to eat and drink toasts. Friends read poems of congratulation to the twins and sang songs they had composed and then other songs. Liuba's husband fell asleep and slid off his chair into the fireplace. Leonid rigged up a screen and we watched a home movie in which several of the party took turns swinging on a rope out over a lake and jumping in.

New Friends and a Younger Generation

Before the revolution Russia followed the Julian calendar, according to which Christmas fell on January 7, followed shortly afterwards by the New Year. In 1918 the Gregorian calendar was adopted and January 1 became New Year's Day. But people still celebrated the old dates too. In 1993 everything stopped for a fortnight for the New Year, Christmas, and the Old New Year. I returned from England in time to celebrate the Old New Year at a party hosted by Nikolai Belyak's Theater of the Interior. I went as Andrei Alexeev's guest. I was introduced to a physicist called, I thought, Rembrandt—but when I queried it he explained that no, his first name was Rem (Revolution, Elektrifikatsiia, Marx) and his second name was Brandt. There were more of these names around than I had thought. Arlen, another new friend, was Armiya Lenina.

In the big room, with photos and sketches on the wall and a clever wooden Christmas tree made from triangular bars of wood hung with candles and presents of gingerbread wrapped in gold paper, a table had been set up for forty people. There were potatoes, and gherkins and sour cabbage, and big cabbage pies, and bread, and juice, and vodka. The troupe, running in and out with food and drink, were dressed in all kinds of costumes, the guests were friends of the theater. At midnight the candles were lighted, and everyone got a gingerbread present. Mikhail Tolstoy, Deputy to the Russian Parliament, big, with white hair, gave the first toast. Belyak read a humorous article on the theater's hoped-for visit to the Venice Festival, the poet Chernov recited some poetry.

Andrei was called upon to make a toast. He got to his feet reluctantly because, he said, he no longer had anything special to say—his old beliefs had gone, all that remained was an intuitive feeling for good and evil. He couldn't embrace a new creed because he had really believed in the old; none of the political parties appealed, the defense of human rights was all that was left to him, and maybe creating the archive, "building a temple." This continued to occupy him for the next several years. There was plenty to do, and his moral integrity was always combined with a strategy of action. He always lived on a shoestring, wearing the same clothes until they fell apart, but soon Zina would move back to St. Petersburg and they would find an apartment together.

And what of my friend Vera, eking out an existence on a schoolteacher's salary in Tambov? My links, at that time, were through her daughter Olga who had come to St. Petersburg as a twenty-year-old to learn a trade as a decorator. And with Olga we move away from "Stalin's children" to their children, born under Khrushchev or Brezhnev. Now trained, but with only a temporary residence permit, Olga was living with a girlfriend in a room on the ground floor of a deserted old apartment block, awaiting renovation. Vera bombarded her with letters (and sent money) to which she rarely replied; then came the distraught phone calls to Galina. One evening we went together to find Olga. "Rats," said Galina, clutching my arm as a cat darted out of the dark and damp entrance. Olga, a copy of her mother in her student days, was smartly dressed, about to go out for the evening with her girlfriend. They had transformed the little room in which they lived. She assured Galina she had finished her technical training; she sighed over her impossible mother and promised to write. I wept as we walked back through the courtyards. The shock of seeing Vera again, in the person of her daughter, brought her back to me, and our hopes and beliefs of the sixties. But it was also on account of Olga. How, I thought, can she possibly get a job that will enable her to buy a room, let alone an apartment? How can she buy the clothes that are part of today's youth culture? But here I was wrong. By the turn of the century, Olga and her husband had an apartment in an enviable location on Petrogradskaya, and Vera was living with them.

The nineties were already a different world for the young, their world, albeit unstable, fast-moving, and unpredictable. It was a time for the energetic, the wheelers and dealers, the ones with practical ideas, self-confidence, and ambition. You really could go to Siberia with rucksacks full of money, buy metals, get them over the border to the Baltic States, and make a million. With language skills and perseverance, you got taken on by a joint venture and paid $200 a month, more than your father or mother, university professors, got paid in a year. Galina's students, or young faculty with language skills, could get grants to spend time visiting universities in the west. (A friend would stand in for a telephone interview if the applicant's spoken English was poor. But what happened, I wondered, when s/he arrived at the American university?) Or they found part-time employment on the side. Dmitry, one of Galina's students who had recently become an orthodox priest, worked shifts in the Vladimirsky church four days a week, hours and hours of going through the services. He was getting paid 5,000r a month (about the same as a professor but "very little" from a youthful perspective) and had his student grant. He telephoned Galina to invite us to come and see the church's valuable icons and pictures. We picked our way through the yard by the metro station where construction had been halted for lack of money ("Russia, get up from your knees!" proclaimed the large graffiti on the cement wall), past the signs advertising a pop concert in the sports hall, and entered the church.

Dmitry, tall and good looking in his pink vestments, explained that he had twenty minutes before a wedding and took us round. Then the wedding party arrived—a young couple, looking nervous, two or three parent-like people, and half a dozen friends in tight skirts and high heels. Dmitry and another priest took it in turns to say the prayers or sing the responses. Dmitry, somehow not surprisingly, had a lovely bass voice. At one point he left the wedding group and joined us. "The next three prayers are rather long," he said, "so I'll show you a bit more of the church," and proceeded to the next icon, returning to pick up his cue in the service as appropriate, and then joining us again when he felt like it. It was somewhat disconcerting. The young couple, duly processed with their aides holding the crowns over their heads, exchanged rings and were pronounced man and wife. The next wedding was due in ten minutes. An anxious father arrived: could it be put back twenty minutes, the main party had got held up and was going to be late. Dmitry calmly explained the rules: more than fifteen minutes late, and the charges are doubled; the father whispered urgently, Dmitry smiled benignly. As we left, to my relief, the car drew up and out spilled the bride and groom and rest of the party: they had just made it.

John Lennon on Vasilevsky Island?

There were those who did not change their lifestyle but now envisaged a shining future. In the autumn of 1992 I had bought a plain pine table and four chairs for $98 at the Baltic hard currency shop across the street. The manager and his assistant carried them over but, even with a front door and hall cupboard door taken off their hinges, the table would not go into the hall. They took it back and sent a young man that evening with just the tabletop. It still would not go into the kitchen. Next day the carpenters came, agreed it was hopeless, and brought their tools after work. They took two hours, sawing, chiseling, and gluing, and said they didn't mind if the firm did not pay them. They were acoustics engineers who had been made redundant. Now they were making ten sets of tables and chairs a month, working with Russian wood and Finnish equipment, enjoying the work and earning ten times what they had as engineers but hoping that one day they would be able to move back into acoustics.

Alexei had his tools wrapped in a cloth embroidered with "John Lennon Rock Temple." Had I really not heard, they asked, of Kolya Vasin, who had a rock and Beatles archive and was hoping to build a temple to John Lennon on Vasilevsky Island? They would take me to meet him. "You do meet interesting people," my daughter Ellika said, on a visit a few months later as we left Kolya Vasin's apartment. And indeed Kolya Vasin was an interesting person, a ceramics artist, then in his forties, big, bearded, happy, with a glass eye. Upon hearing a faded tape of a Beatles record from the early sixties, he resolved to devote his life to collecting Beatles records, photos, memorabilia of every kind—to create a Beatles archive and organize informal concerts of rock music—and so to create a new world of love, peace, and harmony. He lived in one room, in a communal apartment at the top of an old block of flats. The room was a crowded jumble of photos, books, records, and memorabilia; there was a rough table, a bench and a couple of chairs, but it was difficult to see where Kolya slept. Two bicycles took up a bit more space. There was a bowl of roughly cut cabbage and pickles, which we speared with forks, and vodka, and Kolya talked happily of the concerts he and his friends had organized in defiance of the authorities, and of his new project: to build a temple, of rocks, on the water at the end of Vasilevsky Island, topped by two huge revolving transparent but lighted spheres, a temple where rock music would be played and people would gather in peace. They had not collected much money so far. It was against their principles to charge for tickets to concerts. But he was optimistic.

Was life easier for him since perestroika, I asked. No, he said. He had come to realize that there were only two places for him to go—either heaven or an island in the South Pacific. Society did not like the way he lived. Why, he found it hard to understand: he did not harm anyone, and all he wanted to do is to listen to good music. Why should the neighbors, and others, object? "All we need is love," he said, beaming broadly at my daughter and her boyfriend. He knew all the Beatles songs by heart and their phrases, in English, punctuated and sometimes constituted his conversation.

We left the apartment and went to see the rest of the "museum"—in a big basement, in a courtyard where many artists had their studios. The snow was falling lightly, glistening against the streetlights in the little square where the statue of Pushkin stands. Kolya ran into a baker's shop for bread, because we were going to drink tea in the basement. Here there were more pictures, huge scrapbooks, and recording equipment. We drank tea out of big misshapen ceramic mugs and arranged to come to the celebrations in honor of Yoko's sixtieth birthday in two days' time. Then the basement was packed—with innocent-looking twenty-year-olds and bearded John Lennon lookalikes in their forties. People sat round the long table, and a group on the dilapidated couch played and sang old Beatles songs. There was some alcohol, but not much. The TV was there, and a photographer. I couldn't get much sense of the gathering. Ellika and Steve reckoned that a group in the small room was taking drugs but the whole atmosphere was, they said, innocent, like a first-term party at university.

Kolya Vasin lived in his one-room apartment until his death in 2018. The temple on Vasilevsky Island remained a dream. The artists' community in Pushkin Square has largely gone. The apartments sold to new owners. There are still a couple of galleries . . . we'll visit them, and meet new friends, in the next and in the final chapter.

Part
3

St. Petersburg

The New City, 1995 to 2017

11

Great Expectations . . . and Restoration

In 2015 I flew into the new, huge, and still half-empty airport on the edge of the city, not far from the line of defenses that held the Germans at bay in 1941. I was with Marion, my daughter-in-law. She was an art curator and was visiting the Hermitage. At the new airport there is a booth where you can order a taxi, fix the price, receive a receipt, and set off, speeding through a spaghetti junction of new roads, past huge shopping outlets, the Pepsi factory, and car showrooms. But we were even luckier. Once through passport control, I used my mobile to telephone the friend who was waiting in her car to meet us. "Amazing!" I thought proudly, but Marion probably thought it was quite normal.

Perhaps because I was introducing Marion to St. Petersburg, the past came crowding back. As we drove in along the Moscow road, events and experiences jostled each other for a place in my mind—past Skorokhod, the big shoe factory where I had done research on labor disputes in the 1960s, past the constructivist post office and sickle-and-hammer-shaped block, on to the first of the rivers that interlace the city, then, cutting through working-class districts, up Ligovsky, a criminal place in the 1920s, up to the Moscow railway station, where the city's anthem coming over the loudspeakers to greet the trains from Moscow always produces a lump in my throat. Down Nevsky Prospect (too many memories here) and across Palace Square where on November 7, 1961, with friends from the hostel, I too had joined the parade to commemorate the revolution and in 1991 I had listened to those who called for a new democratic Russia. With Marion gazing out of the window at the Hermitage, back to its earlier green and white glory, we crossed the Neva River. Over the bridge we went with its view of the Peter and Paul Fortress, the newly painted mosque, and past the block of luxury apartments that stands where the student hostel had stood, past the zoo where the animals had starved during the Siege and again in the nineties.

But what was Marion seeing? "At times," she said, "I felt that I could be in Paris, London, or another large Western European city. Women looked just like me—wearing a November uniform of jeans, black boots, a fur-trimmed and padded fitted coat, a nice bag and attached to an iPhone. I noticed an older well-dressed woman wearing Ugg boots as we walked across the Field of Mars." However, as she wrote afterwards, "While much of St. Petersburg felt familiar—the waterways of Amsterdam, the wide boulevards of Paris, the shopping in London—decidedly unfamiliar was the language, the industry and the ships on the Neva so close to the center, the petrol smell (no unleaded!) and . . . the curious drainpipes on buildings." We've already mentioned the drainpipes, discharging a load of ice and water with a roar onto the pavements. It is odd how they attract the visitor's attention. But Marion's comments illustrate two truths—St. Petersburg, like all European cities, has its unique features and yet it is indisputably one of them.

Changing Professions

It is easier to write of events, activities, and impressions of many years ago (whether correctly is another matter) than those which still await their sifting in our minds. Whereas in the sixties the lens through which I saw life in Leningrad was that of a twenty-five-year-old from England and in the nineties there was so much new that it pushed the past into the background, today my vision of the city and its residents is clogged with memories, with new impressions, and with images of changing city life in the capitals of Europe. So, how to tell it? Perhaps, first, outline my changing vantage points from the mid-nineties till today.

"Don't worry, Mary," said the high-ranking and respectable member of the city prosecutor's office in September 1998 as he put the fat envelope of notes into an inner pocket, "I am a qualified operative." We were sitting in the busy reception hall of a hotel, and I was anxious. I was glad to be rid of the envelope but concerned lest the transaction had been noticed. Corruption? A bribe? No. Simply the only way to pay the fares for Russian prosecutors, coming from across the country to St. Petersburg to discuss, with visiting American prosecutors, how to tackle police officers' abuse of their powers. But how had I come to be involved?

In 1995 I had changed professions—from university teacher at Oxford to head of the Ford Foundation's office in Russia. The Ford Foundation, a major American philanthropic organization with its headquarters in New York, has offices in several countries. For the past few years it had been supporting human rights, media organizations, and the social sciences in Russia. Now it was opening an office in Moscow, appointing new staff, and expanding its program. I was finishing a book, thinking of perhaps teaching in Russia, when a friend who had sent me the advertisement for the Ford post said, "You'd be able to support an institution such as the European University in St. Petersburg." Wondering if it would it be appropriate to support colleagues I knew, I decided that it would, applied, and was given the job.

We come, later in the chapter, to the European University, and to other institutions or organizations in St. Petersburg that I came to know as a grantmaker. Here, suffice it to say that from 1996 to 2002 Moscow became my base and expanding the grantmaking program across Russia my task. Did becoming a grantmaker, someone with access to considerable financial resources, affect my relations with colleagues and friends? There's no simple answer. None of my friends from the sixties approached me for money, except for Vladimir Yadov, who queried whether the foundation could help improve the toilet facilities in the Moscow Institute of Sociology and was not surprised when I had to say no. But I was anxious to support ventures where they warranted it, and this brought me new friends and enabled me to support some of my more recent colleagues. Only in one instance (and I am glad to say not lastingly) did my new role sever a friendship. Andrei Alexeev sought

Mary celebrating ten years of the
Ford Foundation Office in 2006.
(courtesy of the Ford Foundation)

funding to set up his archive as an independent institution. I thought
the proposal unworkable and backed away. Andrei, true to form, felt I
was wrong. It was only after I had left the foundation, and the Memorial
Society had made a successful application to include part of his archive
in its holdings, that Andrei and I became friends again.

Making grants to institutions or organizations across the country, I
still made frequent visits to St. Petersburg but I sold my apartment to a
young colleague. The spare bed, the pine bookcase and table made in
the defense industry plant, the floor rugs bought in Budapest, the table
lamps, china, and glass from the secondhand shops in the Apraksin
Yard came to Moscow, to the empty flat on Patriarch's Pond which,
with Galina's help, I had chosen and the Ford Foundation had rented.
Alastair took unpaid leave for a year and came to teach at the New Economic School; the children and their partners, friends from St. Petersburg, others from across Russia, and Vilen from Ukraine, made visits.

All the foundation grants were made through registered bank accounts, and duly reported to the tax authorities. But in August 1998 the ruble crashed and the banking system was unable to accept and convert dollar payments from abroad or to transfer the money to Russian organizations. I have the haziest memories of how the office coped. Alastair and I cut short our holiday on a Greek island, and I flew back to Moscow. I remember being unable to guarantee that salaries for office staff would be paid after a certain date, I remember running through the underpass, accompanied by one of the drivers, each of us carrying two holdalls full of ruble notes. We needed to get to Sberbank, the savings bank, to pay them into a new account before it shut for lunch. (Why? Was Sberbank the only bank still operating?) Most projects were simply put on hold, but arrangements for the workshop in St. Petersburg were already in place. In this case, and this case only, a cash payment was made — and the paperwork sorted out afterwards. Surely, I felt, the prosecutor's office could convince the tax inspectorate that all was above board.

So in the late nineties, I was back with prosecutors and lawyers and judges. But now I was supporting projects brought to us by universities or academy institutes, by museums and art galleries, by the new nongovernmental organizations and by lawyers. They all needed money to survive or to engage in new ventures. Through to the early years of the new century it was as a grantmaker that I visited St. Petersburg. Thereafter I came, to teach or do research, sometimes as a consultant evaluating a program, or as a board member of an institution, or simply to spend time with old and new friends. In 2015 I was introducing Marion to the Hermitage.

Two Steps Forward . . . And One Step Back?

How, from these different vantage points, did life in the city change before my eyes? If the mid-sixties to the mid-eighties were years of stagnation, the next decade saw the gradual cracking of the ice, then the sweeping changes that could be likened to the Lagoda ice pouring down the Neva in spring, carrying all before it, tumultuous years that brought excitement, riches, lawlessness, and shocking poverty. The twenty years that followed 1995 allow for no single descriptor . . . perhaps in part because I am too close to them. But, at least for my generation, the first decade was one where hardship coexisted with opportunities for the adventurous. "How would you describe those years?" I asked elderly friends on a recent visit. Two, independently, proffered, "A time of great expectations." So let's call them that.

From 1995 until perhaps 2005 the city's citizens were still struggling to survive. Except for a handful of the new rich, these years were hard on all generations—from the pensioners to the children. To change metaphors, the wind that was blowing in through the now open casement window—and not only from the west—swirled through the streets of a city in bad need of repair and of new ways of making a living. Contract killings took out democratic politicians and business rivals. I've already mentioned the assassination of Galina Starovoitova, the democratic politician, and then Nikolai Girenko, an activist, was murdered on his staircase; Galina's neighbor across the landing, a businessman, was shot dead as he opened the door. Friends were swindled out of an apartment they had bought. But it was also a decade when city politics and the media were a lively affair, and people embarked on new ventures—in business, in education or policy research, and in the arts. Legal aid centers, human rights organizations, environmental groups, and charities set up their tents.

Then, slowly, from 2005 or thereabouts, with the new president, Putin, back in office for a second term, life in the city began to change again. As the state's income rose from the boom in oil prices, as money from different sources began to flow into the city and its institutions, and a younger generation found new ways of earning a living, wages and salaries rose. The dollar/ruble rate stabilized. The drunks, beggars, and street children faded away. Most people were living better by 2012. The palaces were being repainted, the streets asphalted, boutique hotels, restaurants, classy shops, and supermarkets appeared. Museums and art galleries underwent facelifts; the Kirov, now again the Mariinsky Theater, built a new ballet and opera house behind its old building. Today buses and trolleybuses, no longer crammed to bursting, and scores of taxis wind their way through the streams of cars. There are shops galore, including Chanel and Dior in the center of the city, with the kind of shop windows you see in Bond Street, although the customers are very few. However, by 2016, with the fall in the price of oil hitting the state budget, and with rising prices, most were finding their real incomes were either stationary or falling.

What would Peter the Great make of St. Petersburg today? Has it finally realized his dream? In some ways, yes, and without destroying its grandeur and charm in the process. During the White Nights festival celebrating the June equinox, the Neva sprouts fountains of water on the stretch between the fortress and the Winter Palace, while a huge and stately galleon with red sails passes down the river against a back-drop of fireworks. A period of restoration? Yes, but in another sense too. While the last ten years have seen the restoration of the city, and a rise in living standards, they have also seen an end to democratic politics. The Kremlin slowly began to regain control over city governments, over their assemblies and policymaking, over much of the media and TV reporting. A campaign from above began to stifle political opposition, and by 2012 the Duma was legislating against foreign funding of independent organizations or institutions. The expectations or the hopes of those who had participated in the "reform (ad)ventures" of the 1990s and early 2000s have been relegated to the future, and not the near future. Peter would surely have approved.

In another sense too the city of today seems to belong to a different era. The revolution in communications, in technological innovation, the fantastic increases in wealth for some, international travel and trade, and the movement of people have changed cityscapes across Europe. St. Petersburg is no exception. Peter's casement window is now wide open in a new global context. In the past five years, computers, mobile phones, and the internet have made ways of behaving and interacting, whether in St. Petersburg, London, Paris, or New York, more similar to one to another, changing patterns of life in all these cities. No more standing in queues to buy theater tickets, train tickets, airline tickets; we all buy online. In October 2016, Galina, one of her colleagues, and I were standing outside the Troitsky Cathedral instead of at the Troitsky Bridge. No problem. Within five minutes the taxi summoned by mobile phone was there.

Levashovo and Foreign Agents

Why were we there? October 30 is commemoration day for victims of political repression. In St. Petersburg this starts with a gathering by the Troitsky stone, a huge boulder from the Solovetsky Islands in the White Sea, north of Arkhangelsk, a place of exile and death in the twenties and thirties. In the nineties the stone was brought to St. Petersburg by the Memorial Society. The society has two organizations in St. Petersburg, one that focuses on assistance to relatives of those who suffered political repression during the Soviet period and another that is concerned with the historical record and the preservation of sites of repression, the unmarked graveyards of those shot by the authorities in the Soviet period. Levashovo, a site to the north of the city, opposite an army base, sparsely populated by pine trees, was discovered in the nineties. Here, fenced off, were the unmarked graves of those shot, probably in the NKVD cellars in the city, during the Great Terror of the late thirties. No one knows where an individual body lies but memorials were erected—to Catholics, Ukrainians, Poles, Lithuanians, and Estonians as well as to Russians. People have set up little markers on trees or in the ground. One of Galina's graduate students had collected money and put up a plaque to Vladimir Beneshevich, a scholar of Byzantine history, his twin sons, and his brother, all shot in January 1938. Now, on October 30, we were taking flowers to lay by the plaque. We listened to the speeches by the Troitsky stone, then came the release of white balloons, some marked with names, to sail up into the sky and out across the Neva. Some got caught in the tops of the tall trees.

Coaches provided by the city authorities took us out to Levashovo. It is a desolate place. An awful statue of Moloch stands opposite the entrance. A huge bell hangs in the yard. People line up to give it a single pull. It tolls a harsh and dismal sound. We found the plaque and laid the flowers. Little candles stood among the trees on which people had fixed labels with names. The Estonians were holding a service around their monument. Unmarked burial grounds in the forests always create a feeling of coldness and desolation. Sandormokh, the graveyard in Karelia bordering on Finland, where long mounds mark the communal graves, is another such one. At its opening in 1997 it was bitterly cold, people walked among the trees, hoping to feel that they had found the grave of a loved one. When, frozen despite drinking vodka, I climbed back into the bus, an elderly woman asked me kindly, "Did you find yours? We think we did."

The Memorial Society occupies a converted ground floor flat on a side street off Nevsky. Here, with its library and archive, it hosts seminars and exhibitions. But now it has had to register its activities under a new organization. In July 2012 a law was passed that required nonprofit organizations that receive foreign funding and engage in "political activity" (undefined) to register as "foreign agents" (an offensive and derogatory term). Following discussion and protests, and the inclusion of dozens of organizations on the list, the law was amended in June 2016 to exclude groups involved in culture, sport, science, charity work . . . but "political activity" includes any activities aiming at influencing the results of an election or referendum and attempts to change or influence legislation, state policy, or public opinion, including by polling or sociological research. The amendments have, if anything, made life more difficult for policy-oriented NGOs and institutions. When put on the list by the Ministry of Justice, an organization is obliged to state, on any publication, that it has the status of "a foreign agent" or be fined.

Education, Innovation, and Its Costs

In the final chapter we shall come back to the extraordinary changes in today's cityscape and in everyday living, and to our old friends. Here the fate and fortunes of just a few of the new ventures in higher education, the arts, and law, initiated by an older generation, occupy our attention. Once or twice, by way of contrast, a younger generation makes an appearance. By this time, my circle of colleagues and friends included many of them, but they should tell their own stories. Mine, after all, is about those who were young in the early sixties.

The university world is the one I know best. University salaries and those in the research institutes have remained pitifully low. Many of my generation, including those with pensions as survivors of the Siege, have carried on working to make ends meet. Not all have children to support them. For a time Galina taught Russian to Korean students to supplement her income. By the turn of the century, research grants and visiting teaching appointments abroad had become a critical means of providing a living income for all in higher education or academy institutes. It was not until 2010 that salaries for the more senior faculty at St. Petersburg State University, those who held both teaching and administrative positions, rose substantially. Younger generations of university teachers or researchers still cannot live on one salary: they will probably combine a full-time with one or two part-time posts in different educational institutions, they may add earnings from a radio program or rely on Russian or foreign research grants to supplement the family income. Not surprisingly, they have little time for research.

In the mid-nineties, the time of privatization and innovation, of "great expectations," new colleges or institutes appeared, usually with financial support from foreign funders and newly wealthy Russians. The one I know best is the European University at St. Petersburg. In 1994 Boris Firsov left the Institute of Sociology and, with support from colleagues representing different academy institutes, set up a new independent graduate college for the humanities and social sciences. With Mayor Sobchak's approval and support from the city government, it was granted a lease on the Marble Palace, a grand townhouse not far from the Neva and the Fontanka rivers. Originally the home of Alexander II's morganatic wife and four children, in the Soviet period the palace housed various technical institutions and fell into disrepair. But it still had an elegant staircase and one fine room with a painted ceiling. This became the home of the new European University, whose faculty included more than one of my young colleagues from the Institute of Sociology.

Boris Firsov is a very upright person. He refused to pay a bribe when the computer system was installed, and everyone suffered from its inadequacies for several years. He insisted that modern toilet facilities for women should be a priority, and they were. (In the nineties the women at the EUSP had decent facilities while those in the history faculty at St. Petersburg State were still so bad that the dean insisted on no breaks in an international conference until lunch time; then the foreign participants could use the toilets at the neighboring restaurant.) Firsov is a person who understands the importance of patrons. He continued to

Boris Firsov. (courtesy of Boris Firsov)

make phone calls (was it twenty-five?) until he got through to Alexei Kudrin, then the Minister of Finance, and persuaded him to become a member of the Board of Trustees of the European University. I don't remember Kudrin attending a board meeting during the years I served as a deputy chair (this was after I had left the Ford Foundation) but connections matter. Firsov persuaded Mikhail Piotrovsky, the director of the Hermitage, to head the board.

Those initially employed by the five faculties—History, Ethnography (now Anthropology), Politics and Sociology, Economics, and, a little later, Art History—were in the main young researchers who had worked in the Academy of Sciences institutes. Some had gained research degrees in America or the UK. The student cohort was small, coming increasingly from across the country, drawn by the university's reputation and the attraction of studying in St. Petersburg, but by the turn of the century the EUSP also had an MA program, taught in English, for overseas graduate students. The term I taught there, in 2003, the students came from America, Germany, the UK, and from Russia. But all at the EUSP, faculty and students, will participate in a conference or seminar where the working language may be in Russian or in English. A far cry from A. J. Ayer's visit to Leningrad State University in 1961 when the interpreters failed to make sense of his lecture to a crowded hall and all left dissatisfied.

Foreign students' fees made a small contribution toward the university's growing costs. Faculty salaries at the EUSP were initially generous in comparison with those in state institutions but then, despite an active Development Office that raised money from foreign and Russian donors, they began to shrink. And in 2008 its "foreign funding" was targeted by hostile deputies in the City Assembly. The first attack, and the response to it, gives a good example of the changing political environment. A research project on the collection and analysis of election data funded by the European Commission was cited as evidence of foreign-funded involvement in the country's politics. Media attention followed, and then an inspection by the Fire Service found that the building lacked adequate fire protection measures and ruled on its closure. A district court upheld the ruling. Doors were taped up.

A very anxious two months followed. Appeals in support of the university were organized both within Russia and abroad. Money was raised to start doing the fire protection measures. Letters went up as high as the president's administration. When the new semester started classes were held in welcoming neighboring institutions and, to attract attention, on the street. The students organized a clever demonstration around the statue of Lomonosov (the father of Russian science) outside St. Petersburg State University, a demonstration that lasted all of two minutes but attracted the media. They challenged the Fire Service to a friendly football match (I forget who won), again as a publicity measure. Then the wind changed. A less than self-confident representative of the Mayor's Office made what sounded like conciliatory comments at a packed meeting, and the district court suddenly found that enough had been done to make the building safe and lifted the injunction. So who had decided the outcome? Certainly not the deputies or the district court or perhaps not even the Mayor's Office.

In 2016, now with an able young rector, Oleg Kharkhordin, the EUSP was again under attack. Although the university no longer received foreign funding, hostile deputies requested a new State Education Inspectorate, tasked with inspecting the dozens of new private colleges that had sprung up across the country (many of whom, I hasten to say, ought to be closed) to "inspect" the EUSP. The time that an institution will have to spend on responding to inspections, and the documentation required, is mind-boggling: it is an "attack by a paper tiger," in the words of a journalist. Was the bureaucracy quite so bad in the Soviet period? Perhaps not, because then lines of authority and control, imposed from above, were clearer to all and brooked no criticism. Now the system is clogged by webs of officials who are adept at finding lacunae or contradictions in the legislation, at proposing responses that may benefit them personally, and who create mountains of paperwork. Are we back to Gogol's *The Inspector General*? In the case of the EUSP, the inspection resulted in its "closure" by a court order. But by then, President Putin had become involved, had asked a deputy prime minister to hold a meeting to review the situation, an appeal to the Arbitration Court saw the closure halted while negotiations took place, Piotrovsky spoke out . . . and the court delayed a decision yet again. For a year the EUSP found itself without a license to teach and losing its right to occupy the Marble Palace. While it fought the court case, it used its resources to purchase and renovate part of a building in the neighboring Shpalernaya Street. In August 2018, now in its new building and with a decision in its favor regarding the license, its existing students could return and a call could go out for new applications.

The boundary between state and private or nongovernmental is hazy in the new Russia. You remember the dilapidated Bobrinsky Palace where Pashkov's center on industrial relations had a few rooms? In the nineties the center disappeared, and the palace became home to Smolny College, a new "liberal arts college" designed by Bard College (USA) and originally funded by American foundations. But in 2011 it was incorporated into St. Petersburg State University as a separate faculty, and the palace and its gardens were gradually restored to their prerevolutionary elegance. Alexei Kudrin, the ex-Minister of Finance, serves as its dean (in a part-time capacity); its board of trustees includes figures from the university, the art world of the city, and from Bard College, but it is hard to establish just how new a type of education it offers today.

Independent, Nongovernmental Organizations

Not far from the Moscow station, the offices on the first floor of an old but well-kept building were bought in the late 1990s by three nongovernmental (nonprofit) organizations. Funding for their purchase and renovation came from American and German foundations. Today, on the top floor, a newer LGBT organization rents space. The largest of the three, the Center for Independent Social Research (CISR), similar to policy-oriented think tanks or research centers that exist in London, Washington, or Berlin, was set up in the early nineties by a sociologist, Viktor Voronkov, with colleagues previously employed in academy institutes. Known informally as the Voronkov institute, its members, some full-time, others part-time, today mostly younger sociologists, engage in research projects into a variety of social issues (the use of city spaces, labor conflicts, hate crimes, migration . . .). The center produces articles and reports, an interesting journal (when money is available), and hosts conferences and seminars. German foundations and the MacArthur Foundation have been among its most stalwart supporters, but Ford supported it too, and its projects also find Russian funding. In 2015 the Voronkov institute found itself on the "foreign agents" registry and was fined for refusing to use the moniker. It fought and won the case against the fine but . . . on the grounds that the time period for issuing the fine had elapsed.

How should an organization respond? Across the corridor, and sharing the seminar room with the Voronkov institute, is a nongovernmental organization, Citizens Watch. Its founder and chair, Boris Pustintsev, born in 1935, grew up in Vladivostok where, from listening to the foreign radio stations, he became a life-long jazz enthusiast. As a student in Leningrad in 1956, he was sentenced to five years for protesting in support of the Hungarian uprising. On his release he managed to get a degree in languages and then employment composing the subtitles for English-language films. He was an excellent linguist. By the mid-nineties when I came to know him, Citizens Watch had among its aims the strengthening of civic or parliamentary control over the police. This meant establishing working relationships with the city's police leadership and the MVD Academy. Its small board included the well-known defense lawyer Yury Shmidt and city councilors. While its brief is similar to those of organizations in the west, it is reliant—as are the great majority of Russian NGOs—on funders, not members, for its income. Sadly Pustintsev died of cancer in 2014. I have written on its projects elsewhere, but Pustintsev deserves a parting word. His excellent English and his, shall I say, polished manners were a plus. White-haired, always well-dressed, smoking too much, he held his own whether it was a session in Strasburg or in Moscow, in the police academy or in court. But my happiest memory of him is at a jazz club in Soho. He had chosen the venue, but there were no places left. "He's come all the way from Russia," I said. "Is there no way . . ." and a reserved table near the front became ours. I had never been in a jazz club before (nor have I since), but Boris was in his element.

Ten, fifteen years ago lawyers were a growing and flourishing profession. It was not just the emerging business environment that brought new law schools and a new breed of lawyers into existence. Judges upheld appeals, defense lawyers championed adversarial practices, argued for changes in the codes, sometimes won their cases. There were a handful of those from an older generation, such as Yury Shmidt, who were active in high-profile cases in St. Petersburg. A younger group organized a network of clinics offering legal aid to citizens who lacked the knowledge to fight their cases in the courts. This proved popular among law students, and the movement spread across the country. The Ford Foundation was among its financial supporters. The law faculty at the university, which had moved in the seventies from Smolny to a bigger and better building on Vasilevsky Island (this is where Putin and Medvedev studied), also had its students' legal clinic. But I'll leave it to them, and to the other young activists who set up crisis centers or human rights organizations, to tell the story of their generation. I'll make one exception because it takes us back to the sixties.

A few years ago I found myself in one of those old well-courtyards on Petrogradskaya. In the nineteenth and early twentieth century large empty courtyards inside or behind buildings became home to new residential blocks, and then in their courtyards others would be built, hence "the well." Deeper and deeper one goes, looking desperately for the number of a staircase and apartment. Eventually I found the nongovernmental organization that defended workers' rights and its overcrowded office. The chair, in her early thirties, had become an activist as a young shop floor worker, then studied at the labor law department at the university, and then set up an NGO to support employees in disputes with an employer. My memories of department meetings in 1961–63, of visiting factories with Lucia and attending court hearings, came flooding back. How different was it now, I wondered? But, not surprisingly, my hesitant statement that I had studied labor disputes in the same department evoked not the slightest interest. The young activists have more than enough in the present to interest and occupy them. Together we looked at their website, and they told me of how they take cases to court or organize protests.

All in all, it's a picture of innovation, and of conservatism, of new departures and setbacks. The talent and the city's resources could make St. Petersburg one of Europe's leading centers of intellectual life, but it's not there yet.

The Arts—Old and New

The green and white Winter Palace, the winter residence of the imperial family, fronts onto Palace Square and the river. It was here that Catherine the Great, in 1764, housed her new Hermitage museum and art gallery, which over the next 150 years grew and grew. Following the 1917 revolution, the palace and all its contents, including its incomparable collection of art and treasures from the ancient world until the early twentieth century, became state property and open to the public. During the Siege the collection was saved by being transported out of the city, damage to the palace was made good after the war, and the Hermitage lived again. Only part of its collection can be on view at any one time but the Leonardos, the Rembrandts, and the Impressionists are always there. There's not only pictures and priceless collections but also the state rooms and those of the imperial family . . . and the staircase, immortalized in Eisenstein's film *October*.

In the mid-nineties the Hermitage was struggling. The faltering economy and inflation had simply eroded the state budget, its main source of income. Now it could barely pay its staff and preserve its collection, let alone engage in new ways with its own public or the outside world. Artists and sponsors from abroad were anxious to help. In 1997 a newly created State Hermitage Museum Foundation of Canada approached the Ford Foundation. Where the gallery windows looked out on the Neva and received the evening sun the pictures badly needed protection, but the cost was substantial. Might the Ford Foundation help with funding to install a protective film coating on the Hermitage's exhibition windows, thus deflecting the sun's rays and providing added security? I am glad to say that we did, and that at a reception to celebrate the new windows two museum attendants demonstrated, on models, how a sledgehammer might crack the glass but it would not break. I give the portraits in those rooms a little friendly wave when I visit.

Russian Ark, a film made by Alexander Sukurov in 2002 using a single sequence shot, takes you on an unusual journey through the Winter Palace, past and present. If you look carefully you will see the director, Mikhail Piotrovsky, who inherited the position from his father, talking to some visitors in one of the galleries. Piotrovsky is an Orientalist and speaks good English. As you will remember, he chairs the Board of Trustees of the EUSP. Quietly spoken, a little shy, he had no experience dealing with foundations nor, I suspect, with Russian oligarchs but he proved to be a quick learner. He also proved adept at persuading the Russian government, once its finances improved, that the Hermitage is one of the jewels in the Russian crown. Today it has taken over part of the General Staff building which, in a semicircle, faces the Winter Palace. This gives it new gallery space for its own or foreign exhibitions. And now it has its own foundation, the Hermitage Foundation, with affiliates in London, Amsterdam, Florence, New York, and Ottawa. The Hermitage has won its place as Europe's leading art museum.

Piotrovsky was born as the war drew to its end, too young to remember it, but I think of him as almost of our generation. For something completely different, cross over the river to the Peter and Paul Fortress which rents out space to the PRO ARTE Foundation for Culture and Arts, a nonprofit, nongovernmental organization set up in 1999 to promote contemporary arts and culture. Among its early projects was an intriguing citywide exhibition that opened at midnight on one of the white nights in June. Soviet artifacts appeared in unusual places. Knitted women's hats and berets of the Soviet period hung among the plants in the conservatories in the Botanical Garden, Soviet underwear had a different home, other artifacts were in a submarine. PRO ARTE, now funded by the City Council and by the Prokhorov Foundation, is one of the new ventures that has made it.

That is all I have space for on art, but a visit to the apartment-museums brings the city's writers and artists and the city they lived in to life. Pushkin's apartment was preserved after his death in the ill-fated duel in 1837 and has remained a place of pilgrimage ever since. It is quite grand, on the Moika River just off Palace Square. For a sense of how the Soviet elite lived, the large and well-appointed apartment on Petrogradskaya, home to Sergei Kirov, the Leningrad party leader assassinated in 1934, is well worth a visit. From the website, it looks even more spacious than it was in the early eighties when I visited with the Essex students. By then both Dostoevsky's apartment across the street from the central market on Vladimirskaya and the house in the port district where Alexander Blok, one of Russia's famous poets, lived until his death in 1920 had been refurbished and opened to the public. Even when some restructuring has been done, and kitchen and bathroom have disappeared, you can imagine, almost, that the writer will walk into the room and sit at his writing desk.

Those who had fallen foul of the authorities in the Stalin period had to wait longer. Mikhail Zoshchenko, the short story writer who in 1948, together with the poet Anna Akhmatova, was savagely criticized for his writing, lived not far from the Winter Palace. Only with the thaw under Khrushchev could their works again be published. Akhmatova's apartment on Liteiny was opened in 1989; Zoshchenko's in 1992. And today the apartment (not far from Dostoevsky's) where Akhmatova's son Lev Gumilev, the ethnographer, lived, has become a museum. A visit there will give you an idea of how Leningrad intellectuals, those fortunate enough not to live in a communal apartment, were living as their city became St. Petersburg. Kolya Vasin lived nearby in his room packed with Beatles memorabilia, and Yuly Rybakov, the democratic deputy in the nineties, has opened a gallery of modern paintings.

As I write I am aware that this is becoming an introduction to St. Petersburg today. Would Andrei Alexeev approve of my changing the vantage point? Alas, I can no longer ask him. It's time to bid farewell to the city and to its now elderly citizens, some of whom have been with us since the sixties. Let me take you by the hand and we'll walk or take a trolleybus, we shall look at the sights, and visit old friends. But first we bid farewell to those who are no longer with us.

12

Farewell to St. Petersburg

El'mar died from a stroke in April 2003. I was in England when Tamara rang me with the news that he was in hospital, unable to speak and unlikely to recover. The Institute of Culture organized the funeral at the crematorium and the wake at the institute itself. I could not make it and, to be honest, I was relieved. The Russian custom of leaving the coffin open until the final farewells are said makes a funeral even more distressing. I have only attended one at the crematorium, carefully laying my flowers (they must be an even number) by the coffin, feeling colder and colder as people spoke, the lid was closed, and the coffin lowered down through the floor.

Tamara and their daughter Katya scattered El'mar's ashes in the Botanical Garden. Tamara still lives in their top floor flat in the garden but, with bad arthritis, the stairs are a challenge and maintaining the dacha and its plot became too much of a burden. Recently, and regretfully, she sold it. Only two of the group of school friends are still living — Leva and Dima. Volodya Frolov died recently, in the aftermath of a major stroke. Dima has difficulty walking. Leva and Gabriella are often out of town. So, childhood friends from Petrogradskaya, farewell.

Vitaly Startsev the historian died in 2000. Vladimir Yadov, another old friend, died recently. We've already mentioned Boris Pustintsev of Citizens Watch, and Yury Shmidt, the human rights lawyer, died in

2013. Andrei Alexeev died, unexpectedly, in September 2017. I had visited him and Zina earlier that month. They and Zina's sister lived in a well-built, ten-story block standing on the edge of a small park fronting on the river, in an apartment allocated to the sisters' father, a leading engineer, by the factory in which he worked. It has a little balcony where Zina grows herbs and tomatoes and a fine view out over the river to the roofs of factories and to the Alexander Nevsky Monastery and, in the distance, there's the odd golden spire. Andrei had stopped smoking. He stopped on the day the doctor told him that the pain and difficulty he had walking was from poor circulation caused by smoking. But he was active through the internet, publishing his or others' comments on contemporary issues, advocating action to support different causes. And, when he could, he participated in events organized by the Memorial Society.

Others of their generation, I am glad to say, are alive and well. And my women friends, as might be expected, are still with us. So let's set out, to spend time with them and others in today's city.

Moscow Railway Station and Nevsky Prospect

We start at the Moscow railway station, the place where so many arrive, right in the center of the city. The train from Moscow slows down as it passes through its southern outskirts, there are glimpses of the huge old industrial plants, some dating from before the 1917 revolution, and then we reach the rivers and canals. The city's anthem comes over the loudspeaker . . . we have arrived and the crowds of passengers hurry to make their way out through the arches to taxis, buses, or the metro. Now we are standing outside, in the square where a church still stood in the 1930s. Today it's a traffic roundabout, a hub for streets going north and south, east and west. Opposite is the big hotel, still the October Hotel. To our left Nevsky Prospect, wide enough for eight lanes of traffic, beckons us to take a journey down to Palace Square, home of the Winter Palace and the Hermitage.

While Nevsky is wide and grand, its continuation taking you east, Old Nevsky, is much narrower. It has little to offer, but as it reaches the river there's the Alexander Nevsky Monastery founded by Peter the

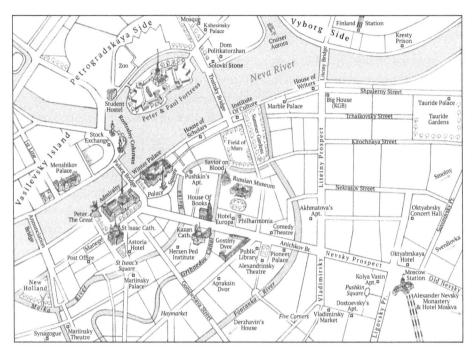

St. Petersburg city center.

Great. This is where the soldiers' billet was during the Siege. Several churches were built on the site, and one still was a working church during the Soviet period. The seminary is here. It may host a conference on some aspect of Byzantine history that Galina will participate in. The cemetery, where Dostoevsky's grave lies among those of other well-known people, is perhaps its major attraction. Across the road is the ugly Hotel Moskva, where British and American academics stayed in the early eighties.

Nevsky itself offers so much—grand houses or palaces that in the Soviet period became council buildings or centers for writers and artists, the imperial Anichkov Palace that became the Pioneer Palace, the famous horses that rear up on the Anichkov Bridge itself, and as one moves on there's Catherine the Great in front of the Alexandrovsky Theater, then the gray and white public library, and Gostiny Dvor, the big shopping arcade, while on the opposite side of the street there's the

"Akimov" Theater, the smart Yeliseevsky food shop . . . and, as we approach Palace Square, much, much more. It is not just that there is so much on Nevsky Prospect, it is also that the rivers that cut across it provide views of yet more buildings of all architectural styles from the eighteenth to the early twentieth century, all with a history to tell.

Up Liteiny and On to the Summer Garden

Liteiny, a long, straight, busy but not beautiful street, runs from Nevsky Prospect northwards to a bridge over the Neva, to the Vyborg side of the river. Here is the Finland Station where Lenin arrived in 1917 and where he still stands. And stretching along the Arsenal embankment is the dark red brick Kresty prison that has held so many over the past one hundred years and still serves as a detention center for those awaiting trial. From the aerial photos the two buildings in the shape of crosses (hence its name) stand out clearly. A monument to John Howard, the English penal reformer of the eighteenth century, used to stand in one of its courtyards. What would he make of Russian prisons today, I wonder? Over the past twenty years I have visited several, in different parts of the country, but in St. Petersburg only the SIZO, or detention center, for juveniles awaiting trial.

In the sixties Liteiny was the place for the best secondhand bookshops. This is where the poet Akhmatova lived. There are some fine residential streets whose houses, of different styles, largely built in the nineteenth century, became home to government institutions. But Liteiny itself, as it approaches the Neva, is overshadowed by the Big House, as it is usually referred to, the big constructivist (but appropriately unattractive) concrete block built in 1932—home to the security services, first the NKVD, then the KGB, now St. Petersburg's FSB. It is here that people were held and interrogated, and many (how many?) were shot during the purges of the late thirties and again in the forties. This is where Nikolai Belyak of the Theater of the Interior wanted to stage *Hamlet*. We'll walk quickly past it, and on to Shpalernaya Street.

The elegant townhouse, the House of Writers, a hive of activity in the nineties, stood here but was destroyed by a fire in the early 2000s. Now a luxury apartment block stands in its place. But on the other corner of Shpalernaya and Liteiny there's a big old red brick house and, on the ground floor, the flat where in 1993 the democratic candidates failed to agree which one among them should stand against the patriotic and popular TV producer Nevzorov; he won the seat. The meeting was organized as an F-Seminar, a discussion series hosted by Felix Yakubson, a documentary film producer who lives in the apartment.

Felix was often to be found in the early nineties with his camera at political meetings, sometimes on the stage filming, sometimes on the street. A handsome man, with his dark eyes and beard and an ability to engage almost anyone in conversation, Felix is by nature a peacemaker. I only knew him slightly then but soon after my moving to Moscow Felix appeared in search of work. When he had time he helped me with the design of the office, we went together to buy pictures for its walls, and we became friends. His Moscow years brought him together with Irina Tarkhanova, a talented art book designer, and now they divide their time between St. Petersburg and Moscow.

In the nineties when the F-seminars took place, a tree growing out of the floor occupied the corner by the window. (Did some of its branches go through the wall and outside?) It was still there when friends old and new came to celebrate my sixtieth birthday in 1998. It was long gone, after a redesign by Irina, when Felix celebrated his seventy-fifth birthday in October 2016. Now there's a new "office" in the basement for Irina's publishing venture and a cold dark room that can be used to show films. We watched Felix's latest documentary there: in a slow train going from Moscow to St. Petersburg, he engages the passengers in conversation about their everyday lives. As always he manages to charm them, to get them to talk. Then we moved back upstairs, and there were cold pies, tarts, salads, a great deal of food of all kinds, and drink, and speeches, toasts, and a long poem written in Felix's honor.

Felix was wearing a kippah, I think because it was already the Sabbath. It was while he was in Moscow that he started going to the synagogue. Now he observes certain rituals. His son, Maxim, also a filmmaker, is a practicing Christian, Russian Orthodox. Maxim has a large family: his wife had three children from a former marriage and now they have five-year-old Kolya, an elf with large dark eyes. One day in the summer when I went to visit, Felix was child minding and Kolya was watching a program, but then he came to join us at the table. We were talking about Brexit. Kolya was bored. Felix gave him a piece of paper and a pencil, suggested he think of a word and write it down, and we would try to guess what it was. Kolya, tongue poking out, shading the paper with his arm, wrote carefully, and then folded the paper into a smaller and smaller package. We had to guess a letter. Kolya would carefully unwrap the package, make sure we could not see its contents, check to see if the letter was there, tell us, and fold the paper up again. It took a long time. Were there, we queried, really three As? We gave up. Kolya unrolled the paper—Atlantida—he said triumphantly. A child with a future, I thought.

Not far away is Tchaikovsky Street and the flat where the Romankov twins lived through the Siege. Liuba and their older sister still live there, and one autumn evening in 2016 Leonid was spending the night there. The two of us left a meeting and walked together to Tchaikovsky Street. Leonid served as a deputy to the City Council until 2002. Since then, he participates in different cultural and human rights activities. As we walked, we agreed we would not raise the topic of Ukraine, and neither did Liuba. She sees the "return" of Crimea to Russia as right and proper, as indeed do many (most?) St. Petersburg intellectuals, including friends from the sixties—but not Leonid. Liuba also sides with the Donbass separatists in their opposition to the Ukrainian government. And, being Liuba, she is not only active in providing support to those who have fled from the fighting across the border into Russia but has visited the Donbass to talk to fellow scientists there. Sharp differences of opinion on Ukraine divide families and friends. Sometimes, but not always, I can guess where friends will line up. Vilen, a Ukrainian but always an outsider, supported Russia's taking of Crimea, is bitterly opposed to the "nationalist" Poroshenko government in Kiev, and left home and family to move to the Crimea; now he is back in Alexandria, in ill health, protesting on the web.

However, that evening Liuba and Leonid and I talked of other things, among them their visit, earlier in the year, to London to see Ralph Fiennes in *The Master Builder*. They had received an invitation from Fiennes's agent to fly to London for the weekend, see the play, and have dinner with him afterwards to talk about Rudolph Nureyev. Puzzled, "Who is Ralph Fiennes?" they had asked Russian friends now living in London. To cut the story short, they came, and when Fiennes's film about Nureyev appears, two young actors will play his friends, the Romankov twins, in Leningrad in 1960.

Liuba is still engaged in research in her laboratory, endlessly busy but always with time to do a good deed. You remember Volodya Frolov, one of El'mar's friends, who has just died? He worked under the twins' father in the Technological Institute. Upon hearing of his stroke, I had written to Liuba and, without delay, she found out where he was, went to visit, and wrote back. "How did you know?" he had asked her. "The news came from London," she said, and they both laughed. But the news was not good.

If we retrace our steps, back across Liteiny, we reach the Marble Palace, home of the European University, and now we have a choice—turn left onto the embankment and walk westwards past the elegant buildings, past the Fontanka River where Lucia, friend from the labor law department, lived, past the iron fencing of the Summer Garden, the blue and white Institute of Culture where El'mar taught, on past more elegant buildings (where Rostropovich bought an apartment), past the House of Scholars, and finally to the Hermitage. All the while the view across the Neva—the *Aurora* battleship, the mosque, the Peter and Paul Fortress—claims your attention. But if the weather's bad, rain and wind buffet a pedestrian unmercifully. In October my umbrella was torn from my hand, and in trying to retrieve it I lost hold of my shopping bag and it was whirled away . . . I thought of Pushkin's famous poem *The Bronze Horseman* where, in a storm, the statue comes alive, the river rises, and the helpless Yevgeny is swept away to one of the islands. But this summer, at one in the morning, the weather was lovely. As the taxi driver, an Uzbek from Samarkand, summoned by mobile phone from the Romankov apartment, was driving along the embankment and I was marveling at the view, his phone rang. "Young woman," he said, "you've left your cardigan at your friend's apartment," and he turned the taxi around. Back to Tchaikovsky, where Liuba was standing on the pavement with the cardigan, and then, again on the embankment, the view became even more spectacular—the Liteiny Bridge was opening, raising its lighted sides into the sky. "Shall we make to Vasilevsky?" I asked. "Yes," he said, as we sped past the Summer Garden, on towards the Hermitage. "We've got a quarter of an hour before the Palace Bridge opens."

From the Field of Mars to the Bronze Horseman

It's but a step from the Summer Garden to the Field of Mars, where the Romankovs grew vegetables during the Siege. Stately buildings, home before the revolution to the wealthy, then to members of the Soviet cultural or intellectual elite, look out across the imperial parade ground. This is perhaps the Hyde Park or Kensington of St. Petersburg. Before us lies the little Moika River and both the Red Palace where the mad Tsar Paul was murdered and, partly hidden by the trees in its park, the Russian Museum, the sumptuous Mikhailovsky Palace chosen by Tsar Nicholas II in 1895 to become the home of Russian art in commemoration of his father Alexander III. The collection included pieces from the Hermitage and other museums and, after the revolution, private collections were given a home here. It is a fine gallery.

In the square in front of the museum stands the famous statue of Pushkin, with his arm outstretched as though he is directing our attention to the right, to the Mikhailovsky Theater of Opera and Ballet, second only to the Mariinsky for its décor and performances. And as if this were not enough, the Philharmonia occupies one corner of the square in front of him and the grand Hotel Europa the other.

Music? If a young Shostakovich were in the city today, would he be planning on staying or leaving? Anna Netrebko came from the south, as a young singer, to study music. The story has it that while cleaning floors at the Mariinsky, she was overheard singing by Valery Gergiev, the leading conductor, and that was the start of her international career. In the nineties young musicians and dancers left for the west. Today? I don't know. All I can say is that, compared with the nineties, a visit to the Mariinsky or the Philharmonia is like stepping back into a world of bright lights, a world of large casts, fanciful costumes, and full houses.

In the autumn of 2015 Galina and I went together to the new Mariinsky Opera House to see an avant-garde staging of *Yevgeny Onegin*, which, as sophisticated elderly opera goers sitting among a largely young audience, met with our approval. We drank champagne (French) in the interval, negotiated the modern lifts, and took a taxi home. Tickets may still be cheap by comparison with London or New York, but they are no longer cheap for Russians—$25 for a piano recital in the Small Hall of the Phiharmonia in October 2016. Yet they are fully sold out, and children are among the audience. The girls still have spindly stockinged legs and their hair in white bows, but their parents, indeed all the adults, now dress differently, in the kinds of clothes you might see in London, and they no longer take off their boots, check them in at the cloakroom, and put on their indoor shoes.

A block away is the Canal Griboedova. Look south, and there, on Nevsky, the huge classical columned Kazan Cathedral, the Museum of Atheism and Religion in the Soviet period, blocks the view. Opposite it there's the four-story Singer building, with its globe on top, the House of Books, now with a café but no longer the best bookshop in the city (for that visit Bukvoyed further up Nevsky). And if you look north, the iconic Church of the Saviour on Blood, with its extravagant carvings and cluster of decorated onion domes, stands on the spot where Alexander II was assassinated in 1881 as his carriage drove toward the Winter Palace. The Soviet authorities masked its domes with scaffolding for years, and it was shut to the public. Now it is open again.

Palace Square and the Hermitage is a short walk away. If you get there by 10 a.m, before the school parties and tourist groups arrive, as did Marion, you may have the Rembrandts all to yourself for an hour. But we cross the road, past the Admiralty with its golden spire, and continuing along the embankment we come to the statue of Peter the Great, the bronze horseman, in front of St. Isaac's Cathedral. Newly married couples pose with their wedding guests here. Peter looks across the river to Vasilevsky Island. We admire the view but as by now you are well acquainted with its buildings and the statue of Lomonosov, we'll take a bus across the Palace Bridge, past the original Stock Exchange, with its classical Roman façade, pass the two huge red columns whose fiery beacons alerted ships to the dividing of the Neva, and cross the bridge that takes us to the Petrogradskaya side of the river.

Petrogradskaya Side

Now we are back in the streets I knew so well in the sixties. The hostel, alas, has made way for a block of luxury apartments, and the market, now but a shadow of its former self, is surrounded by shops selling all and sundry from cheap goods to mobile phones, from farm produce to wonderful cakes in the Sever patisserie. "Sekond Hend" bawls an elderly man, waving a placard outside a hall where clothing from the charity shops of Western Europe is now on sale.

Vera lives here, not far from the market. In 1993, together with her older sister Nina, she came to St. Petersburg to visit her daughter Olga. The situation was far worse than she had feared. Despite her sending Olga food parcels and money, the fridge in the room Olga was sharing with two other girls was empty. Vera and Nina decided to sell all their property in Tambov—their two one-room apartments and their deceased parents' two-room apartment—and move to St. Petersburg. This gave them enough to buy a four-room apartment on the outskirts of the city, and Olga moved in. With Nina now incurably ill, they started an exchange process (initially to be near a hospital) which continued after her death. Over the next ten years, with Olga doing the renovations, they moved seven times, slowly into the center until, in 2006, they had a four-room apartment in the center, on Petrogradskaya. Olga and her husband, who is from Abkhaziya in the south, converted this into a three-room apartment for themselves and for Vera and a one-room apartment that they rent out. For several years they had a Chinese student as a lodger, but once he graduated and moved to Moscow Olga and her husband adopted a little boy. Now he is the apple of Vera's eye.

Vera likes to entertain. A few years ago, on one of my visits, I made the mistake of suggesting that I take the four of us—Vera, Galina, Tamara, and I—out to a restaurant for lunch. Galina consulted a young member of her department. He suggested a new restaurant, At Giovanni's, on the corner of the park by the Russian Museum. Vera grudgingly agreed to accept the offer of a taxi and meet us on the corner. There she was by the ornate park gates. I took her by the arm and we moved slowly, looking for the restaurant. I saw the sign, on a square red-brick building, and happily called to the others. Vera stopped in her tracks. "Girls," she said, "in Soviet times that was a public lavatory." My heart sank. It is now a very nice Italian restaurant. But the meal started badly. Vera announced she would have Salad Olivier, a famous Russian salad, and expressed dismay and disbelief that it was not on offer; Galina claimed to have left her reading glasses at home and to be unable to read the menu. However, somehow, we sorted things out, and everyone was happy.

This summer I gave in, and Galina and I accepted Vera's invitation to lunch. We brought a cake from the nearby Sever shop. There was cold soup, and several salads, and a hot dish and potatoes, and battered vegetables and sausages . . . and a cold dessert. Sometimes we take a break between courses, and all have a rest on Vera's spacious bed. Sometimes Vera reads to us—from letters or a chronicle she writes—sometimes we fall asleep. This time a jazz band was playing outside the early-twentieth-century People's House on the edge of the park, which became the Velikan cinema, and is now the Music Hall. What kind of entertainment is offered there now, I wonder? It wasn't up to much in the sixties. A theater from Tbilisi, offering a Georgian version of Sholokhov's *Quiet Flows the Don* is all that comes to mind, and not because it was good.

Boris Firsov of the European University and his wife Galina also live on Petrogradskaya, in the two-room flat that Boris grew up in as a boy and where at the end of the thirties his father died after a short spell in a freezing detention cell. As a district Communist Party secretary Boris could have been allocated a larger flat but he never sought to take advantage of his position. A year ago he was ill, it took more than a year to recover from a heart operation (again he refused special treatment) but, almost miraculously, he is now active again and writing. I went to lunch—Galina provided so many courses, including a large hot tongue—and we had so much to talk about that it was evening before I left. We started with Galina's wartime experiences as a child, when her school convoy, unable to get through the blockade, had returned to the city. She found herself alone in an empty flat from which her mother and younger brother had left, and that was only the beginning. Then we were on to Boris, as a high school graduate, standing in, with forged documents, to take the entrance exam in physics to get a friend a place at an institute . . . and there was the European University to talk about, and Brexit, and Putin's Russia of today.

The Cityscape of Today

Apart from the new shops, and the traffic, the central city districts still look much as they did fifty years ago. Very little new building has been allowed, but everything is smarter, lights and shops everywhere, and advertisements instead of political posters. A successful campaign against the construction of a Gasprom tower saved the skyline. It is the once-empty spaces on Vasilevsky Island's north and west, or in the northern part of Petrogradskaya, that are now home to new buildings of every architectural style, residential blocks and office blocks and new business ventures. The outlying districts linking the city with the resorts on the Finnish gulf have changed even more, with big apartment blocks, substantial private houses, and shopping centers overtaking and submerging the scattered wooden dachas. Those arriving at the new airport can head for the resorts on the Finnish gulf, avoiding the city altogether via a long bridge that takes them past Kronstadt, the original naval base. A four-lane ring road now circles the city and is linked to it by access roads, but looking as though they have dropped from the sky are surrealist new clusters of twenty-story residential towers—concrete, pale brick, and glass—sometimes painted in pastel colors, standing in empty fields. With their shops and schools and car parks, they provide a new home—one, two, three-room flats for city dwellers and for newcomers. Mornings and evenings a trail of cars, like ants, heads from them into and out of the city. But what, I wonder, do the children do when they are not in school?

Sanctions or not, as regards shopping you could be in any European city. Yes, decent European cheese may have disappeared. Yes, those with cars and time drive over the border to Finland and stock up with scarce products. Prices, often European prices, are rising fast, while wages, salaries, and pensions lag far behind. But for those who are making money, there's no need to shop in Europe. In 2015 I bought two pairs of shoes at the Ecco shop near the Andreevsky cathedral, at London prices, and Galina chose a handbag that completed the special offer. A year later she had ordered a large new fridge off the internet; it had been delivered and the old one taken away. Through a German website, she had bought a really nice winter coat and shoes. She has an account with a taxi firm, which collects from the door and gives its members a discount, but even without that the fares are manageable. There's a lot of competition.

What might a visitor from Europe comment on? St. Petersburg is still a "white city." It has its newcomers from Central Asia who sometimes gather in a noisy group in a courtyard, but very few Chinese and even fewer from India or Africa. There are the foreign tourists of course, but nothing like the foreign resident community that exists in Moscow. The streets may be full of cars, the buses and trolleybuses much emptier, but the metro is still a showpiece, as well-maintained as it always was, and now the passengers all have decent footwear, and half of them are busy on their phones. For several years part of the northern line had to be suspended because of a ground slip; now it's now working again. But beware when Zenit, the St. Petersburg football team, wins the championship. Then Nevsky is swamped with cars, their passengers waving banners, hooting, and blowing whistles, the pavements are blocked by football fans in their blue and white scarves, and the central metro stations are shut for safety reasons.

New cafés and restaurants had started to appear in the late nineties—does the classy Restoran with modern furniture and traditional Russian food that opened behind the Academy of Sciences still exist, I wonder? But it was 2010 or so before Italian, Lithuanian, and Chinese restaurants joined the Georgian, which had always been there, and Shtolle arrived, offering a selection of traditional Russian pies (meat, vegetable, or fruit) to eat in, take away, or have delivered. Walk down 7th Line on Vasilevsky Island today and you are spoiled for choice. Two new ventures, both good, are a traditional Soviet restaurant, whose décor is "Soviet" furniture including samovars, books, a chessboard, and whose menu includes the standard soups. At the end of the street in one of the old eighteenth-century houses, with a garden extension, there's a smart Russian restaurant. During the White Nights, the two weeks at the end of June when all kinds of celebrations take place, it will be fully booked. There's now a very busy rooftop restaurant, just off Nevsky near the Kazan cathedral, with views over that part of the city. All of this is a far cry from what was on offer even ten years ago. But then London has changed too. People in London eat out more, particularly at lunchtime. In recent years cafés and restaurants of all and every kind have sprouted up along the London streets. There is a difference, though. While some of the St. Petersburg restaurants and cafés are always crowded, there are those, even on 7th Line, where hardly a table is occupied. How do they manage to survive?

What else is new? Let's stick with Vasilevsky Island for the moment. There's the Finnish supermarket, Prism, where I could happily do a week's shop; Antante surely has gone out of business. But I would go elsewhere for meat, fish, and Russian dairy products. To the market by the Andreevsky church? Here you are in for a disappointment. It's now a shadow of its former self. Most of the building has been sold off to sellers of tatty goods, leaving a few stalls of fruit and vegetables from the Caucasus and Central Asia; of milk, sour cheese, and pickled cabbage from the countryside; some red caviar, and a few sad fish swimming in a tank. There's very little meat. Only the honey, of all different kinds, glistening, still tempts. Galina sometimes buys milk here, but she can get all kinds of milk products in a supermarket much nearer home. Across the street we go to the old-fashioned pharmacy. It puzzles me that there are so many pharmacies, with their glass-fronted display cases, all with an unmistakably European (but not an English) feel, and the assistants, in their white coats, are a little stern. Perhaps, before the revolution, the pharmacies came to Russia from Germany and never changed.

If we take a trolleybus up to the Maly or Little Prospect, we shall find a branch of Sberbank, gleaming with neon lighting, with comfortable seats, booths with clouded glass for privacy and, of course, cash machines offering different services. Out in the street, and into a shop, maybe belonging to the Azart confectionery factory (Mikoyan to me) — an Aladdin's cave of beautifully wrapped sweets and chocolates of all kinds — for Galina to buy a kilo of Korovka for my grandchildren, their favorite Russian sweet. But we are the only customers, and three assistants sit behind the counters. Everything is available now, the nineties a distant past. Some of the shops have a curious assortment of merchandise—good quality china and glass, then a rack of clothes, hair products, and behind a screen sits a tailor who repairs clothes while, under the counter, for known customers, there's salami from Finland.

We summon a taxi to take us to meet Tamara for lunch at a new restaurant near the Botanical Garden. The Cafe Rinaldo has two sections, one offering Georgian cuisine, the other Central Asian. We opt for Georgian and a table with upright chairs rather than soft couches, which we might find difficult to get up from. We talk the afternoon and evening away, then we walk slowly, three old ladies, back toward the Botanical Garden. The house, with its top-floor apartment, no longer belongs to the Botanical Institute and is undergoing *remont*. It's been in wraps for six months. The bus stop on the opposite side of the street is still there and, while Galina is thinking of summoning a taxi, the 128 bus—the bus that used to take me back to Mytny in the 1960s—comes into view. We wave farewell to Tamara and climb, not very nimbly, into the bus. It takes us past the new shops on Bolshoi Prospect, past the stadium, over the bridge, and home to Vasilevsky Island.

Postscript

It's early evening in Bloomsbury. The sun slips out from behind the mansion block across the street and shines into my study. It catches the glass of a large framed map titled "St. Petersburg 1914." Between the years 1914 and 1917 an annual directory listing residents, businesses, and cultural and government institutions included an illustrated map of the city, folded and tucked into the back of each volume. Over the years the directories retreated to the libraries but a map might find its way to an antiquarian bookshop. I bought mine for 5 rubles in one on Liteiny in 1961. Next to the map hangs a batik—key buildings, bridges, and monuments crowd a watery cityscape of St. Petersburg. The European University at St. Petersburg, which commissioned the batik as a farewell present, is there, and in the clouds above the artist has traced my signature.

The statue of Pushkin, given to me by Pashkov, stands on the bookcase lining the opposite wall, but now a primitive fuse made by a prisoner in the workshop at Perm-36, the camp in the Urals, hangs from his outstretched arm. A little plaster cast of one of the sleeping lions at the palace in Yalta where Stalin met Churchill and Roosevelt lies dreaming at his feet. A Matryoshka doll—Gorbachev, emblazoned with a red Perestroika banner, who unscrews to reveal Brezhnev, then smaller and smaller, Khrushchev, Stalin, and Lenin—stands among photos of children and grandchildren, and on the wall hang two of the Memorial Society's posters for their history competition for schoolchildren.

The sun manages to sneak into the sitting room. The characters in its pictures, as I told my grandson Joe when he was young enough to believe it, come alive at night and step out of their frames. The lion, who rests under a tree during the day with his samovar beside him, paces up and down the corridor, looks in to check that I am asleep, and keeps the noise level down. The women queuing at the Leningrad post office counter painted by Zinshtein, and the three gentlemen whom Yershov has riding on an extended bicycle through a cornfield, are the worst offenders. The women chatter and gossip. The men stretch their legs and try to persuade the young woman resting in her deckchair—who ever since she was painted by Viting in 1938 has hidden her face with her hand—to talk to them. Maybe she smiles behind her hand, but she doesn't take it away.

In the corridor, the boy playing the flute in a St. Petersburg cellar, photographed by Maxim Yakubson, left in the 1980s for India and has disappeared. And, from her vantage point at the end, Shemiakin's *Lady with the Pomegranate* observes the scene with an ironic smile. If I show signs of waking up, the lion has them back in their frames in a matter of minutes. Sometimes, as I told Joe, I check in the morning—are the three men back in their proper places on the bicycle, is the bee still humming in the sky? I look at the lion, under his tree, questioningly. Was that a wink he gave me? I am not quite sure.

Lightning Source UK Ltd.
Milton Keynes UK
UKHW022349120819
347850UK00003B/200/P